Sexonomics™

The Golden Triangle:
Sexuality, Money, Power

$exonomics™

A pathbreaking innovative inquiry
into women's and men's sexual
reasoning and behavior

Dr. A. Lallier
Montreal, Quebec

Sexonomics™
The Golden Triangle:
Sexuality, Money, Power

A pathbreaking innovative inquiry
into women's and men's
sexual reasoning
and behavior

While "Pure love" is heavenly destiny,
human Reason is its unique terrestrial companion.

Dr. A. Lallier
Montreal, Canada

With my forever gratitude to Mrs. Delutis and Mrs. Kim Delutis-Scott,
for their incessant and encouraging effort to help me through the intricacies
and complexities of English grammar and composition.

Library of Congress Control Number:		2012922062
ISBN:	Hardcover	978-1-4797-5443-4
	Softcover	978-1-4797-5442-7
	Ebook	978-1-4797-5444-1

Sexonomics™ is the trademark of Dr. Adalbert Lallier, officially registered by the United States Patent and Trademark Office: Reg. No. 3,914,169; Feb. 1, 2011; and in Canada: TMS 759,064, dated 1988 and 2-9-2010.

This book was printed in the United States of America.

To order additional copies of this book, contact:
Xlibris Corporation
1-888-795-4274
www.Xlibris.com
Orders@Xlibris.com
126252

CONTENTS

Part Two: The Fascinating World of Sexonomics as a Science

INTRODUCTION

Sexonomics' Definition and Purpose: The Economics and Politics of Human Sexuality

Sexonomics, as the fifth social science, is about the economics and politics of human sexuality. It involves the *magic* triangle of sex, money, and power—the art of marketing human sexuality. Like all art, it involves esthetics, risk taking, and a certain air of gamesmanship. However, Sexonomics also constitutes a science; in fact, "Sexonomics" constitutes the first official text in what is meant to become the fifth social science. Since the sexual drive of normal women and men is as natural as their desire for happiness, it is therefore subject to an objective analysis. Sexonomics studies the linkage between human sexuality, material welfare, and personal well-being in a social context in which the equal empowerment of women and men is presumed to be encouraged and promoted.

Typically, women and men engage in sexual intercourse because of the following:

- They seek instant gratification and relief from momentous loin heat ("fornication"). It involves mainly those individuals who are unable to control the intensity of their demand for intercourse. It also involves individuals who supply such a service, mainly as a primary source of their incomes.

- They yearn for an ideal lifetime relationship that is totally devoid of material self-interest ("puppy love," "pure love," or "selfless love"). This group involves dreamy-eyed adolescents and unusually romantically inclined adult females and males.

- They wish to achieve a lifestyle of status and material opulence (sexonomic rationality). Its practitioners are those experienced women and men who market their sexuality in the quest for enhanced living standards and social visibility.

7

We commence our reflections by confirming that most individual women and men, in the course of their lifetime, experience each and every one of these motivations. However, by far the highest percentage of individuals, reflecting upon several decades of their fully bloomed adulthood, quite voluntarily participate in the rational use of human reason when playing their sexonomic strategies and games.

Sexonomics regards the marketing of human sexuality as a rational quest to obtain maximum happiness. Sexonomic rationality represents an objective form of behavior in which the sexual interaction of intelligent women and intelligent men emanates from reason as the control center. Successful marketing enhances the full development of human sexuality and is expected to secure for the sexonomic players, during the course of their adult years, the highest material welfare and optimal personal happiness.

In Sexonomics, the concept of "pure love" expresses an equal "giving and taking" and "sharing" without any material considerations whatsoever; the sexual togetherness of the lovers reflects deep-seated spiritual needs that enable them to reach the highest plains of happiness. On the contrary, Sexonomics regards the term "fornication" as a business proposition—the rational exchange of cash or assets for loveless sex (sex in its "crudest" form) between those who "need to do it" and those who will "provide the service."

"Happy" marriages constitute a particular example of the effective linkage between sexuality, loving, and sexonomic reasoning; the sexonomic investment is paying off. "Unhappy" marriages represent opposite examples; the investment is not paying off and is most likely going to turn into a disinvestment.

The evolution of society reflects the growing significance of sexonomic reasoning concerning linkages between women and men (lately, even in "same-sex" relationships), situations that are rooted in the magic triangle of sex, money, and power. At all levels of social structure, most of these linkages are directly linked to situations in which human sexuality is intertwined with material self-interest.

Sexonomics ranks romantic love as the highest level of human loving. It is lovemaking in its most exalted—spiritual as well physical—sense, the ultimate biospiritual intimacy. Sexonomic reasoning submits that this linkage, unique in its total indifference to material conditions, is only possible between Lotus-women and Quintessential-men.

Sexonomics views "middle-class" linkages as those that are cultivated by most women and men in the so-called democratic countries of the Western world. In these countries, the women across a whole range of social classes have attained progressively equal status with the men and have become free to participate in a whole range of contemporary sexonomic strategies and games. Most women, by assigning varying proportions of significance to power, sex, and money, have become quite skilled in their use of these three determinants of the golden triangle. The rational application of these sexonomic valuations have become important factors in their quest to arrive at the "perfect blending" of their individual sexuality with their personal material preferences. Prearranged marriages, marriage contracts, and family planning may be viewed as legalized expressions of sexonomic reasoning in action.

Yet in spite of the significant improvement in the condition of women at lower levels of the social structure, some past historical forms of the known sexploitation of women still linger on in contemporary society; in literally all societies, some women are still engaged in what Sexonomics terms royal-prerogative prostitution. Historically practiced at the level of rulers and ruling classes in most countries and cultures, this form of sexonomic behavior first gained social acceptability in France, where the female practitioners were (and still are) called *courtisanes*. Unlike in street-level prostitution, these linkages are still socially tolerated, if not encouraged, within particular national or cultural settings. *Royal-prerogative prostitution* usually involves an authoritarian dictum that the "chosen" would-be consort has no choice but to accept a one-to-one relationship at the apex of social, political, and financial power. An "established" male "taker" chooses a female partner (very rarely from the same "class") and engages her in a longer-term sexonomic liaison. He shares the numerous perks and prerogatives of his position with his consort, in return for which he expects his "giver" to act not only as his bedmate but also often as a spiritual partner and, at times, a senior policy adviser. In many opposite instances, it is the women themselves who, choosing to work their way up the social ladder by using their sexonomic rationality, intelligently manage to induce the sovereign—or the CEO—to take them into their royal (or presidential, chief executive) bedrooms in the expectation of exuberant sex that is spiced with the condiments of supreme power. These women view male commanders-in-chief of the armed forces, male heads of state, and males at the apex of political power or commanders-in-chief of the armed forces—be they feudal, enlightened, ideological, or even democratic presidential—as men who exude overwhelming sexual attractiveness for their presumed ability to demonstrate superabundant virility. Coveted by women who are either already in their entourage or are aspiring to enter it, these men are expected to offer the whiff of the power that is thought to reside behind each of those imperial briefs in return for moments of instant sexual gratification. Both patriarchal and matriarchal societies provide ample historical examples of the continuous practice of royal-prerogative prostitution. In spite of the socially unequal status of the male and female partners involved, Sexonomics recognizes that, even though the initial trigger may have been power considerations, it may bloom in a few instances into a situation of a genuine, enduring loving relationship. However, ample is the evidence that it may also induce fatal results if the *courtisane* is discovered as being less than satisfactory in bed—or a powermonger, a political schemer, or even in an impromptu embrace with another man.

Practices that resemble the use of royal-prerogative prostitution as a particular form of applied sexonomic strategy are also amply evident in contemporary society—the emergence of a new sexonomic market (in addition to the *Kama Sutra*'s classification of women into "four orders'), a market in which *Vampire*-women exchange cash and sexual services with *Girandole*-men. In this market, on the one hand, the rapidly increasing numbers of female participants make use of their commanding high posts and substantial financial liquidity to secure for themselves—usually for the short term—the virility of men who are willing to sell their bodies to the highest bidders for substantial cash payments. On the other hand, we see women from the highly educated but not yet materially independent subset of "working women" who are known to prefer wealthy male suitors over those who are not only less well endowed financially—even though the various other qualities of the former are identical with those of the latter group of competing men, viz. charm, talent, physical appearance, sensuousness, sensitivity, scent, creativity, potential—but will also be used as stepping-stones for those females in their quest for shortcuts toward the apex of the social pyramid (see chapter 2 on the modern classification of women and men into *five orders*). Even though this new sexonomic market may entail a standard fee of as much as ten thousand dollars for an entire "one-night stand," sexonomic reasoning accords it a very low sexonomic valuation since it constitutes "sex for lots of cash" without any trace of ideal romantic love. Yet Sexonomics cannot term its female and male participants "prostitutes" since any and all of their sexonomic linkages are conducted under conditions of absolute privacy.

The lowest level of sexonomic activity, street-level prostitution—also called "crude or vulgar sex"—is also of concern to Sexonomics since it permeates, apparently in perpetuity, the social fabric of all countries and regions and cultures. Its main emphasis is on the material gain that is derived from marketing an individual female's (or male's) sex organs in the absence of any feelings of love or desire for a longer-term relationship. Practiced mainly by *elephant*-women and *mob*-men, the two lowest social orders in sexonomic reasoning, its participants often seek to reach for men and women from the higher *orders* who are willing to provide their superior purchasing power in order to satisfy their occasional craving for crude sexuality.

Overall, sexonomic reasoning submits that—contrary to and in spite of the moral tenets of the Vatican and the promise of "eternal and pure" love—in the real world, most women and men are conditioned by the material bond that links human reason with the urge for sex and will, therefore, seek to exchange sex for cash or other assets.

Ample are the historical examples encompassing the highest as well as the lowest stratum of society in which human sexuality has been turned into a marketable commodity—especially whenever considerations of power are involved.

Contemporary society has gone through stages of evolution in which what used to be royal prerogatives have now become fairly generalized practices in the quest of women and men as a whole—to find an instantaneously satisfying sexual partner or to proceed to look for one rationally in the expectation of a long-term relationship. A sampling of the whole range of such choices provides us with the following real-life examples of sexonomic reasoning:

> "Most women and men will exchange sex for money, while only a few women and men are destined to experience forever-pure love."

> "If female prostitution were abolished, wives and girlfriends will eventually claim much higher user fees from their husbands and/or boyfriends."

> "Many women are like Sophie, who married John for his money, even though she did not love him. Every Friday at midnight, she lets him use her body, 'a pleasant but uninspiring chore.' But John is happy, feeling secure about having 'all of his' Sophie forever for himself."

> "Many men are like Michael, who, even though poor, exudes overpowering sex appeal. Only twenty-eight years old, he has had sex with hundreds of longing women of all ages. Michael has just engaged in a private contract with Mary Suzanne, a thirty-seven-year-old vice president of an investment bank, who covets him and wishes to 'lease' his body in exchange for substantial annual cash payments. Tired of having no fixed sources of income, Michael accepts with a commitment to offer Mary Suzanne full sexonomic value in return for his sexonomic price."

Even though prostitution is legally prohibited in many countries, its presence is tolerated because it is a means by which a social sexonomic equilibrium is achieved at a minimum modicum of private and social cost.

Attempts by some women to penetrate the private chambers of male kings or presidents always involve a voluntary offer of female sexuality in return for the expectation of experiencing the presumed unique potency of men who command absolute power. Demanding that priests remain forever celibate contradicts the law of nature that is inherent in human sexuality. It is also an untenable tenet as demonstrated by the behavior of a significant number of the clergy at all levels of the hierarchy.

Human sexuality has always been a marketable commodity because the urge for sex has always been stronger than the lust for power or the greed for money.

Sexonomics is a biosocial science. It considers sexuality as one of the three basic drives in our quest for greater material welfare over our lifetime. It views human sexuality in its contemporary setting as neither moral nor immoral. It does not believe in saints or sinners; neither does it consider itself bound by canon law or the Ten Commandments. It rationalizes about the linkage between human sexuality and material considerations. Open-minded and trusting the genius of human reason, it submits that human sexuality cannot be detached from the material conditions in which we live. It concludes that individual women and men have finally become free to make their free choices with respect to both sexual enjoyment and material self-interest. It recognizes that the double standards of the past (e.g., unlimited freedom for men, total suppression of women) have been significantly relaxed in response to the relentless pressure on the part of the masses wishing to enjoy freedoms equal to those ruling over them. Equal opportunity and equal rights for all mankind and the principles of free sexonomic will and personal accountability have finally been categorized, codified, and generally accepted in the various charters of human rights.

Sexonomics assigns to the individual the task of finding her/his own road to personal liberty and progression to happiness. Sexonomics represents the intellectual dimension of this freedom and expresses it as the rational pursuit (versus the former "sinful" ways) of natural sexual enjoyment and the desire for appropriate material welfare. In its essence, Sexonomics is about an individualistic lifestyle that induces consenting adults to use reason in their desire to maximize their sexonomic happiness. This is so because the freedom of modern women and men to seek their maximum sexonomic happiness is now considered the prerequisite for the maximum happiness of society.

Seeking to facilitate our inquiry into the relationship between human sexuality and material welfare, Sexonomics will attempt to link the *Kama Sutra*, the first historically renowned treatise involving sexonomic reasoning, to the *hierarchical* (i.e., from the highest to the lowest social subgroups) structure of modern society. Sexonomics will commence with a short summary of the ancient classification of women into four subgroups that were called *orders*.* Then it will add its own (innovative and progressive) corresponding classification of men for a total of four such gender subgroups in each. Finally, it will proceed to create, reflecting the changes in the social structure of contemporary market capitalism, one additional subgroup in each of these two distinct gender groups as follows:

Ancient: Kama Sutra —> Modern: Sexonomics

Lotus-women	—>	Quintessential-men
Art-women	—>	Lace-men
Conch-women	—>	Vulpine-men
Elephant-women	—>	Mob-men
Vampire-women	—>	Girandole-men

Note: Even though the *Kama Sutra*'s ancient (prefeudal and feudal) classification of women into four distinct subgroups called *orders* reflected a rigid—usually tyrannical—society in which ascent into the next higher group was literally impossible, Sexonomics will retain the term *orders* in its own description and analysis of the subgroups of women and men in our modern society, even though it considers vertical and horizontal mobility as one of our fundamental human liberties. To facilitate our readers' comprehension, the terms *order* and *orders* will always be written in italics in comparison to the word *order* in its everyday usage (e.g., in order to, court order, law and order).

Each of these parallel subgroups (*orders*) of women and men are deemed to constitute their own particular sexonomic market for a total of five, ranking from the highest to the lowest in terms of sexonomic valuation. To each of these markets, the same sexonomic terminology applies, with the following representing its principal expressions and concerns:

1. Sexonomic demand and supply: it is made up of the respective numbers of women and men who enter their particular markets in the pursuit of their sexonomic partners;

2. Sexonomic valuation coefficients: they measure the success (and failure) ratios of the comparative marketability of women and men who participate in their respective markets;

3. Sexonomic prices and opportunity costs: expressions of the private and public assessment of the perceived qualities of sexonomic partners (involving acceptance or rejection); and

4. Sexonomic utility functions: expressions of the overall level of lifetime success (and failure) in the individual woman's and man's quest to maximize their sexual and material happiness.

As a contemporary biosocial science, Sexonomics is engaged in this study mainly because human sexuality has been subject to repression since biblical times; as a consequence, human beings have developed feelings of guilt, have failed to enjoy their sexuality, and have been forced to dissociate sexual activity from material welfare considerations. In fact, they have been unable to maximize their individual happiness. The mistreatment of women throughout history provides the most convincing example—as well as the most shameful illustration—of this dehumanizing evolution and its persisting dismal state even in many parts of contemporary society.

Sexonomic reasoning is preoccupied with four principal inquiries:

First, it studies the linkage between human sexuality and human reason. By observing how women and men behave in their everyday sexual interactions, Sexonomics seeks to learn how human sexuality is linked to reason and how it can be guided by the latter in the quest to enhance sexual pleasure and to secure material success. We believe that this linkage derives from natural law and that its suppression not only negates human liberty but also leads to seriously debilitating economic and social consequences.

Second, as expressed in the particular demonstration of the Western tradition of individual freedom and personal accountability in the chapter "The Fascinating World of Sexonomic Marketing and Success," Sexonomics looks at how women and men go about finding their respective "ideal" partners; it seeks to pinpoint those factors that make for success as well as those that may cause failure.

Third, Sexonomics is especially concerned about those large numbers of women and men who view themselves as "losers" and many of whom may already have "given up." The optimistically scientific orientation of Sexonomics seeks to assist such women and men to rediscover their innate capacity for a fulfilling lifestyle.

Fourth, as a biosocial science, Sexonomics attempts to inform and to enlighten; it will engage in demonstrating to its readers how to rid themselves of feelings of guilt and how to go about maximizing their lifelong expectations concerning their sexual fulfillment and material happiness. The *Sexonomic Institute* will offer courses, engage in private consulting, and make its findings generally accessible in the form of printed matter, formal lectures and seminars, and weekend study sessions.

In short, whether human beings apply reason to their sexuality solely for material gain or whether they market their sexuality just for "the love of it," sexonomic reasoning promises to be a lot of fun because it will apply the entire range of the human genius to the enhancement of this particular dimension of human quality lifestyles without fear of doctrines, dogmas, and possible persecution.

In the *Sexonomics Textbook,* we shall first redefine, with tongue-in-cheek mischievousness, the female sexual organs and qualities and their male counterpart organs and qualities, stopping for a brief moment to reveal notions and emotions concerning "*saints or sinners.*" Next, we will proceed with a detailed discussion of the *five orders* of women and *five orders* of men (as per our short review on page 6).

With all these introductory things done, we shall then, in our chapters on *sexonomic strategies and games,* engage in demonstrating how women and men should go about meeting with and eventually securing for themselves their own true sexonomic partners with whom they will expect to share a lifetime of fulfilling sexuality as well as the net proceeds from their joint investment into their spiritual and material happiness.

Finally, we shall then turn to *part 2* in order to elaborate on the concept of "Sexonomics as a science"; in its first chapter, we will resume our discussion of the *sexonomic heart* with emphasis on each of the five respective female and male *orders* and with the purpose of enabling our readers to determine which of these sexonomic subgroups—female or male—is most appropriate for each of them. In its second chapter, we shall discuss the age-old concept of the merger of the "sacred feminine" with the "godly masculine" by presenting it in what we shall henceforth term the Golden Triangle. Using sexonomic rationality, we shall illustrate the state of the "perfect union" between the feminine and the masculine and will analyze the consequences of decisions to shift from "pure love" to a human sexuality that reflects the influence of material preferences and/or power plays upon sexonomic choices. In chapter 3, we shall then account for the essential basic vocabulary of Sexonomics. Mastering these terms—and hopefully consulting with us in order to obtain full understanding—should enable our readers to rate their own "sexonomic standing" and their contentment (or dissatisfaction) with it—fundamental requisites if they are to engage successfully in their preferred sexonomic strategies and games (which may include their answering the questions contained in "Do I Know Myself?").

Before we proceed with our inquiry into the female and male sexual characteristics and their sexonomic qualities, we take great pleasure in inviting those of *you,* our visitors who have already developed a sense of urgency about "Sexonomics," to read "Do I Know Myself?", answer its ten questions that involve your personal assessment of the quality of your sexuality and its contribution to your material and spiritual happiness, and possibly transmit your answers to us for analysis.

Your Sexonomics: "Do I Know Myself?"

Basic Questions

    a.   At what age did you commence your full sexual linkages?

    b.   Has your experience been
        i.   mostly romantic (pure love)?
       ii.   mostly biological (fornication)?
     iii.   mostly for material considerations (involving money or power)?

    c.   How much do you know about how the capitalist financial market works (0 means very little; 100 means you're a specialist in finance)?

1. On a scale of 0–100, how do you rate the quality of your past sex life (0 means terrible; 100 means totally satisfactory)?

2. On a scale of 0–100, what do you expect from life (0 means purely romantic loving; 100 implies your quest for maximum material gain from marketing your sexuality)?

3. On a scale of 0–100, reflecting on your past, how do you view the linkage between reason and your sexuality (0 means that your sexuality has been mainly an emotional experience; 100 means that your sexuality is fully controlled by reason)?

4. On a scale of 0–100, have the attempts to market your sexuality resulted in
    a.   dismal failure (0–20),
    b.   unreasonably low returns (21–39),
    c.   adequate performance (41–59),
    d.   rewarding payoffs (61–79), or
    e.   a highly satisfactory lifestyle (81–100)?

5. On a scale of 0–100, how have your partners viewed your sexuality and your material means (0 means that you were accorded highly romantic sexuality but as lacking abundant means; 100 means that you were considered asset-rich but a very poor romantic lover)?

6. On a scale of 0–100, state whether feelings of guilt have ever inhibited the marketing of your sexuality (0 means the absence of any feelings of guilt and therefore a most successful marketing of your sexuality; 100 means overwhelming feelings of guilt and therefore poor sexonomic performance).

7. On a scale of 0–100, state whether accepting payment (cash, assets, or power) in exchange for your sexuality has enhanced your lovemaking ability (0 means it has diminished it totally; 100 means optimal sexual performance on your part because it's cash-and-carry).

8. "Western organized religion generally suppresses sexual desire and performance even though they are naturally imbedded in human beings." (0 means that you strongly disagree; 100 means that you fully agree).

9. Using reason in making your sexonomic choices is very much like investing in the stock market, betting, or playing poker—a rational quest to make quick material gains even if you are involved in a situation of "purely romantic" loving (0 means you strongly disagree; 100 means that you fully agree).

10. On a scale of 0–100, do you see yourself involved as a sexual partner with a male or a female "chief executive officer," political, financial, business, or military (0 means "never" since power and morality are two opposites; 100 means "whenever possible" since "bedding" with a person with absolute power represents the ultimate sexual opium)?

Now please proceed to review your answers and add up your score, for each question.

If the total score for your ten answers is 800 or higher, we congratulate you for your great success in marketing your sexuality and for attaining the status of an early expert in Sexonomics.

If your total score for the ten answers ranges between 600 and 799, then you have achieved high sexonomic standards and are happy not only with your sexuality and its material conditions but also with your freedom to bear them and enjoy them both.

If the sum of your valuations for the ten answers scores a total between 400 and 599, then your subconscious is inhibited and your sexonomic potential has remained underexploited; in fact, you are concerned about the lack of success in marketing your sexuality and its detrimental effect upon your joy in life.

If the sum of your valuations for the ten answers falls into the still lower range of 200 to 399, you deem yourself discontented, even though you reveal valuable sexonomic potential. You are therefore urgently advised to liberate your reason from your eminent feelings of guilt about your sexual and material condition and then engage as quickly as possible in a reassessment of your sexonomic situation.

Finally, if the sum of your self-valuations amounts to 199 or less, you must have grown up feeling very guilty about human sexuality and its material environment, possibly because, as a child, you were manipulated into believing that human sexuality was sinful and that its marketing was evil. If so, you will need to consult psychologists who specialized in Sexonomics, and you will also be advised to take a full program in Sexonomics for concerned adults, all of which should enable you to live a normal life and to fulfill your personal sexonomic needs.*

* If you wish to discuss your findings with us, please contact us through our online discussion board or via our e-mail facility at lieux0525@hotmail.com.

PART ONE

The Romantic Art of Sexonomics

CHAPTER ONE

Saints or Sinners: Women and Men and the Qualities of Their Sexualities

Lady LUSSEY (luscious ulotrichan sensuously satisfying exquisite yum-yum): the female sexual organ, vagina, flower (in the Philippines), or cherry (in Southeast Asia).

In recognition of the fact that even Western class structure still contains numerous onerous outdated characteristics, Sexonomics mischievously proposes to rename the sexual organ of modern women Lady LUSSEY, for the vaginas of the two top orders of women, and simply LUSSEY, for the sexual organs of the women of the three lower orders. This distinction seems called for on the understanding that any individual female person in modern society will deem herself free to seek a promotion into one of the top-ranking orders (while also risking a demotion) during her lifetime. Western society has finally evolved toward almost complete individual freedom, and vertical mobility constitutes a fundamental notion in the analysis of human sexonomic rationality and each individual's desire to improve her/his sexonomic lifestyle.

This freedom—especially of women to interact sexually in our society, having always been severely repressed—shows Sexonomics to be totally supportive of women's *natural* liberty to market their sexuality as an expression of their right to climb upward on the scales of their social structure. Sexonomics considers this natural liberty of women as the ultimate social morality. Throughout history, only a few women were accorded this right as a "privilege" (i.e., in the *Kama Sutra*), and Sexonomics duly recognizes that even today, not all women will share equally in the perusal of this recently acquired right. In consequence, to reflect reality, Sexonomics needs to distinguish between two distinct levels of "qualities" of women: the "higher" level, which comprises the *orders* of *Lotus*-women and *Art*-women, and the "lower" level, which consists of *Conch*-women, *Elephant*-women, and *Vampire*-women.

As a reflection of this particular division, Sexonomics also needs to distinguish between the "superior quality" of the Lady LUSSEYs of Lotus-women and Art-women versus the "inferior quality" LUSSEYs of Conch-, Elephant-, and Vampire-women.

The Lady LUSSEYs of the two higher orders of women and the LUSSEYs of the three lower orders of women have been discovered to possess—unequally—the following *three unique qualities*, whose marketing constitute a legitimate use of human reason: *enticement-and-control quality*, *conception-and-delivery quality*, and *pleasure quality*. Each of these qualities has its own valuation and commands, from the bidding males in their respective sexonomic markets, its own particular sexonomic price. The skillful marketing of any or all of these qualities enables top-order female persons to remain in their respective order without any threat of their being removed by "upstarts" from any of the three lower orders of women. As history teaches us, in a vertically mobile society, the exceptionally successful sexonomic marketing by a small percentage of higher-ranking women in the lower orders will enable them to climb upward into the next higher order of women; with the assistance of their appreciative male partners, these women are propelled up into the next higher societal pecking order—an encouraging expression and remarkable consequence of our individualistic and freely entrepreneurial social structure.

Initiating the description of these three qualities, we wish to state that the primary function, discharge, of the Lady LUSSEY is expected to perform to perfection. But we must make allowance for the actual less-than-optimal discharge of many lower-order LUSSEYs, with their consequent and often serious sexonomic devaluation—a situation that exhibits men's much higher preference for women who do not suffer such a health problem (or are willing to take positive action in order to remedy it).

The enticement-and-control quality: This function reflects the inner essence of a woman's personal chemistry and mystique, the primary purpose of which is to attract a competing male from the respective order of men as well as to secure the advances of the more adventurous and loose-footed males from the next higher order. While the enticement part of this quality emanates directly from the scent and bouquet of a particular female person, the control part (reason) will effectively intervene when the male suitor is viewed as undeserving or as unable to fulfill the expectation of the particular female person. Intercourse may but need not always be the purpose of the enticement-and-control quality. Lady LUSSEYs are known for their exclusiveness and their role as one of the principal determinants of continuously high sexonomic scarcity value. But LUSSEYs imply frequent intercourse with many partners with the effect of a significantly diminished sexonomic valuation; in fact, in circumstances in which women's LUSSEYs are overmarketed and overutilized, their sexonomic valuation will sink to the zero level. Inevitably, they will become the sexual "public thoroughfares" of women who are engaged in the lowest forms of the sex trade. Women who are the owners of such zero-valuated LUSSEYs will, in fact, have ceased being sexonomically marketable in their own equivalent order. Such women will inevitably find no men still willing to bid for their companionship, and in consequence, they will suffer the ultimate tragedy of demotion into the next lower order.

Highest-order women are naturally cognizant of the preciousness of their Lady LUSSEYs. Reserved for the most precious moments and offered only sparingly, they exert a powerful and mind-boggling effect on all males, even those in their parallel orders. When skillfully marketed in such an exclusive manner, the enticement-and-control quality of the Lady LUSSEY will bring to her woman-owner many immaterial and material benefits and will assure her of the presence—and the allegiance—of a compatible and sexonomically valuable male partner from her own equivalent order.

The conception-and-delivery quality: Viewed from the standpoint of both the individual and society, this quality is an essential requisite for the high valuation of the Lady LUSSEY; in consequence, she commands a monopolistic price, both from her regular user and from the occasional privileged visitor. Recently, the weight of this quality in a woman's overall valuation has been steadily rising because of the effect of feminism on modern women's willingness to have exclusive control on the number of children they wish to have; men can no longer take for granted their historically exercised prerogative to sire any number of offspring—an evolutionary circumstance which has accorded to women enormous potential bargaining power, private as well as political. Sexonomics wishes to point out that, unlike the enticement-and-control quality, whose weight may vary a great deal from woman to woman and from the highest orders to the lowest, the conception-and-delivery quality shows little variance among the women in each of the particular orders in Western society. Depending on the level of economic development of a particular society, the sexonomic valuation of its women's conception-and-delivery quality will be high or low. In developed economies, it is high; in developing economies, it is low. Generally, we would expect that the sexonomic valuation of women will be the higher, the fewer children the women in a particular society will decide to conceive. Sexonomics wishes to point out that, in Western society, this particular quality of women has lately become clearly subject to a woman's desire to "do with her body as she pleases"—that is, to limit the number of children by controlling conception (and men's access to the site of conception), a personalized wish that the world of men in politics have sought to manipulate by continuing to make women economically dependent upon them or to "bribe" women with a money-linked increase in their sexonomic valuations (for example, by paying baby bonuses or child-carrying premiums or by increasing day care allowances or by building more day care centers).

The conception-and-delivery quality of the Lady LUSSEY is possibly a woman's ultimate weapon in securing for herself equal rights and the prospect of a lifetime revenue stream which will match that of men. Women's sexonomic rationality would demand that women unify in this quest and withdraw, if needed, their bodies from all men (which must especially include the men in power)—a strategy which would work well with all women except those whose love is "pure" or those who love "too much."

The pleasure quality: If a girl's metamorphosis into womanhood succeeds in demonstrating the naturally beautiful and fulfilling experience of human sexuality, the young woman will assign to her sexuality a normal-to-high priority. However, should she assign to lovemaking an unusually high significance, the sexonomic valuation of her LUSSEY will fall. This devaluation will be the larger, the more willing a woman is to make love solely for the satiation of a purely biological urge; that is, the less able she is to assert the control aspect of her enticement-and-control quality. In fact, her desire to offer herself to anyone (versus the strong urge to have only one permanent lover) will eventually render her LUSSEY a "free good" (an object which has some usefulness but which is so abundantly available that it commands no price or exchange value—the extremely promiscuous of the modern young women falling into this category). A totally valueless LUSSEY is of no sexonomic use to her owner; neither does she constitute an interesting subject of sexonomic study. In short, this kind of woman fails to realize the full development potential of this, her second, most remarkable possession (the first being her fully developed power to reason). In consequence, she cannot hope to achieve sexual fulfillment or to accumulate any material benefits. In fact, she will have to endure a demotion to the next lower order of women.

It is the basic premise of Sexonomics that an intelligent woman will take great care to learn how to assert the enticement-and-control quality of her Lady LUSSEY over the sometimes voracious appetite of her *pleasure* function. Sexonomics postulates that a girl's sexonomic valuation is zero at birth and that, starting with puberty, all young women will naturally seek to maximize their sexonomic happiness right into their mature years. However, of the five orders of women, only Lotus-women are viewed as being fully capable of asserting the primacy of their *control* function even when faced with a Quintessential-man; a Lotus-woman will make her Lady LUSSEY available only in return for very substantial personal benefits. (A question for our readers: How do you rate Madame de Pompadour types of women? Are you inclined to rank them automatically as part of the order of Lotus-women, the highest order—if only because Madame de Pompadour is said to have slept with two kings?) Regretfully recalling the deprecating assessment from the *Kama Sutra*, we must confirm that the *Elephant*-woman's low state in sexonomic society is explained by the fact that she cannot control her forever lust for intercourse; her sexonomic valuation can never be higher than ten out of one hundred, reflecting the minimal marketability of her unrefined rubberlike LUSSEY.

As for the valuation of the LUSSEYs of Vampire-women, the lowest order of women in contemporary society, Sexonomics is speaking of the special case of those women who love no one except themselves, even though they are often quite refined. Loving only themselves, they are unable to offer their male partners any love-induced sexual pleasure and must, therefore, compensate them with cash payments for their nonloving sexual services.

Lady LUSSEYs: Saints or Sinners?

Our discussion of the Lady LUSSEY and her three qualities would be incomplete without reference to some of the adjectival terminology which is typical of how men, even the most literate, view the biological pulsations and apparently sociable strategies concerning the anatomy of the human female. This section in our *textbook* is meant to help explain the implicit subtitle, viz. the "not-so-holy little place."

At the root of this discussion lies the issue of the personal privacy of the Lady LUSSEY/LUSSEY. On the one hand, continuous historical, legal, and constitutional attempts by many generations of women in Western society have been able to secure personal privacy for themselves with slow but remarkable official success; the Lady LUSSEYs or the LUSSEYs of individually successful women have always been the innermost sanctum of their woman-owners, and she had, therefore, been made accessible throughout history by her owner to men other than her de jure partners. We are speaking here not of the misappropriation of the Lady LUSSEY by her de jure or de facto long-term user but of the power and the ultimate freedom of a woman to make her own choice, unrestricted by any outside decision making—to offer herself, temporarily or long-term, to any particular male who will reflect purely her own choice.

In Sexonomics, a higher-order woman is considered her Lady LUSSEY's exclusive natural proprietor. A Lotus-woman—uncompromisingly seeking "pure love" in her linkage with Quintessential-men—will never have to share her Lady LUSSEY in return for material considerations. An Art-woman, also very selective, will normally offer her Lady LUSSEY to Lace-men who will have earned her trust and whose sexuality this woman has profound interest, whether or not she already lives in a "permanent" affiliation. Evidently, "her" men, the "permanent" or the "part-time" visitors of her Lady LUSSEY, are expected first to satisfy fully her pleasure function, "material consideration" being viewed only as "incidental." For the women in the three lowest orders, material circumstances pay an increasingly important role, with the values and forms of payment depending on the following considerations:

- the women's own time pressure and preference (instantaneous or long-term): the intensity of the need to engage in nonloving copulation (a negative sexonomic valuation arises when a woman absolutely longs for intercourse and may, therefore, be forced to purchase it);

- the nonloving bidding men's own time pressure and preference: a woman's innate ability will know how to secure the highest possible material reward—cash or charge—from a male who is desperate for a LUSSEY;

- the woman's desire and consent to "let him do it," because she knows that he loves her and is "good" to her; and

- gender politics power considerations: at all levels of male hierarchy, women's temptation and desire to entice and "conquer" commanding-post men and their presumed serene, logical, aloof, and supposed impenetrable purity of ssmale reason (cardinals and popes included) with the primeval power of the scent of her Lady LUSSEY or LUSSEY.

The sexonomic significance of each of these factors is measured in *sexons*, the basic units that express both the material calculus and the immaterial component of human sexuality. A high fee involves a smaller number of women and puts more emphasis on the purely material element (e.g., prostitution) and a low fee expresses either a larger number of women or the presence of a love component (the person who loves selflessly and purely is presumed to "do it" for free). In case of an equally intensive lust on the part of both partners in fornication, the material considerations will cancel out—a zero-sum sexonomic calculus.

In the contemporary Western world, the evolution of law has made the term "with consent" absolutely legally binding. Even the most vicariously lusting men from the lower orders cannot just go ahead, seek out, and grab a coveted LUSSEY. This fact applies—even though apparently unequally—these days to both the men of power and the men of the gutter. Unlike in the old times when such men were legally unrestrained in their desire to usurp a woman's *natural liberty* to protect the privacy of her vagina, such kinds of men—presidents or paupers—are now compelled to forgo the grabbing and to resort to various nonsexist techniques that will be expected to induce a woman voluntarily to market her LUSSEY, on the spot or long-term. In situations of extreme time pressure, lower-order men will normally offer material enticements in the hope that their bid will turn out to be higher than those of other competing males. Men of "quality"—highest-order men—will continue showing full respect for the privacy of the Lady LUSSEYs of their coveted higher-order women. Such men always have and always will manifest genuine and full respect for the sexuality of their women, a mode of behavior that is also explained by their sexonomic refinement and their profound sense of admiration for quality women. A woman who applies her reason and participates intelligently in the sexonomic market of the appropriate high-level order of men will peruse this admiration and be able to secure for herself maximum sexonomic benefits and highest-level fulfillment from her participation in the full development and loving sharing of her sexuality.

Evidently, in contemporary society, we can no longer judge as moral or immoral a woman's disposition of her Lady LUSSEY. This is so because we live in a free society, whose sexonomic rationality implies that only the natural owner of the Lady LUSSEY knows what is best for her. The net sexonomic return to participating women will be the higher—especially in cases of long-term "rentals" of their Lady LUSSEYs—the more exquisite turns out the performance valuation of their three principal sexonomic qualities.

All in all, higher-order men are known to have assigned—speaking in romantic prose—five *attributes* to the Lady LUSSEY and her three unique qualities, of which the first three express delight, the fourth reveals apprehension, and the fifth conveys a feeling of anguished amusement—male views that a well-informed and perceptive woman will know how to use to her best sexonomic advantage. These attributes are as follows:

> Holy Lady LUSSEY: consecrated, sacred; morally and spiritually perfect; innermost shrine; adorable being; the quality thereof.

Most adolescent males and the very romantic grown-up ones bestow upon the Lady LUSSEY this exalted status and are willing to pay her natural owner the appropriate sexonomic-valuation premium. Orders of women below that of Lotus-woman who attempt to market their LUSSEYs with an air of exclusiveness, of unattainability, of scarcity will achieve a sexonomic valuation higher than the average of their respective order and will enjoy appropriate material benefits. One of the forever intriguing issues concerning men's behavior vis-à-vis women has to do with the question of why men would pay highest premium prices for what they presume are the purest and holiest of women only to get such women into bed as quickly as possible and to subject their "saintliness" to an immediate and effective depreciation and possible moral depredation.

> Wholly Lady LUSSEY: entirely, completely, totally, exclusively.

To the sophisticated perceptive men of the two highest orders, this term signifies the ultimate quality of both "holy" and "holey" in the uniqueness of the bouquet and composition of a Lotus-woman's Lady LUSSEY. This rare and exclusive quality is reserved only for the very top-bidding males from the highest order, the order of Quintessence, and her reservation spot price and long-term investment cost are absolutely the highest. While "wholly" does not imply that this unique kind of Lady LUSSEY will become and forever remain the monopoly of her exquisite user, it is presumed that her natural owner will be inclined to wish to remain with this privileged male for he is not only of the highest quality as a person but also possesses in his Sir MOJJ (male sexual organ, see below, page 15) that unique and extraordinary means of pleasure that will fully satisfy the requirements of even the most demanding Lotus-woman.

Holey Lady LUSSEY: the sexonomic quality of a warm, sensuous, receptive, and luscious orifice in a responsive woman's body.

The acute presence of a delicate and very discreet Lady LUSSEY commands the highest spot price (and the high-value long-term cost equivalent of a male's sexonomic self). All highest-order men long exactly for this quality of a woman and her sexuality.

Unholy LUSSEY: a degeneration of the above.

A female orifice that has been rendered accessible to many men and is viewed by other men as quickly deteriorating in quality—a LUSSEY that is about to become a public thoroughfare. But even the vaginas of these kinds of women will still be visited by male spot users who are desperate enough to seek them out and who will pay the corresponding spot price. However, men of the higher orders and those lower-order men who may have acquired refined sexonomic skills and experience will never seek to conclude such long-term affiliations with LUSSEYs of this kind of ill repute. In contemporary society, the mass marketing of such low-quality LUSSEYs on and off the streets is certainly a sign of the existence of a large number of men who have no taste or are simply unable to control their sexual appetites.

The not-so-holy little place: the cause of continuous trepidation in men.

A LUSSEY that is viewed by most men as not constituting the exclusive domain of her male user or tenant; a vagina that is perceived as not immune to penetration by MOJJs of other competing males from the lower orders; an orifice that loves the occasional fornicating excursion with male members from the lower orders—if only to demonstrate the absolute liberty of her natural owner to do with her as she pleases whenever she feels "like it"; a LUSSEY whose sexonomic valuation bears witness to her natural owner's modern attitudes concerning the frequency of lovemaking with the selection of coveted partners but some of which is undertaken with a certain style, with flair, and with a graceful portrayal of femininity. This apprehensive yet appreciative reference to the LUSSEY's "lifestyle" attests to the historical freedom of women to be active members of the *underground* sexonomic market during an interminably long era in which self-appointed male moralists, anointed crusaders against sin, and politicians elected for their presumed code of male ethics sought to impose upon women forms of behavior that men consider "virtuous" but that are contrary to the laws of nature and concerning the natural liberty of women. Fortunately, in contemporary society, this attribute of the LUSSEY is viewed as typical of the modern liberated woman and is clearly demonstrated in all sexonomic markets, from the street-level soliciting members of the "oldest profession" right up to and including the haute *volée* and some of its most distinguished and esteemed ladies.

Sexonomics notes with great interest that most modern men have by now accepted the distinct possibility of "their" lady companions engaging in the occasional sexonomic detour with other men. These men now appear quite willing to accept this contemporary phenomenon, whereby the adage concerning the "cuckold" and his shameful implication seem by now to have been replaced by emerging feelings of the universal "blood brotherhood" of those men who are deemed to have been fortunate enough to cohabit with "each other's" women. Most men seem to have quietly recognized that "their women" too—wives and roomies included—may not anymore be viewed as exempt from the assertion that women are now absolutely and irrevocably free to engage in the sexonomic marketing of their bodies as they see fit. As a matter of fact, these days, an increasing proportion of married men whose wives are employed do not even prefer to divorce their wives over their "unfaithfulness." It appears, therefore, that this kind of historical agony hailing back to the ancient times, of an uncompromising attitude on the part of men who "owned" their women, has by now been increasingly replaced by the men's desire to be "accommodative" in return for enjoying the increasing competitiveness and purchasing power of their working wives, be they professional or executive. Many working women, who would have been stigmatized just one generation ago (and would have been left "literally unmarriageable"), now even enjoy the freedom and opportunity of moving from the lower orders to the higher orders—as a consequence of the successful sexonomic marketing of their LUSSEYs.

Yet we should also note, with equal interest, that the successful sexonomic marketing of an individual higher-order woman's "not-so-holy little place" has always commanded a much higher "spot price" than has the instant "user's fee" that men would normally pay for the LUSSEYs of the lower orders—an irrefutable fact that cannot be explained solely in reference to biology and Sexonomics.

Sir MOJJ (masculine orotund jazzy joystick): male sexual organ, penis, cock or dick (American slang; these two sexist terms are still being used to express the essentially primitive, mindless and thoughtless, uncontrollable, and forever combative and always-ready-to-explode self-seeking attitude of the male chauvinist pig—in spite of the rising voluntary propensity of lower-order females to engage in frequent fellatio).

Sexonomics reserves the term *Sir MOJJ* for the sexuality and sexonomic significance of the human male in the top two orders of men and the use of male sexual organs in the quest to engage their owners in optimally and sexonomically satisfying linkages with their equally high-quality female partners. For the lower orders of men, the term will simply be *MOJJ*, a vastly lower valuation (caused by overall vulgarity and, at times, by such men's brutalizing physical dimensions).

Sexonomics presumes that women of caliber can and will distinguish between high-quality Sir MOJJs and low-caliber MOJJs in a setting in which "high-quality" may refer at times to "small but sensuously agile" rather than "enormous but crudely vehement."

The sexonomic significance of the *Sir MOJJ* lies in his three unique qualities, the so-called *Three Ps*, each of which, in the eyes and experience of women, possesses its proper sexonomic valuation and commands an appropriate short-run and long-run price. Over and beyond the Sir MOJJ's "primary function," we are speaking of the qualities of *potency*, *perseverance*, and *prolificity*. The skillful marketing of these qualities will guarantee the competing male a high degree of sexual pleasure, an increasingly visible success in his material lifestyle, and possibly even access to the next higher order of men. A discerning woman will know intuitively that the Three Ps of Quintessential-men are by far the ones worth striving for, but most women will be compelled by the scarcity of high-quality men to settle for men of the lower orders and their relatively unimaginative and cruder ways of going about satisfying the sexual needs of their female partners. With respect to all men, we must specifically refer to the men's waste discharge (the "primary function" of Sir MOJJ or MOJJ). When it functions normally, its sexonomic valuation is zero (neither positive nor negative). However, many males, as they grow older, suffer with problems owing to the enlargement of the prostate gland. Consequently, a negative valuation occurs when such problems, in particular in their older years, necessitates intervention, surgery, or even the removal of the entire prostate gland, with serious repercussions on the most important qualities of the organs of male sexuality.

The quality of potency: This function of Sir MOJJ reflects the very personal capacity of a competing male from any of the five orders of men to render unto the women of his choice (and normally from the respective order of women) the physical requisite for an exhilarating and fulfilling lovemaking relationship. The quality of potency derives from the following four naturally imbedded propensities of men: *pukkacity*, *sensitiveness, erethism,* and *dimension.* These four propensities enable a human male to offer his female partner a genuine and full-bodied thrust; a perceptive, responsive, and delicate adjustment capacity; an instantaneous and effective fine-tuned linkage between passionate mind stimulation and a potent sexually aroused lovemaking instrument; and last but not least, a visually clearly demonstrated capacity to reach up to and explore to the fullest even the most secluded niches of the mystique of a demanding Lady LUSSEY.

> *Pukkacity:* the superior impact of the propulsion capacity of a man's solidly built and fully erect Sir MOJJ or MOJJ upon a sexually aroused female in each of the five female orders.

> *Erethism:* the brain-gene-induced and chemistry-induced excitement that fills a man's complete being when his sexuality is fully aroused by his female partner.

> *Sensitiveness:* the quality, in higher-order men, of readily responding to even the slightest changes in their female partners' sexual needs coupled with his instantaneous willingness to effect a stimulating change of pace (or even to break off the lovemaking if so desired).

> *Dimension:* The physical size and characteristics of a particular Sir MOJJ or MOJJ is discussed over and over again by each generation of women, lately even quite openly and with frequent empirical sampling in each of the orders of women. Even though most individual women, when asked, will respond that "size is not important," age-old is the question of whether the Sir MOJJ feels "better inside" when "he" is "long and thick" rather than "short and thin."

Sexonomics has been told repcatcdly, all other performance criteria viewed as equally pleasing, that the former size is accorded the higher sexonomic valuation (a view that is confirmed by the fact that the most coveted dildoes in sex shops are those eight inches or longer). However, higher-order women will often view unusually large size as boring, unimaginative, uninspiring, and usually quite ruthless. In consequence, they will eventually rank as superior the smaller but more agile penises. Lotus-women have been overheard conversing in their own sophisticated ways about the physical attributes of their Quintessential-men and are rumored to be both mystified and enchanted by the "ideal proportion" of "three times eight-and-a-half inches"—circumference of the brain ("top-level"), size of the feet ("perfect balance"), and size of the Sir MOJJ ("truly remarkable in his fully erect potency). In the view of these ladies, this particular size of "their" Sir MOJJ reveals a very special flavoring because, unlike the numerous larger penises, this "ideal" size provides the ideal environment for pukkacity, sensitiveness, and erethism, each of which is guaranteed to please "his" Lady LUSSEY's even most exquisite sexual desires.

An issue that arises from the question of the "proper" dimension of the Sir MOJJ concerns male circumcision. Sexonomics views *unnecessary* circumcision as having a negative effect on each of the Three Ps of the Sir MOJJ, resulting in a diminution of his sexonomic valuation. Modern medicine, having discovered effective remedies and treatment for various inflammation-linked penis disorders, leads Sexonomics to submit that this infant-brutalizing intervention should be discontinued for not only does it cause psychic damage to the male infant—inhibiting the blooming of the potency of a maturing Sir MOJJ—but it also shortchanges the women users of quality performance that, by the laws of nature, should belong to them—a saddening loss. Sexonomics also totally objects to the still widely practiced—especially in some regions of Africa—female genital mutilation.

Of the four propensities of the male sexual organ, sensitiveness is valued very highly by the Lotus-woman; erethism is appreciated, especially by the Lotus-woman and the Art-woman, because it constitutes the male response to the full application of a female's enticement-and-control quality; pukkacity is simply adored by all orders of women in their personal response to a deeply imbedded primeval need; while dimension is also an undoubtedly important requisite over the long term for all five orders of women, even though the perception of the significance of dimension ranges from the refined and thought-provoking presence and joy of a reasonably dimensioned Sir MOJJ in the loving patterns of the top two orders of women down to the vulgar craving by the lower orders of women for the primitive volatility of the enormous MOJJs of their respective counterparts in lower men's orders.

The quality of perseverance. This function of the Sir MOJJ reflects the ability of the competing male from any order of men to prolong, to the liking of his female partner, the pleasure of lovemaking togetherness. This quality involves two conditions: the incessant quest of the male partner to enhance the sexual responsiveness of the Lady LUSSEY and the sincere effort to assist her in reaching her own climax. For the top two orders of men, this quality reaches the state of personal virtue since the members of these two orders can prolong (or even shorten, if such is their lady partner's desire), at will, the duration of lovemaking in direct response to the expressed erotic desire of a Lotus-woman or Art-woman—for a perfect blend of erethism and sensitiveness. Evidently, such ability presumes enormous brain control and commands very high sexonomic value, which is typical of higher-order men. What makes this quality of the Sir MOJJs of the top two orders of men such an unforgettable sensuous experience for their top-order female partners is the explicit care which their lovers will take to please them in contrast to the attitudes of Vulpine-men and Mob-men to whom self-gratification represents the ultimate personal goal of intercourse.

The quality of prolificity: This function of the Sir MOJJ constitutes, in fact, the foundation upon which potency rests and from which perseverance derives its energy source—the capacity of the member of a particular order of men to engage in repeated lovemaking over a short period of time and in the highest possible frequency of lovemaking over his lifetime while maintaining at their optimal level the *four conditions of potency* and also, each time, disposing of an abundant reserve of ejaculating mass permeated with an infinite quantity of vibrant semen—each with vehement forward locomotion. While this quality will diminish in value as the men in all orders become older, its sexonomic valuation remains high quite throughout a man's life since women, especially those who wish to conceive, will gladly pay a premium for those men who can clearly and convincingly demonstrate the quality of superior prolificity.

In addition to his own unique three qualities, the Sir MOJJ shares with his opposite, the Lady LUSSEY, the qualities of enticement-and-control and pleasure.

The *enticement-and-control* quality of men is principally derived from natural law—self-assertion, territoriality, possessiveness, protectiveness. But society-induced forms of behavior also play a fundamental role—prudence, tolerance, approbation, sympathy, love. All of these factors will, in their relations with women, serve the function of courtship and possibly of consummation. Knowing of women's preference for materially secure conditions, the men in all orders will, according to the means which are standard to their particular order, seek to provide these means, if only as the material backdrop to their Three Ps. The higher-order men will also add, as a counterpart of the higher-order woman's personal chemistry and mystique, those personal traits which history has shown to be very effective in the pursuit of courtship and consummation: charm, charisma, leadership, an air of casual indifference to wealth, and manifest noblesse and chivalry. However, the "control" aspect of this particular quality means something different with men; unlike the women, for whom "control" means the securing of an equal exchange (exchanging oneself for an equal or higher-quality male), men view "control" as securing women strictly for themselves—a one-sided monopolistic relationship. Even though this monopolistic relationship will normally command a very high price (for which a modern woman would ever wish to sell all of her sexonomic freedoms?), many men prefer paying for it, possibly as an expression of their deeply imbedded *law of territoriality*.

The *pleasure quality* of men is evidenced in their Three Ps, with the respective highest sexonomic valuation for Quintessential-men and the lowest for Mob-men. Men's Sir MOJJs or MOJJs can never be labeled "public thoroughfares," however frequently they may have been utilized by ever larger numbers of women; however, a sexonomic devaluation may occur if men engage in such activity so often that their prolificity suffers from less-than-optimal performances. Such a situation may apply, in particular, to Girandole-men because Vampire-women, who constitute their sexonomic market, are intensely demanding and unforgiving in their desire to fornicate instantaneously, whereby a significant deterioration of these men's ability to perform at peak capacity will be talked about and will eventually lead to a significant deterioration of their sexonomic valuations. However, higher-order men will never misuse the Three Ps of their Sir MOJJs since they know that the highest-order women insist upon being catered to with superb servicing. The two top orders of men know only too well that such quality can be provided only if prudence is adjoined onto lovemaking patterns and if special emphasis is placed upon mutually accepted exclusivity. Lower-order men's enticement-and-control function is often found to emphasize the appreciation of better-to-do lower-order women in equal exchange for the self-imbued potency and prolificity of these men, especially of the Vulpine order, which provides the largest percentage of the so-called studs.

CHAPTER TWO

Female Sexonomic Players:
The Five Orders of Women

Lotus-woman

The order of Lotus-women is the highest order of women. The few women who belong to this order represent highest value to the world of men and will, therefore, command the highest price during their entire lifetime. This is so because the Lotus-woman offers ultimate value and commands the highest sexonomic valuation as a female person and for each of the three qualities of her Lady LUSSEY.

The Lotus-woman has the following vastly superior qualities: In Indian mythology, she has a body soft as petals, skin tender and fair as fragrant pollen, a Lady LUSSEY resembling a lotus bud about to burst open. She also has a lilylike scent, swanlike gait, low and musical voice; she also possesses refined taste, cleverness, and natural aptitude for command.

Unlike Indian mythology, Sexonomics considers the Lotus-woman in the modern sense of women's qualities: She is superbly intelligent, highly educated, and totally committed to individualism. She is politically astute and works incessantly for a better and more humane society. She is exquisite in her taste for music, art, and couture; abounds in social graces; and performs brilliantly in communication. Daringly a trendsetter and magnificently select in her choice of male companions, she is reserved to perfection in her exercise of the three qualities of her Lady LUSSEY. She will never bed with men below her order counterpart since her bed is reserved for the Quintessential-man because in him, she finds, to her repeated great delight, the virility of a true woodsman and the prolificity of an experienced shepherd while also enjoying the rare dimensions which are so truly appropriate to his own exalted status among men.

These superior characteristics and qualities render the Lotus-woman perfect, the consequence of which is that the number of women in this order is very small. The Lotus-woman has highest value and commands highest price. The market for Lotus-woman is exclusive, and not even the church or the divine right of kings will ever have direct bearing on her status. Her market valuation rests on the recognition that she is unique, someone who commands a natural monopoly and sets her own sexonomic value and price. *Queentessence* is the name of the market in which she meets with the Quintessential-man and in which her extraordinary personality comes to full bloom. The Lotus-woman is not limited to a single occupation or profession since, by her very nature, she is multidimensional. In the world of politics, the Lotus-woman will be a leader of the left or of the right but not normally of the center for she has vision and wishes to give dynamic direction rather than seek guidance or search for compromise. She will never love a man below her order, but she will marry one if, in her estimation, a greater social good will arise from her personal sacrifice (in which case she will choose to have several but very distinctly superior lovers). The Lotus-woman never has any problems making her control quality prevail over her enticement function, and her sexuality never ranks as her first priority. She does not have to prioritize this because whenever she engages in lovemaking, she makes it the very best possible with the superb partner with whom she will know how to achieve the most fascinating highlights and earthshaking orgasms.

Art-woman

This order of women is the second highest and accounts for about 15 percent of the female population.

In Indian mythology, the Art-woman is less regal in appearance than the Lotus-woman but has a tender body and well-rounded thighs; moreover, she is delicate, inviting, and fragrant. Her Lady LUSSEY has the perfume of honey and is fond of select pleasure and occasional variety. Quick and perceptive, the Art-woman knows how to handle intrigue and seeks to advance her self-interest or even move up to the order of Lotus-women—if necessary, through (very intricate) scheming and manipulation.

In the sexonomic definition of this order of women, the Art-woman will normally seek to compensate for her second highest order status by finishing university and going on to graduate school and then engaging in one of the professions, or she will attempt to excel in a field of the arts or media. She is very intelligent and will be susceptible to training in logical method, but she can also easily adapt to the arts in general and will be very effective in teamwork as a group leader. She will perform her functions conscientiously and with resolution but with emphasis on being noticed. A career path being one of the Art-woman's main aspirations, she will, for material gain or for promotions into posts of power, consent to granting sexual favors (even to the select Vulpine-man of unusual entrepreneurial talent and millions of dollars worth of assets, provided he shows himself discreet and respectful of her superior-order status). The Art-woman knows how to delegate authority but will manifest some degree of uncertainty if entrusted with those decision-making powers that are the proper realm of the superior capacity of the Lotus-woman.

As wives and lovers, Art-women will normally manifest an attitude of faithfulness by convincing themselves that sex does not constitute a forever enduring priority in their dealings with men. But they also recognize that rendering themselves relatively scarce will enhance their sexonomic valuation—a necessary condition for their possible advancement to the highest order of women. In seeking this advancement, the quality of enticement-and-control forms an essential part of the Art-woman's overall sexonomic strategy. Properly manipulated, this quality will boost her lifetime sexonomic valuation and will earn her the highest possible sexonomic utility at a level well above the average for her order (sexonomic utility: that combination of satisfying sexuality and level of material welfare which is essential for a woman's or a man's happiness, a value of zero meaning total unhappiness and a value of one hundred indicating optimal happiness).

The esthetically pleasing presence of the Art-woman is underwritten by her manifestly intelligent behavior and will guarantee her a representative sexonomic price in the course of her lifetime.

Her market is limited to Lace-men and the occasional Quintessential-man, but she will know how to prevent lower-order women from trespassing into her domain and threatening to compete, especially for the favors of the former, who are Art-women's natural counterpart. The limited entry into their market and the effort to differentiate rather than to conform and to standardize their personalities bestows upon the market for Art-women the distinguished sexonomic definition of *Artlace* and assures this order of women not only of the allegiance of Lace-men but also of the occasional proposition on the part of those Quintessential-men who have more explicit yearning for the unusual. It also offers the Art-woman a satisfying professional career, a rewarding material environment with very high-quality sexuality, and a social status that corresponds to the rising social importance of her order.

Conch-woman

This order of women represents the average woman and ranks as the third highest. Her sexonomic market is termed *Conpine*, which makes up about 55 percent of the female population. Her natural order counterpart is the Vulpine-man. Most

Conch-women expect to remain in this order throughout their lifetime, even though a few will manage to ascend to the order of Art-women.

In Indian mythology, the Conch-woman has a large and often heavy body with long hands and feet; she delights in flowery dresses but possesses an uneven temper because the fire from her forever lustful LUSSEY often takes hold of her owner and threatens to devour her, especially in times of acute sexual fever (modern-day rumor has it that Conch-women are by far the most numerous buyers of high-performance vibrators). But she does engage in moments of reflection, eats in moderation, and is affordable for a man with average income and average taste.

In sexonomic terminology, the Conch-woman is viewed as a person wanting to please, a person always willing to exchange her sexuality for an improvement in her material conditions. Usually quite intelligent, she looks with envy at the superior state of the Art-woman and incessantly lusts after the Lace-man. She tries very hard, and with supreme effort, she is able to demonstrate that behind that apparent clumsiness, one may discover not only a person capable of efficient organization but also a fantastic lover who, by mastering the appropriate techniques, will seek to respond to inquisitive Lace-men's yearning for fornication uninhibited by the social constraints or deodorants of his own order counterpart. The Conch-woman has no fear of smelling like a woman, but her lustful orientation may cause some problems for the ladies in the order of Art-women, who know only too well that quite a few Lace-men will often prefer the Conch-woman's naturally scented and luscious LUSSEY, even though she may appear less delicate and more frequently used than the vaginas of Art-women. This apprehension emanates from the experience that ambitious Conch-women will do "everything" to please Lace-men and will usually succeed because they train their enticement-and-control quality to find and keep a perfect balance between the sexonomic rationality of their brains and the desire of their bodies to experience abundant and unmitigated sexuality.

Elephant-woman

This order of women is classified as the second lowest in quality. Its sexonomic market is termed *Mophant*, with about 20 percent of the population of women and Mob-men representing the order counterpart.

In Indian mythology, the Elephant-woman is portrayed as having a body with coarse skin, large feet and mouth, slouching manners, pungent airs pervading from her thickly covered cleft. She is forever gluttonous and is often shameless about her private needs and dispositions. In sum, this order of women scares men off, except those of her own kind, Mob-men—the greedy, the crude, the brutal, the uncouth, the merciless, the totally undisciplined.

In sexonomic terminology, most Elephant-women lack innate wisdom to handle their sexuality and are naturally inclined to purvey their bodies by catering to the primitive needs of those men who seek instantaneous prolonged intercourse at the lowest possible cost—men in their unmitigated, uncontrollable, insatiable lust for sex. But even those few Elephant-women who do have the innate capacity to assert brain control over their lust and passion are unable to do so because their ravenous LUSSEY's potent oozing forth of their biological effluents remains an uncontrollable force—unless accorded momentary relief by the doglike rigidity and vehement locomotion of the Mob-man's MOJJ. These attitudes make the short-run market for the LUSSEY of an Elephant-woman an active one for large is the number of women and men upon whom fornication bestows the only meaning in life, with accent on quantity and without any semblance of quality. Entry into and exit from the sexonomic market of Elephant-woman is free and amounts to a "pick-me-up" situation usually lasting barely more than fifteen minutes (including credit-card and wash-up time). The quality of the sexonomic merchandise is mass-produced and therefore low; the smells are pungent, and all deals are arranged in cash-and-carry at the lowest valuation and the minimum prices of MOJJ and LUSSEY. This market completely lacks any semblance of the rationality which a long-term investment into enhancing the Elephant-woman's sexonomic valuation should call for. In both the short run and the long, Elephant-women and Mob-men form an entity exclusive to themselves and usually resemble humans in their original state of nature and with accent on brutalizing physical force. However, for the materially poor Elephant-women and Mob-men, their primitive sexuality does fill their lairs with that peculiar caveman-era warmth that is essential for the survival of family life at their precarious margins of existence. Knowing that there is no way out of this kind of lifestyle, Elephant-women settle for a lot of physically active sex and for endless talking about their two main topics in life: their men's sexual attributes and their forever quest for money. Elephant-women who have the misfortune of marrying Mob-men inclined to acquire material wealth will often suffer at the hands of their husbands/partners; for poor or rich, Mob-men will never renounce their primitive and predatory ways.

Vampire-woman

This order of women represents a modern-day innovation—a very special genre whose members originate from the orders of women below the Lotus-woman. Their common characteristics—in spite of their widely different backgrounds, levels of education, degrees of sophistication, and therefore, manifestly different forms of societal presence—prevail by far in their unpleasant homogeneity and render this order of women an execrable human experience. Many Vampire-women appear outwardly charming, graceful, feminine, and even beautiful and will organize with great skill and astutely assert personal leadership in the realms of communications, entertainment, and political and economic hierarchies. But in their innermost selves, they are predatory, ruthless, calculating, narcissistic, and are at all times preoccupied with the quest for power, domination, and maximum material and pecuniary gain. Their external visibility vis-à-vis men is often that of poise and intellectual brilliance, which is why these women often marry rich or secure very high posts in government and industry—but only until their true nature reveals itself by their incessant drive for ever more dominance over all men and all other women.

This order of women does not exist in Indian mythology; it is the outcome of industrialization (in the West as well as in the East) and of the inherent urge of some women to fight and to destroy men. They are razor-sharp, merciless (especially with the older set of women in all orders), deadly in their efficiency. In their minds, the ultimate human self, the members of this order, will misuse and exploit the trust of the occasional friend (all their friendships are "short-term") and the occasional devotion of their sex partner (always a transient) since they owe no allegiance, no fealty, no gratitude, and know no pity. Clearly, this genre of women is the result of the transition from the social hierarchy of the postfeudal era to an industrialized society in which the rise of women's countervailing power has degenerated into a struggle for the survival of the fittest women against all other women and men. Indian mythology was unable to foresee this evolution and its most detrimental consequence, the emergence of the order of Vampire-women.

The Vampire-woman's sexonomic relationships being essentially short-run (she cannot help revealing the predatory nature of her innermost self), her sexonomic happiness heart line shows a discontinuous pattern with many ups and downs since these women are compelled to keep on moving from post to post and between different societal milieus and business environments. After a number of rises to and falls from power (for a lifetime average of about three to four for a typical woman in this order), she descends into an ostracized and lonely existence without friends and without ever again having a hope of even a cursory love relationship. In fact, she ceases being sexonomically marketable for any order of men except a few Mob-men and the "men for hire," the Girandole-men. In fact, had she no funds whatsoever, she would become a free sexonomic good, an unwanted woman. Even the Mob-man, in his forever lustfulness, would demand a hefty cash payment in order to overcome the aversion to her irretrievably fully rubberized LUSSEY and the corroding acidic matter which oozes forth from the Vampire-woman's innermost ultimately destructive self. The sexonomic market involving this order of women is called *Vampdole*, a situation in which these women must hire men and pay them very high compensation for their willingness to endure possibly great abrasions in seeking to penetrate these women's domineering LUSSEYs. At any one time in the short run, Mob-men and even some Vulpine-men may enter this market when in need of money, only to leave immediately and usually never to return. Only the Girandole-men will remain (see "Girandole-men" below) because Vampire-women pay well when economic times are good (in contrast to bad times, when Vampire-women tend to be "downsized" and are forced to earn income in the rapidly expanding porno industry or are even compelled to turn to covert prostitution).

CHAPTER THREE

Male Sexonomic Players:
The Five Orders of Men

Quintessential-man

This order of men is the highest and therefore the most exclusive. Only a small percentage of men in every generation are destined to become members of this extremely select group since, to qualify, the individual male must not only be born with the appropriate qualities but must come out on top in the continuous struggle for ascent into this order, which status he must then safeguard.

The men of this order are men of effective survival, of leaving their positive imprint on the evolution of human society toward the highest moral plane. Copulation with these men has always been the highest aspiration of all five orders of women in their search to guarantee their offspring superior qualities and direct access into this unique, creative order of men. The basic essence of these men is their universal vision. Their innermost urge and their ultimate goal is their search for an enduring world peace.

In addition to the *Three Ps* (which women require of all men), the men of the Quintessential order also possess the following fifteen human qualities, of which nine are exclusive to them:

> a*rtistry*, assertion, authority, *charisma*, *creativity*, endurance, *knowledge*, passion, self-control, *sensitivity*, *sensuousness*, *spiritual wealth*, tenderness, *truth*, and *wisdom*.

With these fifteen superior qualities—of which nine are exclusive—the Quintessential-man ranks highest, by far, of all five orders of men; his sexonomic heart is filled with creativity and happiness for his lifestyle combines absolutely fulfilling sexuality with the joy of being with the Lotus-woman, his natural complement. Since the qualities of the males in this order of men become discernible during their early adolescence, Quintessential-men represent the highest value for which they always command the highest sexonomic price and enjoy highest-level sexonomic utility throughout their lifetime.

The market for Quintessential-men is *Queentessence*, which they share exclusively with the order of Lotus-women. In exceptional circumstances, one or the other top-quality Art-woman, on her way up and visibly an enticing sexonomic prospect, would be offered a highest-quality sexonomic partnership by men of this exclusive order who are inclined toward risky adventures—an offer that such Art-women will find irresistible and will therefore happily accept. The happiness of the Quintessential-man is also explained by the fact that he will never suffer from a malaise known as the "vulva syndrome" (the fear that the Lady LUSSEY of "his" woman might be visited by a Sir MOJJ other than his own), this being so because, in his view, "his" woman would never consider cohabiting with any other male.

Lace-man

The intricate web of the fabric of social hierarchy and of the ranking of women and men in their liaisons and power relations puts special onus on the actions of Lace-men, the second highest order of men—a small but visible and thoroughly organized group—which is involved in communication, administration, and marketing—negotiation, arbitrage, and manipulation. The task of Lace-men is to implement the decisions and to see to the realization of the goals which emanate from the order of Quintessential-men—a task which accords to Lace-men the *appearance* of power and which, therefore, commands respect and follow-through on the part of the ranks of Vulpine-men and Mob-men. It is this apparent disposition of real power that renders Lace-men a very interesting group of individuals to Art-women and the other three lower orders of women.

To sexonomists, the second highest order of men is of profound interest because the men in this group are usually well educated, have job tenure (as they are indispensable to the efficient operation of our socioeconomic system and its powerful political hierarchy), and maintain linkages with which they seek to compensate for their not having first-order status and having to demonstrate, in their day-to-day interactions, their loyalty to the order of Quintessential-men. As a consequence of their own high ranking, the competition for Lace-men as lovers and husbands is very keen (though not as openly vicious as that for the top order of men). This is so because Lace-men also appear concerned about moral standards, adhere to the basic principles of chivalry, emphasize the work ethic, and have direct access to the real sources of power (in the pre-1789 times of the French monarchy, it was the Lace-men at the Court of Versailles who provided trusted passage to the various courtisanes of the kings). Functioning at the second highest level of command, members of this order of men are also quite accessible to lusting women from the royal courts as well as to some of the more select and enterprising women from the order of Conch-women, women who take much pleasure in copulating with their Lace-men masters whom they consider marvelously refined and untiring lovers.

In addition to the Three Ps (which women who love Lace-men will naturally insist upon), Lace-men possess a score of qualities that endear them to all orders of women, except the highest. Six of these represent the less substantive but still very important qualities of Quintessential-men: assertion, authority, endurance, passion, self-control, tenderness. But they also possess qualities that are uniquely their own: technical and administrative skills, organization, patience, manipulation. Furthermore, at the lower end of their total qualities, Lace-men share with the next lower order, Vulpine-men, the traits of combativeness, group affiliation and loyalty, and a touch of cruelty that is induced by their basic instinct for survival.

The sexonomic happiness heart line of Lace-men is high, reflecting their standing and significance in the hierarchy of the industrial-financial society. But let us note that during Lace-men's entire lifetime, their sexonomic status remains well below that of Quintessential-men. The lower esteem which women accord to Lace-men is attributed to the Lace-men's less exalted background (even though many possess very high intelligence), to their possessing immeasurable energy rather than charisma, and to their lacking the seven superior qualities which are exclusive to the highest order of men. Nevertheless, viewed from the vantage point of Art-women and Conch-women, there are definite offsetting advantages in securing for oneself a Lace-man; he will rise quite rapidly into posts of command in business or government, always being physically well conditioned, and will offer his women visibility, social status, and an interesting network of linkages. Even in his later years and well past his prime, the Lace-man possesses the sexonomic capacity to offer full sexonomic value to the women of his order counterpart.

All these traits make for a high lifetime value of the Lace-man with the appropriate quality price that women will have to pay in exchange. The market for Lace-men constitutes *Artlace*. Since the numbers involved are small, the product is select and individually differentiated, entry is quite restricted, and collusion is widely practiced in order to afford this order of men its distinct identity while also enabling some of them to move up to the level of Quintessential-men. To qualify as a lover or as a wife, the bidding woman will have to pay a high price, which may include her contribution as a professional woman; Lace-men prefer associating with professional women who have a normal disposition (versus that of Vampire-women) with respect to sexual and other affiliations with men since they view an Art-woman who earns, saves, and otherwise shares her best in advancing the interest of "her" man and family as a crucial step toward qualifying for eventual admission to the order of Quintessential-men.

Vulpine-man

The member of this order is caught in the balancing act between the two top orders of men and the two lowest orders; there is literally no access to the former, whose women are almost totally off-limits to him, while he is also faced with the forever acute danger of being shunted down to the order of Mob-men and their vulgar subsistence. In consequence, the Vulpine-man has had no choice but to develop and equip himself with the means and the pursuit of the tactics of dynamic survival; he is tough, sinewy, crafty, calculating, shrewd. He also forms peer groups within his own order in seeking to apply pressure toward working out a mutually advantageous and livable compromise among themselves and with the order of Lace-men, whose cooperation and self-interest the Vulpine-man depends for his sustenance and possible advancement one notch higher.

The Vulpine-man normally sleeps with his own kind, the Conch-woman. But he dreams of the Art-woman, intrigued by her scent and her apparent power over the men of her own order. The favorite subject of his dreams involves physical conquest, which is a source of enormous satisfaction and pleasure. Potent, persevering, and prolific, the Vulpine-man seeks to perfect his lovemaking techniques as a substitute for his relative lack of education and only bare semblance of culture. He is sought after by numerous Art-women, especially those in need of much stronger muscle and much more enduring performance than their own husbands can muster—women who, starting in the forties, can afford to pay hefty bonus prices for this kind of special servicing (normally by the younger set of Vulpine-men, who can be unusually physically good-looking even if quite rough and ill-mannered and from whom come most of the members of the order of Girandole-men). On the opposite side, it is Elephant-women who naturally aspire to bed with Vulpine-men as the only direct means of possible escape from their dismal environment. But the set of Vulpine-men is very acquisitive, and even the occasional momentous affair with these men can turn out to be expensive and quite beyond the means of even a well-to-do Elephant-woman, in spite of the propensity of such women to offer thoroughly lustful fornication of unlimited capacity.

Vulpine-men have the appearance of males who possess a vast outpouring of the Three Ps. Their performance is derived from the volatility of their superb physique and often offsets the visible absence of Art-men-like finesse in both preplay and direct intercourse. When engaged in the odd tempestuous lovemaking with the Art-woman, the Vulpine-man may be unusually sensuous and considerate, even though he knows that a permanent linkage will almost never arise. He therefore seeks solace in his own order, manifesting the qualities of discipline and hard work and expressing his loyalty mainly and foremost to his order peers.

Only the very few wise Vulpine-men will have accumulated for their old age those substantive material resources that are required—not only to more than offset their physical deterioration, but also to provide the purchasing power that is needed to attract those younger Conch-women who will offer their sexuality in exchange for immediate material benefits—and thereby earn a possible shortcut to instant riches. In bedding with older Vulpine-men, ambitious Conch-women will engage in effective sexonomic merchandising since they are out to maximize their material self-interest, in return for which they will need to let loose only a very tiny dose of pure loving—a perfectly acceptable situation in their order of women.

The market for Vulpine-men, with Conch-women as their natural counterpart, is termed *Conpine*. It involves fairly large numbers (about 55 percent of the male population) and manifests upward social mobility but contains sexonomic value and price structures that are significantly lower than those of the order of Lace-men. Entry from below is rendered difficult by the restrictive practices that emanate from these men's innate antagonism versus Mob-men, which is partly based on the fear of the latter's massive and concentrated physical sexual power. Entry from above—involving disgraced and demoted Lace-men—is tolerated because it is infrequent and adds to the order of Vulpine-men a touch of the luster of the Lace-man's culture and suaveness.

For a woman seeking a fair degree of stability and very frequent and powerful intercourse, even though at times monotonous, Vulpine-men represent a fairly reasonable acquisition at an affordable price; their relative lack of polish and imagination and often manifest forms of crude behavior are more than offset by their usually quite sizable and always potent MOJJs. In addition, the Vulpine-man's family structure is normally stable, albeit patriarchal in expending much effort to bring up the daughters and the sons in the hope that they would qualify for entry into the next higher respective orders.

Mob-man

Irrevocably locked in with his own kind, about 20 percent of the male population, the Mob-man manifests the characteristics of his mentally and sexually primitive existence—salacious and insatiable, vulgar and voracious, retrenched but explosive. Violence rather than social compact establish an unstable power structure within, and forces of greed and repression rule over his underdeveloped capacity to reason. This order of men is deemed impenetrable by lawmakers and law enforcers; many of its wealthy members will have acquired their riches from dealing in vice, while its poorer members will at times raise their fists in seeking to demonstrate to the higher orders of men that the real, the long-run power rests with the order of Mob-men.

In his relation to women, the Mob-man is usually uncouth, inconsiderate, vulgar, and angry; but he is a rugged, volatile, and tempestuous lover. Interestingly, these very qualities command a remarkably high price for someone in the Mob-man's state as a member of the lowest tier in the order structure of men, especially for Conch-women and the occasional Art-woman on the lookout for a mind—and body-exhausting male. However, whenever these instant liaisons do come up, they are quickly terminated since no woman except the Elephant-woman will find it possible to endure this man's composite of smell, virulence, and vituperation.

Generally speaking, the valuation and the spot rental or long-run purchase price of the Mob-man are low since his only main sexonomic asset is his ability to engage in crude and powerful but brutalizing sex, a service that only very few women from the higher orders will wish to purchase. For women in general, the Mob-man is indeed a very poor investment since the market for Mob-men constitutes a mass merchandising scenario in which Elephant-women are their order counterpart. Mob-men are deemed homogeneous (one is as predictable as any of the others, and his MOJJ, having no personality, is of low long-run sexonomic value); not only are their forms of behavior identical, but their lifetime relations with women lack permanence and are devoid of any respect or dignity. To Mob-men, women are simply "cunts." Except for the occasion when a very sex-starved woman from the next higher order—in mysteriously seeking the ultimately brutalizing sexual experience and the pungent smell of the male animal at his most prehistoric—offers to pay an inordinately high spot price—in return for guaranteed performance, bordering upon sadism, for the rocketlike thrusts of the Mob-man's sinewy and usually enormous-sized MOJJ, the Mob-man sticks to his own kind. But this self-enclosed attitude does not deter him from being forever on the lookout for a higher-order LUSSEY, which will temporarily make him forget his low-order status, a pleasant change of pace that may either cost him some of his assets (if he is rich) or even enable him to earn some money (if he is poor). He knows from more than hearsay (in past times, many a Mob man worked as gardeners and groundkeepers for *Lady Chatterley*—types of "high-caste" women) that even top-ranking Art-women engage in conversations and tantalizing speculations concerning the absolutely frightening proportions of his MOJJ and his man-in-the-state-of-nature disposition to offer satiating female animal pleasure—perceptions that often induce him to engage in frequent masturbation. His contentment in cohabiting with the occasional Conch-woman while lusting after the Art-woman is triggered by his status as their employee, who finds the scents of their LUSSEYs absolutely irresistible. However, in normal times, he settles for his order counterpart, the Elephant-woman, for her two affordable and enticing qualities: her low acquisition and maintenance cost and the naturally gluttonous appetite of her LUSSEY.

Girandole-man

This order of men represents a very special genre whose members originate from the "fallen" members of the order of Lace-men as well as from Vulpine-men seeking to advance in status. Their common characteristics, in their unpleasant and self-centered homogeneity, prevail by far over the occasional distinctness of their varied backgrounds, levels of education, degrees of sophistication, and at times even genuinely pleasing physical appearances and render this order of men useful only to the women of the Vampire order; otherwise, these men's lifestyles are reminiscent of an execrable human experience. Even though quite a few of these men appear outwardly charming, polished, well-mannered, and conversationally quite astute, in their innermost being and their societal function, they are men for hire. Their sole orientation and singular quest in seeking to maximize their lifetime sexonomic utility revolves around their Three Ps—the conscious, unimpeded, continuous attempt to train their sexuality as to derive maximum efficiency and optimal performance from their potency, their perseverance, and their prolificity—as their unique way of earning their livelihood.

Never part of the real labor force and absolutely never engaged in producing any real goods, these men are purveyors of male sexuality in its purest animal sense, in markets that involve mainly the three lower orders of women and with particular attention to Vampire-women, who have the material means to render the lifestyles of these men quite opulent (when they are in heavy demand) in exchange for sensuously propelling but mechanically repetitive thrusts, vibrant and revolving but sometimes tedious locomotion, and the eventual firework-like explosions in the various LUSSEYs of their cash-and-carry partners in fornication.

Girandole-men are incapable of human loving because they had grown totally immune to it since they know that any soul-touching emotions would inhibit their sexual performance and since they had learned early enough in their sexonomic careers that the women who hire men solely for sex not only absolutely insist on efficient performance but also consider any expression of feeling or of commitment as a serious breach of their instant-term contracts. These men are both narcissists and loners. They are the former because they must have bodies in fine shape with the respective broad shoulders and small but firm asses, both of which take torturous hours of lengthy practice to develop and then maintain once the wear and tear from the constant sexonomic abuse makes itself forcefully visible; they are the latter because they are in direct competition with one another, their market being quite restricted and dependent on the economic fortunes and the biopsychic conditions and pressures of the women to whom they sell their sexual services.

Literally and incessantly rubbing off against scores of women (and their genitalia)—of whom quite a few hold socially visible posts of command or are engaged, often with much renown, in the more exalted professions—these men acquire unusual polish and may also get to sound knowledgeable about the arts, fashion, and even the main course of international affairs and worldwide finance, courts of action in which most of their female clients are found. But in their innermost selves, these men are empty, hollow, and lifeless and are not only incapable of but are also totally devoid of feeling and emotion—the ultimate calculus of sexuality in return for money and material gain.

The demand for the services of Girandole-men fluctuates with the economic ups and downs of society. When the going is good and is expected to be better still, the women makers of this expansion will feel good, will earn more income, and will wish to relax more frequently with the result that their demand for the sexual powers of Girandole-men will increase, leading to higher sexonomic spot prices and in an upgrading of the sexonomic valuations of these men. On the contrary, in bad times, this demand will decrease, their spot prices fall, their valuations decrease, and their servicing will devalue (except in the case of those Vampire-women who will copulate more in seeking to be lifted out of their depressed state). These ups and downs will render Girandole-men's sexonomic fortunes very vulnerable and will lead to total demise in their old age; another pile of live corpses on the sexonomic heap of completely wasted and socially unproductive human beings, men whose lifetime investment in maximizing returns from purveying their sexualities will have kept them luxuriously afloat at peak times but will have been destined to sink them into the morass of sexonomic emptiness.

The overall lifetime sexonomic valuation of Girandole-men is low since only instantaneous buyers are involved (even though significant cash may change hands) and because women spot buyers of these men would never marry them. These men are simply not a viable sexonomic investment—that is, an investment involving not only sexual pleasure but also spiritual togetherness and a joint quest for a better material life. Linkages with Girandole-men are a poor investment, also because they lack even a minimum trace of the one basic and common requisite which is the essential quality if a relationship between women and men is to endure: pure human loving. Unfortunately, the evolution of industrial society and, within it, of women leaders in business, finance, administration, and politics—with the singular quest to achieve remarkable success in their own fields but many of whom manifest a complete negation of their personal feminine mystiques—has led to the rapid expansion of the market for the sexonomic services on the part of the Girandole-men, in spite of its unpredictability and instability and its being so totally contrary to the natural disinclination of most human beings to live the empty lives of sex-selling drones.

CHAPTER FOUR

Sexonomic Hearts and Happiness: The Spirit of Sexonomic Enticement

This Chapter is about sexonomic happiness and its graphic expression, the *sexonomic heart*. The description of the degrees of happiness involves every order of women and of men in their interactions in their respective markets. Since the sexonomic heart is our symbol of the ultimate meaning of the togetherness of women and men, its graphic portrayal should enable our readers to assess their own situation and to place themselves into the sexonomic heart that is appropriate to them. Should our readers find that they are placed below the level of hearts for Lotus-women and Quintessential-men (hearts that are completely filled with and represent the ultimate level of lifetime sexonomic happiness), their reading of this chapter and the (subsequent) chapters on sexonomic strategies and games should enable them to undertake the steps that will be required in order to move higher, into the next higher order and thereby to the next higher level of fulfillment. The discussion in this chapter is a generalized description that reflects the experience of hundreds of women and men. For the convenience of our readers who wish to be more fully informed about the meaning and significance of the *sexonomic hearts* of each of the female and male orders, *chapter 1* of "Part Two: The Fascination of Sexonomics as a Science" provides a detailed description and analysis.

The Sexonomic Happiness Heart: Women

The sexonomic happiness heart of women expresses the lump sum total of sexonomic enjoyment and benefits that accrue for women during their lifetime. Quantifiable in intensity of feeling as well as in pecuniary terms, the experience of the heart (which may range from perfect state of happiness to an explicit condition of misery) demonstrates the human female's biological, spiritual, and material success (or the lack thereof) from engaging in the fascinating strategy and games for sexonomic success. Generally speaking, the feeling of happiness starts out with the positive anticipation of a female adolescent, which also reflects the men's relatively higher sexonomic valuation of younger women. However, the initially higher takeoff will be expected to decline, slowly or rapidly, depending on the particular order of women. Beginning with the metamorphosis of a virgin into full womanhood, this decline will go on gradually until menopause and will then fall more rapidly. We must note, though, that every woman may, by sheer personal effort, succeed in slowing down this rate of decline; as a matter of fact, she may even raise her own level of happiness above the average for her particular order, and she may even move up to the next higher order of women (particularly if she proves exquisitely astute in marketing her enticement-and-control quality). Up until recently, and literally in all cultures, female virginity has always commanded a high valuation, privately and publicly. This fact is demonstrated in the high value of the sexonomic happiness heart during the adolescent stage of a human female; the historically intensive demand for virgins (even in Western society up to a few years ago but reemerging today because of the fear of HIV) added a "virginity premium" to her sexonomic market price (assuring her of additional material benefits being paid by those men to whom the "untouched state" of a woman is of greater significance than her overall qualities, including that of the art of experienced lovemaking). In consequence, for centuries, the stigma of a visible devaluation had to be endured by women in the period immediately following the loss of their virginity, a sexonomic loss that can only be made up during the course of many years. Overall, however, also in the recent past, the historical intensity of the demand for virgins has decreased because acquisitive men (versus the lecher types) nowadays prefer working women over virgins, leading to decreasing the sexonomic valuation of "untouched" LUSSEYs.

Expressed in sexonomic terms, the sexonomic happiness of the heart of a modern human female comprises her (a) happiness from sharing her sexuality with her male partner(s); (b) spiritual benefits, which she derives from these physical linkages, and (c) material gains, which may directly or indirectly be the consequence of taking up and maintaining these links. This state of happiness is both evolutionary and additive; for any given period, a human female's sexonomic happiness may be higher than, equal to, or lower than that for any other period. But her level of happiness will rise at a diminishing rate until, when about thirty-eight to forty years old, the female person reaches her second sexonomic apogee. During the period of the rise, a high proportion of the women's utility valuation will be material interest (younger working women will "sell" their sexuality, while older career women will tend to "buy" the sexuality of men in their respective sexonomic markets).

The sexonomic happiness of a typical average female heart for its entire sexonomic lifetime may be viewed as depicted in illustration F-1 (page 38). Looking over this drawing, we note several interesting things:

- the first apogee reflects the historical fact of the virginity premium, which young female adolescents command;

- the second apogee indicates a woman at her prime sexonomic value—mature, professional, with fully developed intellectual and physical powers, and most likely a wife and mother or an enticing lover;

- evidently, a woman's entire level of happiness will be higher or lower depending on her particular state of happiness concerning her lifetime sexonomic relations with men—the aspects of sexuality, material benefits, and the feeling of contentment arising from being successful in both; and

- since the highest sexonomic happiness and welfare absolutely fills the whole heart in the illustration (a state which only Lotus-women can ever achieve), it follows that the empty, unmarked part of the heart in illustration F-6 (page140) represents unfulfilled sexonomic dreams or aspirations or simply a lack of sexonomic talent—a situation that is typical of lower-order women and their much lower level of lifetime sexonomic happiness.

Sexonomics Utility Function Graphics

Illustration F-1: Average for all orders of women

- Much lower level of happiness than the Lotus-woman

- All values are positive; range is zero to seventy sexons.

- Most of the happiness accrues between the ages of forty to fifty.

Illustration M-1: Average for all orders of men

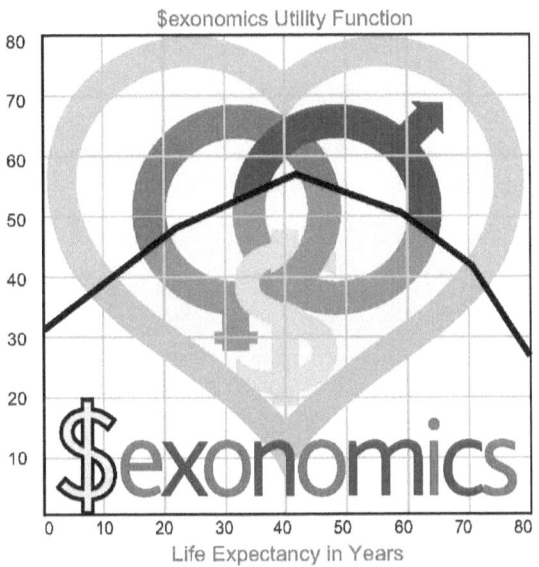

$exonomics Utility Function

Life Expectancy in Years

- The much higher proportion of lower-order men demonstrates that most men are sexonomically unhappy and unfulfilled most of the time.

Sexonomic Happiness Heart: Men

The sexonomic happiness heart of a human male reveals the lump sum total of enjoyments and benefits that accrue for him during his lifetime in exchange for his marketable sexuality. The level of this happiness can be measured in quantifiable or pecuniary terms. Generally speaking, it starts low, indicating that women have little use for male virgins or otherwise inexperienced adolescent males, except for those young men who are known to own or expect to inherit sizeable assets. But with late adolescence and the beginning of sexual activity as a young man, the human male's sexonomic happiness heart level starts rising (even very steeply for his manifestly untiring prolificity and the wild boar–like rigidity of his MOJJ). In the life of a healthy and normally acquisitive male person, it will then level off in its rate of ascent to hit the peak around his midfifties. Then, and so much unlike the sexonomic happiness heart lines of the orders of women in their postmenstrual state, men's sexonomic happiness heart lines may either continue to rise or level off but never steeply decline, depending on the material conditions of the particular male in his particular order of men. This is so because women will have always known how to express their preference for men with ample material means over those without such means.

The set of wealthy older men whose Three Ps are still in a well-functioning state command higher sexonomic valuations and enjoy higher sexonomic happiness heart levels than do most of the younger men who are relatively poor even though at the peak of performance of the Three Ps of their MOJJs. Most Conch-women and many Art-women will seek to marry rich men within their own respective orders and will, in fact, forgo precious youthful male potency in exchange for the older man's coveted material assets. But the more enterprising among them will wish to marry up into the next higher order and would even sacrifice the wealth of a lower-order man for the higher quality of a higher-order man. However, such women will forever suffer from the fear of being caught cohabiting with lower-order males, followed by an instant sexonomic devaluation and subsequent relegation to their previous lower order.

In times of great shortages of men in all orders, the sexonomic happiness heart levels of the remaining men in all orders will shift upward—the effect of their overall scarcity and higher valuation by the competing women. In consequence of this rising shortage of men, their overall market values and market prices will go up in the short run and will remain so in the normal run, even though their real value will remain unchanged. After all, once men's Three Ps function at peak levels of efficiency, they still cannot move even one notch higher—but the market valuation of their performance will go up if their Three Ps take on the appearance of increasing scarcity. In fact, in such a situation, we speak of revaluation; women will generally pay a higher exchange value (a higher price) for "getting their man" without even realizing that they are suffering with a "value illusion," which means that the spot price they are paying (in terms of cash or of their own opportunity cost) is much higher than the real value received in exchange. In this type of situation, men will be said to be collecting an overvaluation rent (a fate which many women have to endure whenever they pick a man who they know is not worth the price) with the unfortunate consequence that an unwarranted sexonomic transfer of wealth from women to men is implied. This phenomenon works across all of the five orders of men, with the consequence that a larger than usual number of higher-order women will reach down to the lower orders of men in the hope that their investment into these lower-quality men will pay off with his instantly available sexuality and the potential of his long-run personal development.

Expressed in sexonomic terms, the sexonomic happiness heart level of a human male comprises his (a) happiness from sharing his sexuality with his female partner(s); (b) spiritual benefits, which he derives from these physical ties (every loving woman or man knows how sweet it is to sleep next to one's very own beloved); and (c) material gains, which may directly or indirectly be the consequence of taking up and maintaining these ties. This function is both additive and evolutionary; for any given period, a human male's sexonomic happiness heart line may be higher than, equal to, or lower than that for any other period. This line will rise at a diminishing rate until he becomes fifty-five years old and reaches his sexonomic apogee. During the early period of the rise, a high proportion of a man's utility valuation will be derived from a successful marketing of his sexuality as well as from his professional advancement. In traditional society, much of his happiness was also derived from love, marriage, and the founding of a family toward which he would channel the monetary fruits of his labor. However, in the contemporary world, the frequency of marriage proposals on the part of younger men has experienced a significant decrease—the effect of the increasing sexonomic devaluation of women.

The typical average sexonomic happiness heart line of a human male during his entire lifetime may be shown to express itself as portrayed in illustration M-1 (page 38).

The readers will note that the male sexonomic happiness heart line has only one apogee, when a male is perceived of as having highest sexonomic value—mature, professional, with fully developed powers of intellect and leadership, in prime physical capacity, and possibly a father and contributor to the social good. Evidently, the whole function may be higher or lower depending on a particular man's state of happiness concerning his lifetime sexonomic relations with women—satisfying sexuality, rewarding material benefits, and the feeling of contentment that arises from having achieved success in both.

Also note that this line does not cover the *entire* sexonomic heart. This is so because this particular line is *made up of the average* of all five orders of men and indicates the much lesser relative valuation of the lower orders of men.

Note: Please be reminded that the specific analysis of the sexonomic hearts of each order of women and men will be continued in *chapter 1* of "Part Two: The Fascination of Sexonomics as a Science" for our readers who wish to explore more fully the illustrated imagery of the differences—and the causes thereof—in the level of sexonomic happiness in each of the female and male orders.

CHAPTER FIVE

Men and Women as Sexonomic Subjects

This discussion is based on hundreds of personal interviews and an in-depth analysis of the views expressed in them, of the reasons that make women and men sexonomically attractive. Highlighting these reasons will enable our readers to assess their own sexonomic appeal and thereby proceed with a much greater chance of success with partaking in sexonomic strategies and games—a complete outline of what to do in the quest to maximize one's own sexonomic utility function. This deliberation will take into account the existence of the five sexonomic markets and will describe how women and men should proceed on the road to personal success in the market appropriate to their own qualities and sexonomic valuations. Obviously, the higher the order of women and men, the more intricate the web of strategic moves becomes, requiring the full utilization of the complete set of the players' sexonomic endowments over the course of their participation in a particular sexonomic involvement.

MEN AND WOMEN AS SEXONOMIC SUBJECTS

With the termination of our discussion of sexonomic conventions and the rules of the game, we may now proceed to our discussion of how women and men view one another as objects of sexual desire as well as subjects of pecuniary or material considerations. Obviously, this discussion will go well beyond the perception, in its generalized physical reference, of men and women as sex objects in that it will reflect the much higher intellectual level of sexonomic reasoning. These deliberations emanate from many private conversations and formally staged and taped interviews with individuals as well as with groups in a sense that reveals a general perception of how modern women and men view and think of this particular subject matter.

1. Men as Sexonomic Subjects

As proposed in the introduction, the exploration of the question "Why do women and men seek out each other?" revolves around the three main themes that are of primary concern to Sexonomics: sexuality, money, and power. For starters, we shall treat the question of why women want men, a discussion that is based on many hundreds of interviews that we have conducted with women of all age-groups and social strata during the past several years.

Necessarily, our main emphasis has had to do with what goes on in a woman's mind before she consents to bed with a man, be it for short-run pleasure or as a deliberate act toward founding a family, a step which manifests all the characteristics of a long-term investment decision. But we were also interested in discovering the concerns and apprehensions of women with respect to their wishing to hold on to "their" men and the many sacrifices they must often incur in wishing to succeed.

In the course of these interviews, the following main topics were covered:

- How does a quality woman rank a *man's sexuality, power, and material means* (relative to other requisite characteristics) and why?

- How does a quality woman use the *three enticing functions of her* Lady LUSSEY in her quest to secure for herself the "ideal man," and how will she proceed to protect his allegiance (her investment) against trespassing by other competing women?

- How does a quality woman view her *ideal man*, and what are his essential characteristics?

- Will a quality woman ever wish to be *bedding with a man* without being in love with him? Would she do so for reasons other than passion and why?

- Finally, is *needing to have a man* compatible with a woman's desire to be free?

Men's Sexuality, Material Wealth, and Power Defined

Men as sex objects: Most women define a "male sex object" as a man with a fantastic physique in the nude, who exudes irresistible charm and is presumed to be able to make love as often as the coveting woman would like and as long as it would please her. But "sex appeal" is much more than just the genitals and the gyrations; it presupposes the physique in terms of motion, something that happens as the result of touch, a situation out of the ordinary, his expression and voice modulation, his energy beam. His scent must be mind-awakening, or else the sensation will not descend and arouse the innermost desire in her being, but he must also be clean, kind, gentle, and affectionate, and with the sweetness of the expression of the soul in his eyes. Finally, he must have both intelligence and chemistry, unless it is simply the matter of the right man coming toward you when your hormones overwork. What still remains, however, is that certain barriers will have to be crossed, or else lovemaking will not take place.

"Playboys" often qualify as sex subjects because they are in the right places, looking good and demonstrating that they are "with it"; moreover, in his case, the women know that it will not last forever and that it amounts, therefore, to a fair exchange. He makes her feel wanted and puts her on the pedestal, while she is looking good being picked from the crowd of competitors and feeling good for enjoying his successful lifestyle. Besides, women have always preferred promiscuity to innocence in men, although they are often contented just to fantasize about men without even aspiring to get horny.

Men and material wealth: Unlike power, which turns women on (because it is *so* masculine!), rich men are more fun; a woman prefers feeling like his mistress than having to think that he may be mooching on her. Moreover, like in the old times, it feels so nice to be receiving presents, especially if one believes that there are no strings attached. While no woman would marry only for his money, she knows that more wealthy men are more attractive than poor guys, and often she is socially prevented from approaching even the most interesting of the latter set of men. "Beautiful" women are known to wish to marry wealthy men for dynastic/biological reasons, men who they presume will make and keep their children beautiful and will accord them all the chances in the world. In these cases, the loving does not come from instant loin heat but will emerge slowly, developing from the bottom up and demonstrating that a kind, considerate, and civil man of means can, in fact, have a very special glow, a man that she can really "learn or grow to love."

Marrying into wealth accords the woman a comfortable lifestyle and assures her of extraordinary personal liberty. Unfortunately, rich men often fail to recognize their wives' intelligence and will, therefore, treat them without the appropriate sense of touch—and even rudely—a risky situation, especially for superbly intelligent women who consciously prefer to choose to marry money instead of a male with "class."

Lately, the market for wealthy men has considerably tightened because of the inflow of a large number of lower-order professional women of the predatory kind, a situation which has demeaned the situation of many of the competing older women and in which the presumed financial security and striving for freedom from material want have become very elusive. The growing disparity between the increasing number of young women engaging in the hunt for the relatively forever smaller numbers of rich men has necessarily resulted in a noticeable depreciation of all of these women's sexonomic valuations, with the end effect of decreasing their long-run sexonomic utility functions. Having no other men to turn to but those whose means are few, a large proportion of these women, the older and the younger—faced with being losers in the battle for the men of means—will become increasingly discontented and would rarely, if ever, make good wives, even if they did succeed in getting married.

Men and power. Men with power turn women on since the exercise of power makes men look masculine. Such men are perceived of possessing enormous sex appeal and are therefore much sought after as "high-level sex subjects." Men of power are not those who have a longer and thicker penis but those who are very successful in all walks of life, those who are admired because they radiate strength and command obedience from other men—a man who is a pillar among the other men. Such a man will also peruse his innate power in order to fight the elements and will seek to prevail over them. Necessarily, in such men, their brainpower will rule over the power of their loins and will direct their gyrations during intercourse. Such men are capable of conquering other men as well as their own frailties and weaknesses. Because of his exquisite physical appearance and the apparent full control over his movements, a professional dancer is usually much more powerfully attractive to women than a wealthy businessman.

Men's *power*, as viewed by women, expresses itself in many different ways:

- *the power of a purely physical sexual attractiveness*: this power is what makes a man biologically a sex object;

- *the power of reason*: undoubtedly the supreme sexonomic quality of a human male;

- *the power of the achiever and conqueror*: a presence that is delightful to watch manifest itself but very difficult to bear if it is aimed at a woman and is likely to lead to a power struggle and a division into the conqueror and the conquered;

- *the power of conviction*: a characteristic that makes for forthrightness, approbation, and sympathy but can also easily spill over into inflexibility, unwillingness to compromise, and even doctrinaire rigidity; poor is the woman who runs into a man, however superb, who turns out to be an adherent to a set of absolute, irrevocable principles;

- *the power of the aura of inexhaustible energy*: the other of the two supreme qualities of a man, this characteristic provides succor, comradeship, and protection and is at the base of chivalry, of the survival instinct, and of procreation (our sample demonstrated quite clearly that women would prefer men without wealth or only with an ordinary capacity to reason to men whose energy field is weak and who are, therefore, simply not good enough sexually);

- *the power of imagination*: the requisite for a forever exciting love relationship and the foundation for an interesting and continuously self-regenerating togetherness; a man endowed with this power will never be boring in bed or have hang-ups about life;

- *the power of positive aging*: sexuality in the youth being different from sexuality when a person is older, this power will enable a man to become a better, gentler, more delicate, and more complete lover, which he has to become because a woman of forty suffers more from the lack of sex than does a girl of twenty; this kind of man will not fritter away his energy just worrying about getting older but will convert it into a forever lasting source of joy of life by keeping his body and spirit in a prime energy-generating condition; and

- *the economic power*: unlike the accumulation of wealth for the purpose of pursuing an opulent and hedonistic lifestyle (from which group of men come those who would wish to buy women rather than earn their companionship), economic power permits its holders to organize inputs and engage in production and distribution in order to augment this power and to adjoin it onto a forever increasing financial base. Having command (usually as employers) over other men and women and able to acquire any resources (including and especially land), the men who wield economic power also give direction to innovative technology and are in fact makers of society. The higher-order men of this kind will prefer women whose understanding and devotion they will know how to attract and whose full support they will know how to secure. Their women will always be superbly intelligent, but they will never be meek, maladroit, or loath to take risk; neither will they ever sell themselves unto their men's economic means. In America, the women of the frontier represent this type of strong, committed, principled companions to whom the loving relationship with such men also constitutes a family partnership and possibly the building of a private family empire. Unlike the lower-order predatory men of economic power as portrayed by television, the real-life higher-order members of men with economic power are as constructive as they are honest, even though, throughout their lifetime, they will often suffer with a bad case of double allegiance (their work versus their family); but they will be and will remain totally committed to the woman of their life. The higher-order men of economic power are usually very reserved in their private lives, possibly because they need to offset their forever exposure to the public during their business hours, which explains why they chose their women with discretion and with utter privacy in mind.

Men's Sexuality, Material Wealth, and Power Compared

Having arrived at the end of the discussion of the main headings in this chapter, we now need to proceed with a comparison of their total significance as shown in the illustration below. More than one hundred women of all ages (classified in two subgroups, those below forty years of age and those above forty years of age) were interviewed about their views on the following questions:

- How do women, particularly women of quality, view these primary requisites of quality manhood?

- Will women's perception of the ranking—into the present "five orders" as well as within each of the orders—change over time?

- Is there a difference between the men's ranking by younger women and their ranking by older women?

- What is the sexonomic significance of these requisites and their rankings over time?

- Does each order of women, from the highest to the lowest, have an equal perception of the absolute significance and of the relative ranking of each of these "fundamental elements"?

Of all the answers, only one—a fifty-five-year-old mother of three and grandmother of seven—left no room for doubt; the deeper meaning of loving a man is derived not from his penis or his money but from sharing in his personal power, even though sometimes overwhelming.

The responses of the sampled women show an almost clear split between the older generation and the younger set. With only very few exceptions in this particular sampling, these two groups of women ranked the relative weights of the component elements of the perceived "power" of men as follows (the numbers in parentheses signify the relative order of ranking for all categories—1 for the highest, 8 for the lowest):

Fundamental elements of men's "power":	Older women:	Younger women:
Sexual attractiveness:	(4)	(2)
Reason:	(3)	(4)
Achiever:	(5)	(3)
Conviction:	(8)	(6)
Aura of energy:	(1)	(5)
Imagination:	(7)	(7)
Positive aging:	(2)	(8)
Economic/financial power:	(6)	(1)

This sampling reveals the much more pronounced materialistic inclination of the younger set of women, but it also shows the greater concern, from the older set of women, about the ability of their men to cope with aging.

Women and the Enticing Roles of the Three Functions of the Sir MOJJ

As discussed above (pages 19–22), the three functions or qualities of the Sir MOJJ are the essential biological requisites for the success of men in their sexonomic strategies and games concerning their cohabitation with or lifetime investment into being with women. Like the plumes of the males in the world of birds and their effect on the mating-hungry female birds, the men's complete biological apparatus and the qualities of its full potency represent so much more than just a sex organ. *He* is a man's principal instrument of negotiation and bargaining—an instrument whose natural endowment can still be vastly enhanced by the conscious portrayal of all of *his* naturally imbedded and/or individually developed (let us remind ourselves of the purpose and functions of the *Sexonomic Institute!*) attributes: the Three Ps (potency, perseverance, prolificity), enticement-and-control, and pleasure. Of these, the quality of potency derives from the four natural propensities of men as men: pukkacity, sensitiveness, erethism, and dimension. While optimal performance perseverance and prolificity are a function of external inducement and of a Spartan attitude concerning exercise and healthy dietary habits as well as of a philosophy of life, which is an effective combination of both the *Kama Sutra* and *The Ten Principal Upanishads.*

Listening to these interviewed women, the assumption that these attributes are fully part and parcel of the male Eros and will be brought fully and effectively into "play" in the quest for a complete merger with a particular coveted female was fully confirmed. These women considered it absolutely essential that all these men's qualities had to be and would be superactivated and rendered supereffective when a man is believed to have met *his* "dream woman." In *her* presence as *his* loving mate with sparkling eyes would feel very embarrassed and terribly ill at ease if unexpectedly caught in the nude with his Sir MOJJ fully exposed in the presence of a woman with whom he has absolutely no interest. The natural (unspoiled by culture) biology of primitive human sexuality apparently still manifests a powerful effect upon the joyful dimension of an enchantingly humanizing moment of sexonomic bliss in the respective orders of women and men in modern society.

In our sample, many men expressed surprise at the number of women, especially younger women, who seemed never to get tired fondling, caressing, and even kissing a particularly pleasing Sir MOJJ. But many other men expressed dismay over their penises being labeled "ugly" by scores of women who would then still go on and express their desire to be made love to exactly by such MOJJs. Men who had been burdened with this kind of dismal situation claim that this type of making love does amount to very "hard work" because they must first convince their MOJJs that *they* should rise to the occasion and proceed to "do the job" well, even though *they* know that their looks are not appreciated by the lustful but otherwise deprecating female. Be that as it may, even for men, hard work at lovemaking will pay off, for with abundant erotic interest between the partners, *she* will eventually respond to *him*, impressed by his quality performance and even forgiving him for the duration of the act despite his ugly-duckling looks.

In the eyes of the sampled men (do recall that each of these men had affairs with an average of at least ten women), women wishing to make love accord definite preference to the pleasure quality of a Sir MOJJ. This is so because women suspect that men will use their enticement-and-control quality with the aim of bringing women under their domination (like many women, men will "withhold" in the hope to turn the terms of the sexual encounter in their favor). This attitude is expressed mainly by the set of younger women, who prefer the pleasure quality of men because it is meant not to lead to anything more than intercourse. It is this enchantment with the enticement quality of superior men that induces thousands of women, the younger and the older, to yearn for intercourse literally following their first encounter with such men, an encounter which they simply do not expect to endure. Instant loin heat over the power to reason? Or the outpouring of a primeval need that cannot be explained by science?

In plotting their sexonomic strategies, the sampled men viewed their Sir MOJJ's qualities as merchandising devices. Of these qualities, that particular one will be played up in the course of several sexual encounters with a woman who appears particularly interesting or particularly exciting. In their experience, pukkacity and sensitiveness command the highest value, followed by prolificity, erethism, and dimension. Perseverance is considered a naturally abundant requisite, and its presence is taken for granted by women who believe that "men need *her* literally all the time!" Its absence becomes the principal reason for a quick cessation of the sexual togetherness and an inducement to seek recourse with men who will demonstrate its capacity. While most women were quite unanimous in ranking these priorities concerning their male partners' Sir MOJJs and their qualities, a substantive difference of opinion was revealed concerning the significance of the intrinsic qualities of men's enticement-and-control quality (see pages 16–17). Of these, love, sympathy, and prudence are viewed as "requisites of a loving man" but not so the qualities of tolerance and approbation, which many women do not view as a requisite when engaged in making love with the so-called real men, with their "cocky, self-assured, and warrior-type attitudes. Moreover, whereas self-assertion, territoriality, and possessiveness are thought of by older women as the innermost essences of masculinity, most younger women will accept self-assertion and will tolerate territoriality but will reject possessiveness and will subject it to a hefty sexonomic discount if the men appear so heavy-handed in their encroachment upon a woman's liberty as to pose a threat to their otherwise liberated behavior.

Men of prolonged experience with women will not openly admit that they are more than aware of the women's rankings by priority of the qualities of Sir MOJJs. They will not because seeking to "earn" these rankings might involve many years of hard work and of trial and error, including recurring experiences of alternating pleasure and pain. However, once accumulated, this knowledge constitutes a very private domain of each competing male, his personal monopoly and reserve in his sexonomic strategies and games.

Wise women know an experienced male when they see one and will be intrigued. Fact has it that, as far as pure sexual performance is concerned, Girandole-men, the professionals in sex-for-hire markets, possess absolutely and relatively the vastest reservoir of this kind of specialized knowledge, which will permit them to please any woman but only in the shortest run. This is so because, by the nature of their trade, Girandole-men cannot allow themselves to reveal the so exclusively male characteristics of self-assertion, territoriality, and possessiveness and will never wish to generate feelings of love and sympathy. These men's insightful knowledge of women's sexual needs and their rankings of the qualities of Girandole-men's MOJJs amount to a vast reservoir that is meant to serve as a technical means for instant gratification. However, since Girandole-men have lost their capacity for "pure love," they and other men for hire fail to achieve the highest apogee in sexonomic utility and must be contented with their largely unfilled sexonomic hearts.

Do men, like women, suggest that the "main sexual organ is contained in the head"—that is, that the men's control function is, in fact, located not in their scrotums but in their heads in order to better control their pleasure function? Judging by the men's still openly practiced habit of taking on most of the costs of both courtship and divorce, Sexonomics would have to conclude in the negative. This conclusion seems both logically and empirically tenable, but it also finds expression even in the present ethos concerning men's behavior—you want a woman, you will pick up the tab and will postpone worrying about the consequences. Education and women's movements have caused a dent in this attitude and more and more working women will now wish to (a) invite a "coveted" man and (b) pick up the tab. But Sexonomics suspects that there will be no wholesale change in the orientation of men since even Lace-men have problems holding on to their reason as the sole and exclusive control center of their Sir MOJJs.

The world of women—professing that men's reason cannot possibly prevail over their sexual urges—seems convinced that the expression "using one's head" is exclusive to their domain. The decision by women to market their sexuality "always comes from the head."

Ideal Men

Literally all women in our interview sample conceded that ideal men ("dream men") exist only in women's fantasies and that, in reality, it would take about four superbly qualified men to make up even a semblance of the "ideal" image. The vast majority of older women in the sample admitted to having been very idealistic in their late teens about men, a viewpoint which revealed itself very clearly in their description of the essential characteristics of a quality man. They also declared that a woman who has an exceptional man will find it terribly hard to be unfaithful to him or to love another man even in the course of an entire lifetime. She would accept unfaithfulness on his part because nobody else can compare with him (in her mind, but possibly also in the eyes of society). But the set of younger women in our sample (younger than thirty-five years of age) was much more skeptical about the image of "ideal men," possibly because most of them had, starting as young adolescents, already shared in sexual experiences with a much larger number of men than had the set of older women by the time they had reached their midfifties.

The younger women's "dream man" time period also appeared by far shorter and limited to their midteens and with a much more pronounced dose of pecuniary self-interest. But interestingly, both groups of women proclaimed that not only was there an enormous shortage of quality men but that the well-to-do men were much greater "fun" to be with because they could do things that poorer men (even though with similar other qualities) simply could not afford.

Looking for the "ideal man," the set of older women were very emphatic in pointing out the following "musts" as primary requisites:

First of all, he must be a lover and not a lovee, but he must not overdo his loving, or else he will make his woman feel unfree.

Second, he should manifest a feeling of strength as well as of power; the former will make a woman "feel like a woman," while the latter will "turn a woman on," which makes these men "higher-level sex objects." A man's strength permits him to treat "his woman" like a princess while knowing exactly how not to "overpamper." A man's power lies not in his penis but in his success in competitive undertakings and achievements (judging from the responses by the interviewed women, these men would include composers of pop music, top-level aerial skiers, leaders of the business community, and even priests at high levels of hierarchy), whose "achievements" were referred to by these women as indicating "virility," "masculinity," risk-taking capacity, and the ability to take command (over oneself as well as over others). Interestingly, none of these women viewed only money or solely potency and pukkacity as the main determining factors. But neither did these women have any problems thinking about or even wishing to have affairs with such men—necessarily in conditions of utmost discretion—while insisting that they would remain with their loving and caring husbands (with whom they "enjoyed very pleasant and sometimes even exhilarating lovemakings"), this being so because these "mind-arousing affairs" would never be meant to last.

Third, a man (husband) who turns out to be a "doormat" will forever become a social embarrassment to a dynamic woman with strong fighting qualities because his attitude may lead to awkward situations and, personally, because it degenerates into a boring relationship. But most of the interviewed women professed that they would still remain with such husbands if they were kind and considerate and were also "men of means."

Fourth, literally all of the interviewed women insisted that their "chosen" men would have to manifest, at the very least, the following main qualities: frank and open; clean, decent, and looking "nice"; gentle touch, very tender, pleasing scent ("from underarm to rear end"); intelligent ("he must be intelligent to give you intelligent children"); excellent companion ("he would know when a woman does not feel like being trespassed upon and will know how to respect such a situation while continuing to be an interesting and challenging conversationalist or playmate"); healthy and normal ("no major vices" as a basic requisite for an exciting long-run sexual togetherness); hardworking (one of the surprising revelations in these interviews was the frequency of women who insisted that "their men" would absolutely have to be creative in doing their own things, that they should not "hang around" their women all the time, and that they should be "themselves"); should dress well, should not be stingy with gifts, and should have the genuine desire to "pamper his woman"; instead of being an "absolute" virgin and sentimental romantic, he should enjoy some "kinkiness" in lovemaking as a manifestation of his sexually liberated state as well of the presence of his incessantly imaginative mind; should be charming, handsome, and should reveal himself as having the "proper" mix between delicacy and passion; lastly, he should also possess that "special" quality which makes him uniquely interesting and sexually appealing to a particular woman.

A very important concomitant attribute of the "ideal man" is his perception of the woman who has particular and exclusive interest in him. The younger set of women expressed their readiness to "be everything" to such a man, to be what "he would like me to be," adapting to his likes. If he is perfect, "we would happily give to him whatever he wants from us, even if we had to readjust" (even to the extent of eating less to lose some weight, restyling one's hairdo, changing the color of nail polish, making time available to really pamper him, even taking care not to annoy him), and we would give him double of whatever he gives us. "A woman in love will give the ideal man everything he wants. She will find out what he wants and will make him happy." This applies to all men, even though all men are different.

However, the older women of means appeared more skeptical and far less inclined to compromise. "The ideal man is he who accepts me as I am. If he does not like the real me, he is wasting my time and I am wasting his. Besides, since there are no ideal women, neither are there ideal men." But the less well-to-do member of the older set of women will adjust much along the lines of the younger set of women; this is so because she views the "ideal man" as a man of means who will take care of her personal needs and financial security.

Bedding with Men

If a woman is not too much in love (being "too much in love" makes her lose some of her own sexonomic powers) and, therefore, in full power of her wiles, she can certainly apply them in the expectation of success (that is, a happy marriage). She will bed with a man if she wants a short-term relationship, but in the long run, she wants much more than just to fornicate—companionship, which is far better than loneliness; freedom, usually from oppressive parents; financial security; a home of their own with children of their own. But women often succumb to the need of being with men because at various stages in the course of their lives, they are vulnerable. But most often, women bed with men out of necessity—marriage without true love but for economic reasons. Surprisingly, however, even if they make love without having an emotional desire to do so, they may feel better afterward (diminishes feeling of guilt of "not giving enough" to a unilaterally loving husband).

In contemporary society, masses of women are induced by their loin heat to bed with men, even though they do not love them. Neither do many men bed with women because they love them. But those few that do are "very precious"; they are the "good ones" to whom to get married. There is, however, an exception in that not loving them back might lead to a forever widening vicious circle situation; since he, like all other men, needs sex, giving it to him will abate the feelings of guilt for not loving him but will intensify the feelings of guilt for pretending that the lovemaking happens out of loving and not as a necessary sacrifice. However, a man who continues loving his wife, even though she does not reciprocate and even exploits him, is considered a wimp, one whose wife will eventually leave him.

The theme of men of all ages "needing sex" keeps on repeating itself and is taken by both the older and the younger women as a natural inclination, a need to which the women will cater as a matter of natural course; *she* is the natural place for *him*. But providing this "natural" place now has its price; *his* owner must pay a compensation, which is higher, the less *her* owner loves him (recall our earlier statement concerning LUSSEY as a "free good"; *she* will be offered for free when *her* owner's love for her man approaches an infinite intensity. Or LUSSEY may be offered—either for free or for cash—in the spur of the moment in order to satisfy her owner's instantaneous craving for fornication with whomever). In a longer-term situation in which the woman partner's love is not reciprocated, a sense of obligation is likely to permeate the woman's psyche. In such caring situations, his own appearance and behavior—looking nice and clean; acting with consideration, gentleness, decency, very tenderly; and never wishing to impose his lovemaking needs on her without prior consent—will be helpful in that she will not have to use more than just a touch of vaginal cream (and will also likely never have to fake an orgasm).

In these interviews, two themes kept on recurring in both age-groups of the sampled women. The first was the perception that "men need it" and that most women will let their vaginas "be used" (for a whole range of reasons, from the natural inclination to be their men's lovemates and thereby help them out in their needs to the provision of a scarce resource to a man intensely wanting it and willing to pay the appropriate price). The second seems to be a deeply imbedded feeling of longing for the "ideal man," the man for whom the loving woman would "do everything" (on the assumption that he really manifests, over time, the existence of the whole set of appropriate, deserving characteristics). Only two of the interviewed women had been "fortunate" enough to have met such men, of which one eventually resulted in marriage. The woman who had married her "ideal man" had never since wanted anything or anyone else because "he had given me everything a woman would possibly want to be perfectly happy. Even after he dies, I would never even look at another man." The other woman had met her "ideal man" and "given herself to him," even though he had come from a totally different social environment for which reason she knew that nothing permanent would come of this relationship. But while "it lasted, I was hanging on to this absolute dream of a man without whom

I would not have considered my life as a worthwhile experience." Even though, to her own admission, she then went on to marry a man who she did not love but who was good to the child she had conceived with her ideal man." She eventually procreated two more children with her husband and appeared quite happy about being married all her life to the far less than ideal man (she was eighty-three when telling her story to the author), possibly because during all those years, she was feeding on her memories and did, in fact, on many occasions think of her first lover while giving her body to her husband to enjoy.

The interviews concerning *bedding with men* confirmed the perception that the more women consider copulating with a man whom they do not love, the greater is the promise of an explicit or implicit material incentive. In this sense, women tend to view their sexual organs with a sense of rational and objective purpose; there is nothing mysterious about their reproductive system, nothing heavenly or holy that should be put on a pedestal and kept there by those "idealistic but silly men" to whom *she* is the inspiring source of life, the "holey" crevice offering safest refuge or highest fulfillment, or even the substantiated myth of the ultimate conquest. In these women's view, *she* is there to be used for her owner's pleasure and material benefit. Since *she* is there and not even beautiful to look at (how often will women have wasted many hours of self-viewing in trying to find out what about *her* looks makes her so eternally attractive to men until they eventually give up trying to understand!), her owner may as well learn to view *her* as a primary physical tool of personal hedonism, as the natural requisite for the procreation with those men, who will provide care and succor in her old days, and as the principal organ for a materially rewarding long-term investment.

Needing a Man—but Also Wishing to Be Free

A socially preeminent woman in her "best years" voiced the following viewpoint:

"A dream man you do not need that often, but the dream man would sometimes be a man of whom you had not dreamt before. Your own dream man is someone who does the same business that you do, for which reason you really understand him and have a closeness; then you can love the part of him that you think is the greatest, and he will love that part of you that he thinks is the best. However, I am not sure that such two people make the best companions, and I will think twice before marrying him. I'd even just prefer making love to him."

This lady then recounted that she had once had a lover who was "simple and good, intelligent, sexy, kind, and all that" but who had been brought up differently and with a different set of values. That she had "taken him" because he was a pillar when everything else in her life had crumbled. She had never loved him and thought that she was quite callous to him, especially when she ditched him because he was developing some sexual "hang-ups" and was showing himself too shy to do certain kinky things. She ditched him because sex had become too much hard work for her, even though "everything else had been quite perfect," but also because he had become redundant once she was finally able to solve her own problems. She would forever have lasting memories of the preciousness of that man at that time, even though the sexual desire was completely gone. But she was still feeling very guilty about sending him away as soon as she knew that he would be of no more use to her.

The admission of having "hurt" a man does not come easily from a woman's lips. This is so because, except for most of the very young and inexperienced women and the very few who go through their lives idealizing about the perfect male companion, women with several serious involvements with men do not like admitting to failure or being regarded as callous, self-seeking bitches, especially not if they are observed in the act of repeatedly ditching the "good guy" types of men. Much rather, women prefer talking about the following perceptions and guidelines concerning the availability and behavior of men in everyday situations:

1. Most men will come running if promised the joy of an enticingly offered Lady LUSSEY.

2. Most of the men who do come running will seek to minimize the cost of this enjoyment, but the really selective ones will pay even an inappropriately high premium price (as a function of the offering woman's consciously portrayed uniqueness).

3. Most of these men are sought after for purposes other than their sexuality if the women "in need" are talented and ambitious but have few or no means (as is manifest in the revelations of the younger set of women of relatively simple background who are in a hurry to get ahead and are willing to swap sex for financial support, moral support, intellectual counsel, or just for a great lover who would relieve a particular woman of her condition of stress in very trying periods). But after realizing their goals, most of the younger set of women will have no qualms about sending these—by then redundant—men on their way.

4. Once these goals have been achieved (education, technical expertise, professional standing, steady and fairly high-level income stream), a woman will then want not someone "special" who will stand by her and support

her but someone "absolutely wonderful" as a great lover and companion, someone who will be even more important because she will have no more need to compromise herself or her basic moral values.

5.   Unlike fine wine, not all men get better with age, but men do qualify as ready-made husbands if women (especially of the older generation) absolutely need to get away from their parents' bondage or believe that marriage will buy them the freedom to be themselves.

6.   Most men are "incredibly" naive and cannot see through women's wiles, but they absolutely need a home, which only a woman can give them.

7.   Most men are afraid of intelligent women, especially professionals who work in a very competitive milieu (e.g., lawyers); this is so because men are afraid that women who want power will also wish to run their husbands.

8.   Since most men cannot resist the scent of a Lady LUSSEYs honey, women with talent, poise, and education will know how to offset the dearth of their own material means; usually, they will also win out over their less endowed competing sisters, even though the overall surplus of women over men is increasing.

9.   The promise of a Lady LUSSEYs "honey" is not only the best means to attract the desired man but also the safest means to keep him in line and guessing.

10. A wise woman is that very intelligent woman who will very subtly let a man have his way; she will run those things which will not interfere with what he believes are his domain. She will also know that men get bored very quickly with "dumb broads," especially those which are very bossy.

11. Men are there to serve five purposes: financial security, fascinating and fulfilling sexuality, equal-opportunity companionship, standby in all emergency circumstances, aloofness in his privacy if he is told that he is not wanted.

12. Finally, a really wise woman is that superbly intelligent woman who will not fall into the trap of thoughtlessly accepting any of these listed perceptions and guidelines. And she will know that neither will intelligent men. Clearly, only Lotus-women and some Art-women have this kind of wisdom.

How can these perceptions and guidelines serve the purpose of reflecting upon the statement about women "needing men but also desiring to be free"? Aren't these two principal wants of women sexonomically mutually exclusive?

Five natural liberties of women are involved here:

- freedom from having to make love to a man who is unwanted at that moment or at any time,

- freedom not to marry an unwanted man,

- freedom from material want,

- freedom not to have to account to the respective male partner for any meandering with other men, and

- freedom of choice of and in any sexonomic markets.

The open manifestation of any and all of these freedoms will permit all women to earn and demonstrate their true sexonomic valuations and thereby to proceed to the maximization of their sexonomic happiness.

Are these freedoms incompatible with a woman's desire to "have a man"?

Viewed in sexonomic terms, the answer depends entirely on the nature of the relationship between a woman and a man, which, as we already know, can range from "pure loving" to "pure material self-interest." Expressed in these terms, we are faced with the following situations:

Women as "sexonomic losers": the "pure but unreciprocated loving" of a man by a woman. Clearly, this situation is one of "unequal exchange," of voluntary self-enslavement; she will give much more than she will ever receive. If "freedom is meant the exercise of a rational choice in the expectation of a maximum (sexonomic) gain," then we must conclude that this type of woman has abdicated every one of her basic five freedoms in exchange for a man whom she will most unlikely be able to hold on to. She will need to make love to him whenever he feels like it; she will most likely never even be proposed to; she will have no guarantee of material succor; she will forever have to fear that man's wrath for ever casting, however innocently, her eyes upon another man; and she will most likely find herself tied down to a sexonomic market of a much lower order than the innate value of her qualities would call for. This type of woman may be named a "sexonomic loser."

Evidently, a Lotus-woman will never find herself in this predicament. An Art-woman might if, in the course of one of her unusually intensive loin heat periods, she encounters a civilized-looking but superpotent Vulpine-man. A Conch-woman will need to exert enormous willpower in order not to be entrapped in this destructive liaison, while a typical Elephant-woman will stoically endure it, having nowhere else to turn. A Vampire-woman will not fit this sample because she is totally devoid of any feeling of love and self-sacrifice.

Women as "sexonomic hopefuls": Sexonomically hopeful is a woman who knows how to compromise several of her needs concerning freedom in exchange for the expectation of a vastly improved sexonomic utility function. Typical of the Art-woman, she will assert her enticement-and control function and will choose the man she will wish to marry (even reaching down to the very gifted Vulpine-man, whose pukkacity she will have learned to appreciate with much delight but whose clearly perceptible innate talents would have to be subjected to development). This kind of man will likely look up at her superior qualities and will be contented to be a "good" husband and even homemaker, happily hanging on to the higher order into which he was elevated by his wife. But he will also grant her liberties which he would never allow a Conch-woman if he had remained in his order of birth, while he would do his natural best to surround his wife with the material requisites of well-being.

These liberties will include an explicit agreement to make love only when both feel like it, an understanding that their family partnership in marriage is exclusive of extramarital affairs but not prohibitive of external linkages, and a compact never to prevent the other from attempts to improve her/his sexonomic happiness. Evidently, an Art-woman, who is typically wise at heart, will never forsake her own sexonomic market for the next higher one unless she has met three innermost conditions (which are exclusive and privy only to herself)—that her own husband's development potential has been exhausted, and she has definitively left him behind; that she will find a Quintessential-man who will have genuine interest in her own development; and that she will be able to sustain herself among the members of the order of Lotus-women. Also evidently, while she will need to assist a man from the order of Vulpine-men to take his proper place as her husband, in the order of Lace-men, she will not have to go through any of these efforts if she decided to marry an original and unadulterated member of the order of Lace-men. With such a man, all the agreements referred to above (explicit with a Vulpine-man husband) would be implicit.

Higher-order women and men have a much greater appreciation of the terms *liberty* and *freedom* and their significance and will, therefore, not even need to discuss or explain most of their dimensions, unlike the women and the men of the lower orders.

Women as "sexonomic winners": To become a "sexonomic winner," a woman will expect to live in union with her ultimate chosen man. Living with such a man, she can indeed "have a man and be free"—a situation restricted to the orders of Lotus-women and Quintessential-men, at times also applying to the highest-ranking Art-women with their Lace-men.

2. Women as Sexonomic Subjects

Our inquiry into the question "Why do men want women?" rests on the premise that the sexonomic reasons are the same as those for women: sexuality, power, money. But in the case of the men, we have discovered that not only does this sequence not always hold but that the weighting of these three motives also differs from those by women. For example, of the hundreds of interviewed men, the largest number by far emphasized sexuality (72 percent), a significant number singled out money (24 percent), and only a few saw women as a means to power (2 percent, the remaining 2 percent having no opinion). But we note with interest that in the minds of most of these men, women's "sexuality" involves "companionship," which is much more than just "sex appeal" or a courtship that solely has intercourse as the ultimate goal. Most of these men expressed the desire to "have themselves their woman for life"—one who, even though not perfect, they would love and cherish and who would in return bear and raise their children while also being "good" to their husbands and sharing with them lifelong care and devotion. While the men's initial insistence on "the quality of sexuality" constitutes a prime requisite in their younger years, starting with their midthirties, they assign increasing priority to their women's other qualities, of which companionship, kindness, and a happy and creative disposition are especially deemed the most significant.

Across all orders in the sample, "sexuality" in the longer term is clearly viewed as cement which comprises more than just one single dimension, with the terms *family*, *partnership*, and *to be cared for* being singled out as the principal bases of such togetherness. The younger men (below twenty-five years of age, who made up 32 percent of our sample) viewed these requisites as preconditions for their settling down in their midthirties for long-term associations, but they did not appear optimistic about their chances of finding women of such quality in their own peer group. But even more so, the men in their midforties or older seeking to marry for the first time or to rebound into a second marriage—caught between their old-fashioned idealism about women and their anxiety to get on with their marriage plans—seemed terribly concerned about the manifest unavailability of women of such quality, as if the women "on the rebound" had caused their previous associations to fail. Interestingly though, and in spite of their apprehensions concerning the "right quality woman," we note that only a very few of the younger men in the sample foresaw being married without ever cheating on his wife, a view which applied about equally to the previously unmarried men as well as to the men on the rebound. When asked whether they anticipated their women being unfaithful in the course of a longer relationship, both groups of men answered in the affirmative, but the younger age-group appeared more willing to accept infidelity as a matter of course.

The men in this sample were aged eighteen to eighty-seven years and admitted to having bedded with an average of at least ten women, a number which included their present and past wives; about one half of these men claimed to have "taken" a virgin. While about 90 percent of these men claimed to have had four basic motives for engaging in premarital sex or in extramarital liaisons (lust, conquest, curiosity, ease of access), literally all of them stated that being with their women had often involved "costs" much higher than the rewards from the enjoyment of sexuality—the costs of "preplay time" (the initial investment into commencing a relationship), "playtime" (beginnings of the payoff—kissing, necking, possibly petting), "consummation time" (engaging in intercourse), "fruition time" (expecting to build a longer-term relationship), and in hedging against possible failure, "debarkation time" (the emotional and pecuniary costs of severing a relationship).

In all of these situations, the largest part of these "costs" involved the dispensing of material means (usually in form of cash considerations, gifts, trips, lodgings), which could turn out to be quite expensive if the courting male was in great hurry to move onto phase three (consummation) but would secure for the bidding male a greater than equivalent chance of success. When sexually overaroused but unable to consummate with their preferred women, about one-third of these men did not mind using the services of prostitutes, provided they were clean, understanding, not in too much of a hurry, and really worth their price. In periods of prolonged frustration with their "favorite" women, these men would even return to such prostitutes for sex as well as to vent their grievances. But many of these men also expressed not only genuine feelings of fear of women but also increasing disgust at themselves. At the base of these feelings, three concerns kept on resurfacing: the increasingly manifest aggressiveness on the part of women, personal inadequacy owing to a presumed or real lack of personal and material competitiveness, and alienation.

In our inquiry concerning women as sexonomic subjects, five main areas were highlighted: men's view of *women's sexuality, material wealth, and power;* sexonomic significance of the *qualities and functions of the Lady LUSSEY/LUSSEY; ideal woman; bedding with women; needing to have a woman but also wishing to be free.*

In addition, several other areas were also explored concerning issues which had arisen from manifest forms of male behavior vis-à-vis women and which were deemed directly pertinent in discussing women as sexonomic subjects: the "umbilical cord" syndrome; the "games only boys play" phenomenon; homosexuality and its sexonomic significance; and life-threatening VD. Having direct relevance to basic sexonomic indicators (women's SEVACs, sexonomic values, and sexonomic prices), these areas may be viewed as primary considerations in women's sexonomic strategies and games. In this sense, the exploration of these areas will be deemed to constitute the requisite for the enhancement of a woman's sexonomic image as well as the determinants of women's sexonomic success.

Women's Sexuality, Material Wealth, and Power Defined

Women as sex subjects: In a man's fantasies about women's sexuality, his potency is very closely linked with territoriality; when intercourse is about to happen (whatever the position), he will seek to possess "his" woman and will manifest this feeling by wishing to share with her to the maximum his three prehistoric and forever enduring urges—pukkacity, sensitiveness, and erethism. During those moments, her Lady LUSSEY becomes the natural abode for his Sir MOJJ as well as the exclusive receptacle for the mass of his explosively discharged semen. So vastly powerful is this urge that the feeling of territoriality prevails, by far, over society-induced mores and legislations concerning human fornication; men (and reciprocally, women) will forget about ecclesiastic and secular conventions, marriage vows or marriage contracts, and publicly professed morals or implicit faithfulness when they find themselves face-to-face with the loin heat–generated urge to engage in instant intercourse. In providing such an accommodative crevice of pleasure, the Lady LUSSEY's unique monopolistic position forces the man's hands, arouses him, and reinforces his territoriality instinct—possibly nature's own strategy of not wishing to let any of the precious semen go to waste generated by artificial devices.

However, territoriality has its major drawback in that the respective woman may not wish to be considered the sexual "domain" of one and only one particular male; in fact, she may find that her LUSSEY may well serve the purpose of cohabiting with several MOJJs, one at a time and with replacement over time. If, through this momentous act of releasing instant loin heat, the man then proceeds to seek a commitment that the woman is not willing to give—since she may wish to reserve her LUSSEY for intercourse with other men—the woman will normally find herself in the "saint whore" type of situation, which will entrap her.

How can a man handle a circumstance in which he feels that he must absolutely have "his own" receptacle while the woman must be free to choose? Clearly, "pure" love would appear as one of the possible two answers as it refers to the "sacrifice principle," while cash payment or assets over time might be considered the other well-documented solution (which could also be called a "long-term LUSSEY rental contract"). In real-life situations, Sexonomics will expect the enticement-and-control quality of most women to find a solution to this kind of problem. If her solution will accept a pecuniary settlement in exchange for granting monopoly rights to the user, the value of the cash payoff will be the higher, the more acute his loin heat and the greater his concern for exclusive territoriality.

How do men's loin heat and territoriality tie in with women's sexuality? Simply speaking, whenever a man needs *her* (remember, it is women who raise men, but it is men who are made to believe—often by their admiring mothers—to be needing *her* all the time!), he will be expected to pay the appropriate sexonomic price. Once he is engaged in paying the appropriate price (on the assumption that he gets the equivalent exchange value in return), he will assume that he acquires monopoly utilization rights. The woman is a "saint" if she sticks with the deal and reserves her LUSSEY for *his* exclusive use, but she becomes a "whore" when she breaks the contract and grants user's rights over her LUSSEY to other men.

What does any of this have to do with women's sex appeal?

The linkage between women's "sex appeal" and women as "sex objects" creates an inseparable effect on all men, something akin to Gillette's double-blade razor; only one is sufficient to guarantee a clean cut, but two will do the job better and faster. This is so because—unlike women, who, as per their own admission, consider a man's "sex appeal" as something much more than just his genitals and gyrations (see pages 59–70)—*men in heat become cross-eyed about the one and only unique outlet that promises instant cooling off*—the LUSSEY. Evidently, gentlemen of "standing" will arrange never to be "caught" lusting only for an ordinary LUSSEY of the lower orders in such situations that priority should be assigned incognito to the owner of a LUSSEY who fulfills the conditions of convenience and confidentiality at the respectively appropriate sexonomic price (arrangements that underlie the popularity of all levels of prostitution throughout history) with special material provisions for especially furtive routes that may have to be taken to satisfy these men's need for such enjoyment. For women, bedding with men is said to be a "total" experience that is unlikely to happen without the many requisites that make up his "sex appeal" in its broadest sense. On the contrary, "average" men are usually directly aroused by the sight of a particularly esthetically pleasing female body; in consequence, they will yearn for instant sexual gratification, especially if the sexonomic marketing of a bidding woman's other personal qualities (voice modulation, energy beam, cleanliness, gentleness, affection, "soul in the eyes") offers an enticing civilized backdrop. But alone, the setting is insufficient to arouse the male suitor since his instincts and thoughts revolve around her LUSSEY—a forever primitive, prehistoric, territorial craving—an inborn tendency that is expected to persist well beyond the postmodern era of social evolution.

In his fantasies, a man will dwell his mind on her breasts, wondering about their size, shape, suppleness, and the speed and frequency of the blooming of nipples; on the distance between the navel and the pubic area, including speculations concerning the skin texture in that terribly erogenous zone; and on the panorama of the woman's crotch (e.g., will she open up with discreet delicacy and invite him to share in the personal fragrance of her exquisite Lady LUSSEY, or will she tear open her thighs and shock him with the dripping of uncontrollable self-possessed lust?) A man of high sexonomic quality will certainly not delve long on the latter possibility for even sexonomically lower-quality men will quickly take refuge from a woman whose apparently insatiable sexual appetite would seem to threaten their own territorial integrity.

In the eyes of a perceptive man, even the highest "backdrop" qualities of a woman cannot compensate for the unappealing sight and unpleasant odor of a LUSSEY (in spite of his possibly finding her breasts curiously arousing for their shape, vibrancy, and the promise of lactic potency). Unlike playboys, who—being in the right places and demonstrating that they are "with it"—will act as externally induced magnets for most women, even though their genital area may not at all be all that sightly—playgirls will very quickly lose their male admirers or adherents if discovered to have unsightly and provocatively greedy vaginas.

Will higher-order men fantasize about women's sexuality? They most certainly will. But while their fantasies are equally directly body-oriented, they will pay much more heed to the backdrop of the composite of her. The enticement proffered by her other personal feminine qualities are viewed not as a determining factor in seeking instant sexual gratification but as the required sexonomic basis for a long-term loving relationship—well beyond the pleasing esthetics of the courted woman's anatomy and sex appeal. It is only in cases of such discerning higher-order men that women will command respectively the highest sexonomic valuations. With an allusion to our *sexonomic strategies and games*, we must therefore once again emphasize how terribly important it is for women to continuously seek to enhance not only their biological sex appeal but also her potentially equally tantalizing personal attributes. But we must also warn our female readers that too much emphasis on her sex appeal and too little input into the development of her spiritual qualities will have a depreciating and possibly demeaning effect on her image if she fails to camouflage her sexual preferences and transparencies from the forever prying eyes of the public.

With regard to "pure sexuality," the difference between the sexonomic valuation of a Lady LUSSEY relative to a plain LUSSEY reveals itself in the public behavior of the respective orders of women that they represent. Women of the highest two orders will never manifest in public their desire to fornicate; instead, they will wisely first entice and then, over a prolonged time period, slowly and deliberately lift the veil of her personal charms, all of it in strictest privacy. Neither will ever act in a manner that might threaten her with AIDS. On the contrary, a woman of low sexonomic valuation simply cannot wait in her urge to be stung and will bare herself greedily and within the instant, not even realizing that the only men to be aroused in this situation of vulgar forms of intercourse are men of equally low sexonomic value.

Women and material wealth: "Wealthy women whose husbands cannot do a good job servicing their sexual needs will seek their contentment by purchasing the cash-and-carry professional expertise of gigolos." One of the lesser explored forms of human behavior, the relation between women and wealth, and men's perception of this relation, are of great significance to Sexonomics because of the vast preponderance of well-to-do widows and the enormous inflow of well-paid women into even the highest professional ranks and realms of business and government. Much more than ever before, men are presently publicly wanted for their sexuality, a vast new market in which the rules of the game reveal conditions and contracts similar to those in the markets in which the buyers of sex are men and the sellers are women. As we have already professed, highest-order men are "not for sale," which leaves us with the conclusion that most men in the market in which wealthy women are demanders come from the orders of Vulpine-men and Girandole-men. While women would marry rich for many reasons which have no direct relevance to money (pages 85–88), men, especially the younger set, will seek out wealthy women mainly for material comfort, the power which money thus earned is believed to give them, and last but not least, narcissism (being "in love with oneself" can be a very expensive proposition).

Just like their women counterparts (the younger set of women who consciously seek out rich men), these men have no feelings of guilt or shame. Consequently, they act in accord with the material aspects of sexonomic reasoning. They know that, for the money, they must provide companionship and sexual gratification. Evidence has it that these men are dismissed as easily from these relationships as are the counterpart women from theirs. Lately, however, a new brand of man for hire has emerged—men who sell their semen or entire bodies to women wishing to have a child but no father, a phenomenon which has become particularly visible in the women's age-group of thirty-five to forty-five years. But evidence also has it that, unlike the women—most of whom hold on to their incomes (and inheritances) obtained from the usually older males with their much shorter life expectancy—the men who marry "rich older women" are much more likely to squander their incomes (and eventual inheritances) on much younger women. While scores of rich men's widows still manage to retain their material wealth, other such widows—exploited by their Girandole-men lovers—eventually die impoverished.

Relative to the market for rich men, which, as we have seen, has tightened considerably, the market for wealthy women may be considered much softer, which is explained by the numerical disproportions—there are many more wealthy and available high-income women than are equivalent men, especially in the set of older women. In sexonomic terms, this kind of situation favors the younger set of men because they will have a much greater chance of success if they do not mind approaching "older women." Looking ahead in time and seeking to choose the appropriate sexonomic strategy, eligible young men would be advised to give serious consideration to becoming professionals in the market for wealthy women—provided that the money they will be making and the narcissistic life they will be enjoying will be worth their eventually sinking forever deeper into the lowest order of men, Girandole-men.

Women and power. Are men turned on by women with power? As we have seen above, what turns on women are men with power. Power makes men masculine, and men of power have sex appeal. But men of power are not those who have a more potent penis but those who radiate strength, command obedience from other men, and will also prevail over elements and those whose brains rule over their loins. But women are the "opposite of men," and Sexonomics will first prudently seek to clarify the term "power" as men see it in reference to women, and it will only then proceed to seek an answer to this question and to discuss the reasons.

Evidently, when men speak of "women's power," they rarely, if ever, mean the muscle power of the women's physique, even though there is ample evidence that many women have and will physically abuse men whose bodies are smaller or weaker (many mothers will hit their children, and a significant percentage of girlfriends and wives will beat their boyfriends or husbands or otherwise cause physical harm to them). Fortunately, this is not generally how most women behave, but the sexonomic valuation of those who do will suffer and, in extreme cases, even diminish to zero.

Neither do men, as yet, often get to discuss women "in power" (the equivalent of the dominant men in the realm of "traditional" sets of control and influence) since the number of these women, both absolute and relative to those of the men, is still too small to allow reasonably intelligent generalizations. To be sure, those women who have left their imprint in these realms of "male predominance" have tended to surround themselves with personal aides, assistants, counselors, and fortune-tellers, using all of the man-developed and applied means of keeping themselves in power, ranging from all orchestrations of PR and persuasion to dissuasion, manipulation, coercion, corruption, and even threats of violence. In addition, many of these women (not unlike their men counterparts) have also left behind an outpouring of stories concerning their sexual appetites and exploits (e.g., countless are the stories of goings-on, ranging from Cleopatra through to the imperial court of Catherine the Great—with their modern-day equivalents in the "intimate" biographies of some of the eminent "ladies in power" in contemporary society). In these accounts, we note two interesting kinds of behavior by women in power. On one extreme, the "imperial" types, who command literally absolute power and indulge in sexual excesses, either because their power corrupts the control center of the pleasure quality of their royal LUSSEYs or because they wish to demonstrate their total secular powers over all men by bedding with a score of them. On the other extreme, women who had risen from somewhat lower status to posts of prestige and power by marrying ruling sovereigns will—while still married to them—proceed to select men from the lower orders who manifest extraordinary sexual potency and are capable of exerting enormous influence upon such women's LUSSEYs and, with it, upon the direction of state—or corporate—policy (the so-called Rasputin trap).

Does *power* make women "feminine" (in the sense of power by itself making men "masculine")? On first sight, Sexonomics needs to point out a possible logical contradiction. On the one hand, power is said to be a "masculine" trait; men are viewed as the "stronger" sex (in reference to their greater physical power); on the other hand, women are characterized as "feminine," which connotes, in traditional language, the "weaker sex." Sexonomics interprets the term "feminine" differently—as a complement of "masculine," which implies that man and woman make up one complete and equal set of human beings. This is contrary to the old-fashioned emphasis on the "higher state" of men and the lower "status of women," a frame of mind which had given rise to women's movements' premise that women and men are forever engaged in a competition for power and are therefore irretrievably locked in two separate entities that are presumed never to be able to merge into a single harmonious togetherness.

But we are left with the question of whether "femininity" is compatible with "power." Studying women's behavior, we distinctly recognize two types of power which are innate to women, powers which are inborn in their nature as women and which we shall name "feminine power"; and we also discover one additional type, the power that women acquire by emulating men and competing with them, a power that they will use as if they were men, which we shall name "secular power."

Even at the highest-level orders of men, the two "feminine" powers are the Lady LUSSEY and her three qualities and women's power to reason as women (viz. women's wiles). These two "feminine" powers are of great significance to sexonomic reasoning as they emanate directly from the uniqueness of Lady LUSSEY and her three qualities and reveal themselves in women's desire to maximize their sexonomic happiness. Sexonomics submits that the major source of the power of women over men (not over other women) is found in the Lady LUSSEY's enticement-and-control quality, conception-and-delivery quality, and pleasure quality as well as in the intelligent and rational use of these qualities with the singular purpose of enhancing their owners' sexonomic happiness heart levels.

- A woman's enticement-and-control quality is a powerful instrument in her strategy concerning the maximization of her sexonomic utility function in her relation with men. Since, as we have established, most men "need" *her*, the lure of an enticingly but sparingly offered Lady LUSSEY will be found to be irresistible to most men, resulting in highest sexonomic valuation and level-respective sexonomic prices and values. This biological power of women over men's loin heat–weakened capacity to reason can be enhanced by the women owners' putting restrictions on the availability of their Lady LUSSEYs, a function of their control quality. The women's enticement quality, unique to women, ranks higher than the men's power of "purely physical sexual attractiveness" because, speaking in large numbers, women are able to manipulate their enticement quality much more easily and more effectively than men are able to do with their quality of physical sexual attractiveness.

- The women's control function also serves as a very powerful means of manipulation for, applying it in its entire range from pure reason to unmitigated lust, this function will effectively impose a limit beyond which a LUSSEY seeking to engage in an anticipated exquisite fornication will be forced by her owner's reason not to do it if she is to suffer sexonomic devaluation. By applying her control function, the woman will consequently forgo the enjoyment of potentially arousing and fulfilling sexual encounters—the price she will have to pay in the short runs in order to maximize her overall long-term sexonomic happiness (we have already discovered that a LUSSEY, made too frequently available, will demean her owner's status and will eventually relegate her down to the next lower order of women). But the application of a woman's control function will induce all perceptive men to slow down their advances. Most Vulpine-men and most Mob-men, blinded by the vehemence of their lust, never notice the thinking processes that go into those women they are after. If they did, they would discover that thinking women have much more to offer than only their pleasure quality.

Evidently, the control quality cannot but emanate from the woman's ability to reason, her principal inborn power, a power which can be even more enhanced by society's commitment to render the women completely free to come into their own and to develop lifestyles appropriate to all thinking women—a complete and total negation of the traditional presumption by most of our men-created and male-run institutions that women not only do not count as souls but are also incapable of rational thought.

- The conception-and-delivery quality of a woman is the other positive instrument of power that women can play up in seeking to enhance their chances of success in their sexonomic strategies vis-à-vis men. This power has lately taken on a social dimension in countries with very low birthrates and has also been used as a political instrument by well-organized women's groups. In the hands of individual women, the consent to conceive represents a much more potent sexonomic bargaining tool than does the desire to conceive. Used effectively (its skillful application will prevent the bidding male from feeling estranged), it may serve as a primary means for the enhancement of the woman's lifetime sexonomic utility. This quality in women is at the base of family planning, but it does have two significant drawbacks—competing women, many of whom are willing to "conceive" without any restrictions (especially women in the age-group of thirty-five and above), and the loss of sexual enjoyment over time (since "being careful" every time will inevitably lead to a deterioration of the quality of biological sexual fulfillment).

As the conception-and-delivery function represents a positive instrument of women's sexonomic power, the pleasure quality of the Lady LUSSEY may be viewed as potentially always a negative device, an irrational force. Clearly, a woman who wishes to do *it* most of the time will soon demean herself and will soon command no sexonomic price whatsoever. The power of passion may be viewed as the most crucial aspect in a woman's sexuality and sexonomic rationality, but it is negatively correlated with the power to reason. Whereas reason may be viewed as the foundation of the sexual act as well as its most fulfilling dimension, a bidding female who misunderstands and misuses this particular capacity will eventually engage in no sexual activity whatsoever; neither would she if her power of passion should become an uncontrollable force and overwhelming force upon all bidding men, even to the extent of inducing them to retire from their respective sexonomic market.

Do any of the remaining men's powers also apply equally to women (pages 67–68)?

- *The power of achiever and conqueror.* Gone is the historical image of women as the "weaker sex." While still expected to deliver babies and as intensively vying for achievement and the conquest of commanding heights, many women now perform combat roles and some women even meet their deaths in disintegrating spaceships. It is even said that teleologically inclined women are seeking to work for a universal society in which the world government will be composed only of women with the purpose of "undoing" all the historical evils that had been perpetrated by men upon mankind and the planet earth. But the true basis of the women's power is to achieve and to conquer lies—not so much in the individual woman's finesse to induce an initially unwilling male to engage in fornication weekdays or weekends, but in the increasing ability of women in large numbers to organize themselves into pressure groups. This, with an unrelenting quest toward securing the highest posts of effective management, more and more accomplished political acumen, and a very substantial material base that will provide the necessary finance. In spite of the basic animosity between NOW on the one hand and REAL-women on the other, in particular with respect to their views about and relations to men, all women's groups have three goals in common: *POW* (power, opportunity, wealth). While most members of NOW, known for their disdain of men, will apply external pressure on the body politic in order to realize their goals, the ladies of REAL-women are much more suave and realistic; while enjoying their men, they will work, at the threat of "withdrawal" within their families, to achieve the same. Having recourse to this ultimate means, women will convince most men that the goals are reasonable and well thought-out. The threat of withholding sexual favors will only rarely fail and will qualify as the ultimate bargaining tool if other women and women's groups declare their solidarity. Unlike NOW-women, whose basic attitudes scare men off, REAL-women are wise enough to express the "withdrawal of the honey," not as a threat but as a condition—an effective sexonomic strategy in which women's power to reason will have prevailed over their own personal passion qualities.

- *The power of conviction*: While men of "character and conviction" are deemed forthright but are also known at times to turn into rigid doctrinaires with respect to sexist forms of behavior, many women in Western society are known to engage in intrigues and machinations which are said to be "typical of women," at the base of which is found the moral imperative of the self, unique to women. While professing the sanctity of motherhood, a significant percentage of women also insist upon abortion on demand and the freedom of concubinage (even with other women's men); while wishing to have at least one child, most are unwilling to settle for more than the maximum of "one precious hour per day" with their child or children. Implied in this attitude is these women's willingness to do anything, including cohabitation, that will be useful in helping them in the achievement of their long-term sexonomic goals (a trait which is particularly visible in the younger set). However, even though their goals concerning power may presently be considered as comparable to those of men, in the choice of their means, individual women may be said to combine both traditional sexist doctrinairism by exploiting the fallibility of men by "getting there through their men's stomachs" (which is still a widely popular strategy technique for most older women) and an increasing public orchestration of their demands (the preferred tool of women's movement organizations). Thus, what we have is a mix of old-fashioned convictions and modern pragmatism, which involve mainly and foremost material considerations. However, the weighting has shifted: traditional views ("we must stand by our men") have given way to opportunism ("men owe us, therefore any corrective action is right action") with the odd example of compromise ("we are not against men; we are only concerned about redeeming past evils"). These manifest kinds of behavior have had a serious negative effect upon many men—even many "good guys"—and have rendered them increasingly more perplexed if not resentful. The recent rapid increase in overt homosexuality and the rising unwillingness of large numbers of men to get married may be traced back to their concern that "terms of exchange between the sexes" were changing against men. Yet this increasingly unfavorable situation has been mitigated by the fact that two significant phenomena—in comparison with the successes of women activists—have worked in men's favor. Not only has the ratio of the numbers of women to men been increasing, giving the men much more opportunity to make the "right" choice, but women's liberation has also resulted in a massive outpouring and marketing of women's sexuality in contradiction to the resentful views of many of the doctrinaire leaders of women's liberation movements.

- *The aura of inexhaustible energy*: A woman's personal energy field, like a man's, provides succor, comradeship, and protection in that it is directly linked to procreation and survival. But women's rules of the game are different from those of men, and much of the energy of women is expended on playing their sexonomic games. While the men, in order to cover up their basic predatory orientation, often manifest chivalry vis-à-vis other women as well as most other men, women are more ruthless with other women than they are with men. In spite of the official slogans of women's movements concerning the "universal sisterhood" of all women, individual women have become even more accommodative in their private relations with men while expending much more energy than ever before in seeking to outcompete other women. While many individual males have been the fortunate beneficiaries of their women's aura of inexhaustible energy, the last three decades have amply demonstrated the extent to which this enormously potent and creative force in women has been wasted by the incessant infighting among women's groups—a situation that has led to a deterioration of women's sexonomic valuations and is inhibiting all attempts to create and maintain intergender harmony, the basis for all social progress.

- *The power of imagination*: A woman's power of imagination is every bit as creative as that of a man's. It contributes just as much to an exciting love relationship and an interesting and continuously self-regenerating togetherness. But women who possess this power will use much of it in a teleological manner—anticipating, planning, plotting, and even conspiring. Having learned from the exploitations of the past era and recognizing that they have it in their power to prevent this past from being carried over into the future, women have necessarily become more "forward oriented" individually as well as a pressure group. In their homes, their power of imagination covers a whole gamut of wishes, from family planning to sexual fulfillment and material stability; in public, this power is harnessed into the achievement of priority goals like abortions on demand, equitable laws on divorce settlement, and equal income for equal education and effort. For men, women with this power are worth a very high sexonomic valuation, even though sharing their lives with such women can, at times, prove unsettling enough to require great wisdom, infinite patience, and serene tolerance. The power of imagination is linked directly to a woman's sexuality: a wise woman's will know how to proceed to entice her occasionally pessimistic lover to reemphasize his potency and pukkacity. In an erotically charged but precariously apprehensive moment, she will express admiration for the beauty of his fully erect penis and will also, if she truly loves him, commit her entire being to their lovemaking and make him rediscover his quality as a "great lover." A truly loving woman will have no difficulty at all with this kind of encouragement, even though her man will not at all times be ready to satisfy her fully awakened needs. Female wisdom and the enticement quality go hand in hand and will transcend those of literally any males, from the entire range of his first moments of doubt, to the ultimate crescendo of joy with "his woman's" Lady LUSSEY.

- *The power of positive aging*: Unlike most men, most women always worry about their aging and the respective negative sexonomic consequences. Many women start worrying much earlier than do others, even in the professional ranks of Art-women, where reaching the age of thirty-five years becomes the shock threshold. The lower-order woman, terrified by the first signs of the aging of her body, will seek to cover it by expending substantive resources upon trying to look younger than she really is, and she will never realize that the lifelong overutilization of her LUSSEY had caused irreparable physical and sexonomic damage. The higher-order woman, cognizant of the fact that quality men view her with a fascination that transcends beyond her physical appearance, will use wisdom in order to make her aging process appear as the result of the continuous development of her feminine mystique. The Lady LUSSEY of a wise woman will not have been exposed during her younger years to the careless and gluttonous wear and tear that arises from her uncontrolled overutilization. Her owner will have kept herself youthful by naturally caring for herself and for her intimate parts and will know how to grow into a remarkable fifty-year-old who feels radiant, bears a scent of vaginal exclusivity, and continues to manifest her magnetic femininity—knowing only too well that she can offer her lover so much more than just one of those explosive but raw and uncultured LUSSEYs of a typical early twenty-year-old female of the lower orders. She is also aware that the sexonomic value of an intrinsically well-kept mature woman will command a premium, which in return will make her feel and appear fresher and younger than most of the worried thirty-five-year-olds. Women of quality age much more slowly than the average woman and are of great significance to sexonomists because they are endowed with an inside time clock of unusual effectiveness, a mechanism whose intensive study may provide the knowledge required to retard the aging process of all other women.

- *The economic/financial power.* The economic power of women is the sum of the women's purchasing power as consumers, of their incomes from employment, professions, and entrepreneurship, and of their titles of ownership of inherited or otherwise accumulated assets. Historically, the significance of this power was manifest in products and markets specialized in catering to the needs of the elites, whose behavioral preferences reflected themselves in conspicuous consumption and conspicuous leisure and in markets for luxury goods, unlike the women of the masses whose priorities necessarily centered on staples, bland diet foods, and mass-produced manufactures. These women's lifestyles were vastly different in all respects, including men: in the distant past, the well-to-do women would only rarely divorce, for their husbands were men of means and standing. In return for their letting their husbands (many of whom were not loved) use their bodies for their pleasure as well as for procreation, these women enjoyed high material living standards and usually considered themselves free to engage in numerous extramarital affairs, while their poorer sisters had no choice but to stick with their husbands because they had nowhere else to go while being equally careful not to be caught cheating on their husbands. In Sexonomics, these two groups have significance in that these women's choices of men and material things reveal the rationality of sexonomic reasoning. But in contemporary society, the far more interesting group of women with economic power are women who are members of the professions, administrators and executives in government and industry, and, broadly speaking, the women technicians, white collar workers, and union leaders. Similar to the male holders of economic power, these women organize inputs and engage in production and distribution in order to augment their profits, increase their holdings, and eventually use these powers for the achievement of personal goals. As we have already seen, the successful ones of these women—those from orders other than Vampire-women—amass assets in order to augment their power of production and distribution, to acquire resources and land, and to increase their command over men and other women. While their overall numbers are still too small to permit, these women are to be labeled "remakers of society"; many of them have already left their imprint in industry, finance, and government.

Some of these women come from the order of Lotus-women, while many belong to the order of Art-women; surprisingly, a significant proportion of technical and union personnel have lately risen from the order of Conch-women. The women from the two highest orders will seek out men of respectively equivalent qualities and will effectively combine their creative entrepreneurship with the traditional role of women of that status. Having the well-nigh perfect balance of creative talent and femininity, these women know how to handle economic power at even the highest levels and represent for the select bidding males from the counterpart orders the highest sexonomic value with great potential as investment into a lifelong family partnership. These women are strong-willed, committed, and principled companions who will give birth to equally strong-willed and talented daughters (the hitherto unspoken of historical continuation of the bloodline of women of exceptional quality). Women who have no difficulty handling economic power are usually very reserved in their private lives. If married, they are fully devoted to their husbands and children; if unmarried (most likely, by choice), they will excel in the public domain or will forever be ready to support worthwhile social causes. Viewed from the present vantage point, the remaining women in the domain of economic power are women whose incoming numbers are significant but who, by their very natures, cannot be expected to handle power effectively in the long run—Vampire-women. Attracted by the prospect of power and dominance, often backed by unusually high intelligence, and driven by an enormous desire to succeed, these women (as we have seen on pages 27–28) are not only unable to control their sexual appetites but also have negative and destructive attitudes with respect to men. Unfulfilled in their private life and increasingly unbalanced in their income-earning undertakings, they represent low sexonomic valuations and, therefore, poor investment into a lifetime partnership. Increasingly desperate to overcome their frustrations, many of these women will eventually seek the illusion of happiness by buying the short-term services of Girandole-men.

Women's Sexuality, Material Wealth, and Power Compared

- How do men and especially men of quality view these fundamental determinants of quality womanhood?

- Which of these determinants are accorded the highest weight, which the lowest, and why?

- Is men's perception of the order of this ranking likely to change over time and why?

- Do younger men rank these qualities differently from older men?

- Are these rankings and their weights different for each of the orders of men?

- What is the significance of these rankings over time?

- What is the sexonomic significance of all of these?

As we have already noted, the sampled men accorded the highest preference to women's sexuality followed by women's material means but with women's power lagging far behind. But even with men, we notice a distinct split of opinion on the weighting of the component elements of the power of women as women. In our table, the number in parentheses signifies the relative order of ranking for all categories making up women's power—1 for the highest, 8 for the lowest:

Fundamental Determinants of Women's Power:	Older men:	Younger men:
Sexual attractiveness:	(5)	(1)
Reason:	(1)	(4)
Achiever:	(7)	(2)
Character:	(4)	(6)
Aura of energy:	(3)	(5)
Imagination:	(6)	(7)
Positive aging:	(2)	(8)
Economic power:	(8)	(3)

The results of this sampling of the set of men reveals that the younger men prefer women who are sexually attractive, dynamic, and materially inclined; the older men in the sample prefer in their women reflective capacity, harmonious aging, and a strong energy field. Interestingly, this order of ranking would have to be corrected if a sample comprised only lower-order men, whose overall preference, both older and younger, revealed a much greater closeness to the rankings of the "younger set" in our sample.

The sexonomic significance of these rankings and of all these questions? Simply put, younger women who aspire to maximize their sexonomic utility functions will wish to study present and emerging patterns in the assessment by men of women's qualities over time. In so doing, these women would proceed to learn how to adjust to the changing expectations of men and thereby know how to maximize their own sexonomic happiness. The trend so far has revealed an evolution toward a much greater emphasis on material self-interest; women are expected to pull their own weight in the sense of material acquisitiveness in spite of the fact that their sexuality still remains the primary bargaining instrument. Those women who do not, possibly in the expectation of "old-fashioned" romantic and idealistic relationships, will be left behind by their more predatory and competitive sisters in gender.

Studying behavioral patterns of women as university students confirms the fact that most of the intelligent set of younger women (as well as many of their mothers who are unhappy with their marriages) started adapting en masse to this recognition about twenty-five years ago as an investment—not only into securing for themselves their own material means of sustenance, but also into rendering themselves visibly more competitive in their search for their own long-term male partners. It appears that men's appreciation of women's qualities across the generations will retain the same order of priorities, except that more weight will be assigned to women's economic power at the cost of the loss of women's sexual powers. At this vantage point, this changeover would seem the logical outcome of the expected depreciation of women's sexuality and the appreciation of their material base owing to their earning incomes and accumulating assets.

Necessarily, however, the question does arise concerning what the men will do in their desire to enjoy optimal sexual pleasure if "their" women are too busy to provide the time and the milieu? It seems likely that a new breed of women will have to emerge in large enough numbers to cater to these outpouring needs of frustrated future husbands; "neoconcubinage," as a profession, which may include women who will earn their livelihoods by providing the services of surrogate mothers. Sexonomic rationality would even suggest that—should society find itself threatened with extinction owing to the unwillingness of professional women to beget offspring—neoconcubinage, polygamy, and surrogate motherhood may become the norm that will replace the morals based on the Christian ethic.

Men and the Three Enticing Functions of the Lady LUSSEY:

The relative weighting of the three functions of the Lady LUSSEY (enticement-and-control quality, conception-and-delivery quality, pleasure quality) will depend entirely on the purpose of the association with a particular male, but for maximum effectiveness, each of these qualities will be displayed jointly or individually in its fullest bloom when the right occasion arises. While the promise of an ample material reward may to some degree arouse a LUSSEY from her passive state, she will be superactivated only when a woman believes to have met her "dream man."

As revealed during the interviews, women distinguish very clearly between the desire to have sex, on the one hand, and sexual intercourse, which arises from human loving as an investment into a long-term relationship, on the other. The former leads to the almost exclusive perusal of the Lady LUSSEY's pleasure quality (with an adequate application of both enticement and control for, after all, a man is not only a requisite for lustful fornication but also as an exclusive but often unwanted source for conception), while the latter will eventually concentrate on the conception and delivery function as the basis for family planning.

Interestingly, all women in the sample revealed that "good sex is hard work, even though it pays off handsomely" and that, if it is to work, both partners would have to be equally liberated sexually; if one is not, especially the male, then the other has to "work so much harder," which will ultimately diminish the pleasure. Most of the women also admitted that they were willing to put in this extra effort if they "really needed that man," like "hanging on to him when everything else crumbled." There was also fairly general agreement that, in emphasizing the pleasure quality, the first time *it* happens, both partners tend to be sentimental and that both would have to engage in *it* with maximum joy in order to make *it* "really good." A lot of practice is required by partners united in the enjoyment of their sexuality and wishing with equal enthusiasm to make *it* perfect. But they do not necessarily have to love each other equally; rather, they must be willing to work on *it* equally and to perfect it for one another's complete satisfaction.

Since good sex is perfected in practice, great sex will become the basis for a long-term relationship. To achieve such a relationship, a woman cannot keep on going from person to person; humans simply never get sex as good as when they roam around as they do with someone with whom they sleep all the time. There are also additional requisites; their other interests also have to jibe for if they do not, the reciprocity in their sexuality will ultimately disappear and the couple will break up. On the other hand, good sex alone and equal willingness to work at *it* are not a sufficient basis for marriage, but sexuality is important if there is to be a marriage and if it is to endure. In this sense, there will have to be a balance in the application of all three qualities of the Lady LUSSEY—the enticement-and-control quality, in order to induce the man to propose and to get him to wish to make love while leaving the woman in control of the situation; the conception-and-delivery quality, as a response to the naturally patriarchal instincts of the man; and the pleasure quality, which is the proof that the woman loves the man in her partner (her "lion," "tiger," or even "jackrabbit" but never her giraffe, spotted hyena, or porcupine). However, both the young and the old women in the sample stated repeatedly that the main sexual organ in all women was contained in the head and that the pleasure function would eventually be subordinated to the control function, especially if very potential material gains were involved. There was general agreement among the interviewed women who did not love their men or husbands that it was in their material self-interest to let their bodies be used by their men; the more often, the greater was the promise of material rewards and compensatory allowances or just for the retention of the acceptable status quo. Strangely, though, these women would not call such exchanges (money or goods for sex under the guise of marriage) "prostitution" but "using their heads."

Sexonomics has discovered that the three qualities of the Lady LUSSEY serve several purposes and that they are put to full use by their owners in a conscious act to maximize their sexonomic happiness. But whereas the pleasure quality, preoccupied with instantaneous gratification, will be paramount in the more youthful years of a woman as well as shortly into her menopause period, the other two qualities will prevail in the long run through the primacy of her brain as the control center and the ultimate determinant of sexonomic rationality and choice.

Ideal Woman

Of what significance in Sexonomics is the notion of the "ideal woman"? Is this notion a concept, an abstraction, or possibly even an illusion? Or does it reflect the real-life experience of men and their beings and doings and, therefore, a human quality that may be subjectively and objectively quantified?

Intuitively, the image of the "ideal woman" calls for the highest sexonomic assessment as we have already established in our ranking of the orders of women; overall, Lotus-women approximate most closely this image, which represents, at the same time, the highest norm toward which quality men are deemed to aspire. Sexonomics necessarily views the image of the "ideal woman" from several vantage points since, clearly, a woman of such perceived exceptional sexonomic quality will command from her male suitors a much higher sexonomic price than would women of perceived lower sexonomic quality. Higher valuations will result in higher sexonomic prices and exchange value equivalents (quality women will command quality men in exchange).

Sexonomics submits that there are two notions of "ideal woman," the absolute and the relative. The former reveals itself in any woman in the order of Lotus-women; the latter refers to the highest sexonomic quality that a woman can reach in a particular order, a quality that may permit such a woman to rise into the next higher order. Since the Lotus-woman represents the ultimate sexonomic quality in women, she, in fact, represents the ideal woman for the men of all orders; but she is attainable only for the Quintessential-man, the only men who are fully cognizant and appreciative of her uniqueness. The Lotus-woman represents concrete reality to the Quintessential-man but is only an illusion to the men of the lower orders. Lower-order men will have a perception of the superior qualities of higher-order women, but, except for very few of these men who will have ever been engaged in intimate liaisons with higher-order women, they will not have experienced them, meaning that, for most men of the lower orders, the "ideal woman" image of the women of the higher orders remains an abstraction. For example, Vulpine-men will dream of the Art-woman for she represents the almost unattainable "ideal woman." But since cohabitation with her will occur only very rarely, Art-women do, in fact, remain an abstraction for most Vulpine-men. However, since they bed and live with Conch-women, Vulpine-men will learn how to rank during their lifetimes the several Conch-women with whom they will have been intimate and will, therefore, be objectively able to decide which of these Conch-women will deserve being labeled the "ideal woman" within the order of Conch-women. A similar statement can be made for the assessment of Elephant-women by Mob-men, the former being the natural sexonomic counterpart of the latter.

Clearly, as the Lotus-woman represents the ultimate ideal for all men, she is attainable and represents an objective fact only to Quintessential-men; but she is unattainable and remains, therefore, an abstraction for all other lower-order men. As we have already remarked, all lower-order women comprise women with demonstrably inferior sexonomic qualities relative to those of highest-order women. However, even women of lower sexonomic quality do exemplify "ideal women" to their own men, those of the lower orders. Viewed in sexonomic terms, higher-order men will always rank lower-order women on a much lower SEVAC range (than they would the "ideal women" of their own higher order), this being so because lower-order women are assessed in terms far less than perfection since such women are much less desirable and, therefore, unwanted. The Vampire-woman is the farthest removed from the ideal woman image of the Lotus-woman, both absolutely and relatively, and even Girandole-men have a remarkably tough time idealizing Vampire-women in spite of their intimate cash-for-sex relationship.

Looking in concrete terms at the notion of the "ideal woman," we discover that, in the eyes and psyches of most every mature man, this image still constitutes for him a real-life living aspiration right unto his death. A fortunate male person happily recalls how his mother loved him and cared for him, while his little sister looked absolutely like an angel, even though she was at times behaving like a pest. He fondly remembers his first, puppy love in elementary school, a little girl who was irrelevant to and useless in the games the boys played, who but did make his heart beat faster whenever she stood on the sidelines watching, admiring, and cheering him on; he still caresses the feeling of warmth (in recalling that at sixteen years of age in the old times [nowadays as early as about eleven] which followed her invitation to "show me what you've got and I'll show you what I have" and how this invitation resulted in his first timid kiss. Then following several years of nervous and awkward exploration, the abstract image of the heavenly ideal transcended into the concrete reality of an ideal but living human being, a grown-up young woman. And finally, reaching back into his forever fascinated memory cells, he reminisces about the inner glow of happiness following his marriage ceremony with his first greatest love, joyfully reliving the eternal moment of the eventual complete merging with the virgin who had been destined to become his wife (because he would have died if she had not)—the blessed fusion of two human halves into a complete physical and spiritual whole—a marriage that was supposed to last forever because this perfect girl, his ideal wife, the first and only one, represented the substantiation of the image of human perfection.

However, and most mature men know, in spite of this idyllic vision that has endured throughout history, only a few men have ever been destined to experience sharing an entire lifetime with their "ideal woman." Some mothers die in their sons' infancy, and others reveal themselves terribly possessive; while still others enjoy fondling their infant sons' delicate parts, fascinated by the erections so many years before their proper time. Some little sisters will turn into absolute tyrants, while these days, many girls as early as in third grade may wish to do much more than just to show "what they have" to quite a number of boys. And lately, a substantial number of thirteen—and fourteen-year-olds consciously seek to lose their virginity and then proceed to have sex with boys and, eventually, of men of all ages, often in exchange for material considerations.

In the minds of these mature men, one of the visible consequences of the latter state of things has been the replacement of the image of brides who glowingly wore the pure white of true chastity by the present-day fake portrayal of a preciousness which had never been—a situation which usually reveals no loving but explicit materialistic or pecuniary preferences.

The younger men in our sample did not waste their sexonomic time pondering about the existence of "ideal women." Most of these men claimed never to have seen one, while the remaining few allowed for their existence but thought it futile to seek them out. In their eyes, most younger women had forsaken the mystique of femininity in return for instant sex and the highest possible cash flow. The typical reaction of the typical young male reads as follows: "Why should I waste my time idealizing about women if I can use it much better by screwing every one of them? Instead of a commitment, they only wish to fornicate as the expression and confirm their full equality." But quite a few of these younger men expressed an increasing feeling of uneasiness about the quality of women which they would eventually wish to marry, admitting that the sexonomic value of women in general was rapidly decreasing and that they'd rather do without women than to marry "below one's minimum self-imposed standard."

Several of the more intelligent younger men in the sample also claimed to have discovered that the women of their own age-group quite vehemently objected to the notion of "ideal women" for not only was there no such woman, but, even if there were one, living up to that exalted standard would put an unbearable burden upon them and would rob them of their freedom. Interestingly, however, literally all of the interviewed young men did not personally assign to themselves the blame for the deterioration of the sexonomic qualities of women and their severance from the concept of the "ideal woman." Almost without exception, they claimed that (a) it was the women's own fault and own choice, and (b) the men bore no guilt; they were, at worst, accessories in these times of transition in which women, organized in groups and acting under peer pressure, did as they pleased, even though usually not to their advantage.

Sexonomics necessarily views the image of an "ideal woman" from several vantage points since, clearly, the ideal woman will command from her male suitors a much higher sexonomic valuation than would women of lower perceived sexonomic quality. Higher valuations will result in higher sexonomic prices of the "ideal woman" in any one of the particular orders that will eventually elevate this kind of quality woman into the next higher order.

In our perception, the image of the "ideal woman" corresponds to the Lotus-woman. The Lotus-woman is qualitatively vastly different from the women of the lower orders. She represents the ultimate ideal, concrete and real exclusively to Quintessential-men, but she remains an abstract image for lower-order men. Evidently, higher-order men will never seek to attribute the "ideal woman" image to lower-order women.

Most of the set of older men in the sample asserted that the image of the "ideal" woman" had never left them and that this image kept on resurfacing every time these men had fallen in love and were expecting a particular relationship to endure. One of these men, sixty-four years old, revealed that he "had *seen* heaven in seven women, *embraced* it in five, and *merged* it with three." And that he considered his life completely and totally fulfilled. Each of "his" women had meant perfection to him, each at a particular phase in his life, and each having a personality unique unto herself, but all three possessing the same set of qualities that had rendered them "ideal" to him. His first love had shared with him "the first merging of the bodies and souls," but she then perished during the war. His first wife had given him twenty years of "heavenly happiness" and two children but then died from a brain tumor. His present wife had "helped him overcome his despair by bringing back into his life cheerfulness and sharing with him the disposition for mature happiness." The delicate sense of touch in "his" three women was rooted in their inborn natural strength and unmitigated magnetism. Imbedded in their feminine aura was the continuous flow of their optimism concerning human creativity and survival capacity, of their unrelenting power to do "a man's job" when needed to stand by their husband in the trying times of war and peace. Their intelligence and foresight enabled them to give their children much more than just "one precious hour" per day, creating an environment propitious for learning and development throughout their adolescence. The completeness of their commitment to loving their husband and to share fully in the sensuousness of their sexuality—at times with kinky interludes but never with the attempt to lock him in, respecting his traditions while enticing him to open up to and absorb their ways and words of wisdom, and finally, their quest to create in their marriage a lifetime partnership based on devotion, trust, and an incessant belief that it is in the nature of women and men together to make sense out of life and to channel their energies into the joint quest for the maximization of happiness.

Compared with the much more manifest ideal imagery of the older men, those very few younger men in the sample who allowed for the image of the "ideal" woman professed that such a woman had to be "fantastic in bed, a real playmate in the joys of living, frugal with her boyfriends' material means, and possibly earning a high income of her own." In addition, she would also stand by him, offer him a home, and would not nag him about his old affairs, going fishing with friends, and evenings out nor interrupt his concentration when watching baseball or living through countless hours of weekend football. She would definitely want at least one child and would always be totally supportive of his career aspirations. She would be competitive in her own right and would even join in beer bashes with the boys. But she would not make a habit of drinking beer or liquor for hours solely in the company of her girlfriends. And she will never, never have been picked up in a bar and will never have gone to a hotel room with a guy she had just met.

Several of these younger men proposed a down-to-earth even though vulgar-sounding definition of the "ideal woman": "She is the very opposite of a woman who is all washed up." Whereas the "ideal" woman's sexonomic valuation and utility functions are infinity, her opposite at the other extreme of valuations has a zero or even negative sexonomic utility function; she ceases being sexonomically marketable.

Concluding our reflections upon "ideal women," let us single out one particular issue that has historically been part and parcel of the ethos of civilized manhood and, therefore, of serious concern to Sexonomics and sexonomists—the issue of the presumed "frail," "delicate," and "vulnerable" nature of women in general and of the "cultured" set in particular.

Men of traditional upbringing that, up to a few years ago, reflected a mix of the initial Puritanism of the bourgeois class in its quest for power with the vestiges of late-medieval chivalry were raised to believe that women ("their" women) were in need of protection (we should perhaps remind ourselves at this time of the definition of *chivalry*—a moral form of behavior in which such men sought to protect all women from all men except themselves!) exactly because of this perception as imbedded in this worldview. The "weaker" sex, women would "need to endure" the advances of men, would "have to "suffer" through the sexually potent years of their (otherwise terribly refined) men, would "be forced to go through the agony" of childbirth for the sake of guaranteeing her husband an offspring and the continuation of his bloodline, and would "totally and irrevocably" be faithful to her husband and his material acquisitiveness—all of these usually at the cost of endemic migraines and the repression of her sexuality. Legally, the deal seemed fair; the wife conducted the life of a chattel, while the husband provided the means of material and social enjoyment, paying special attention not to endanger her delicate state of being. But in real life, this situation not only gave rise to the double standards in our social evolution (which was described above, pages 3–5 and 18–26) but also created a myth about women that simply did not correspond to reality and assigned an aura to women that was the exact opposite of their manifest sexual needs.

Reflecting on the fact that even the "finest" of women have naturally induced and sometimes even blatantly explicit cravings for sex, Sexonomics can only premise that this mix of the puritan and chivalrous orientation did, in fact, express the desire of the rising new elite of men to not only to put constraints on the freedom of women but also to lower "their" women's sexonomic valuation—a Lady LUSSEY whose disinclination to engage in fantastic lovemaking for its presumed suffering at her core is a Lady LUSSEY that will not earn the full value equivalent of a LUSSEY that finds absolute delight in making love and in bringing maximum pleasure to its male partner. By keeping their women's sexuality repressed, the men of the bourgeois elite devalued the quality of their women's Lady LUSSEYs, but they did then turn to their maids and other "less refined women" in seeking, at the respectively much lower sexonomic cost, to enjoy the earthy pleasures which their own women were not able, or not allowed, to bestow upon them.

It seems very strange, at this vantage point, that generations of (self-declared) "men of substance" would decline to view their wives as *full-bodied women*, whose vaginas had exactly the same needs as did the vaginas of the women of lower sexonomic quality—discreetly hidden from the world at large but craving to be discovered, explored, opened up, and eventually penetrated with the maximal vehemence a man's pukkacity would allow. Even every Lady LUSSEY craves such treatment for, in spite of the societal constraints upon her behavior, her owner's sensuousness and eroticism are naturally abundant, very much like those of her gender sisters from the lower sexonomic orders. These admiring and caring men throughout recent history failed to realize that—by viewing their women as frail, delicate, and vulnerable—they shortchanged their women's Lady LUSSEYs of the innermost essence of their being and brutalized them by withholding from them, especially during their most receptive and lustful moments, the enjoyment of the Sir MOJJs enticement and performance qualities. The rationality of sexonomic reasoning clearly suggests that the "ideal" woman, especially, is *first* a full-fledged *woman*—whose Lady LUSSEY will wish to fully enjoy even "kinky sex" when she feels like it, even though her owner would never admit her yearning for it in any form or language—and, only second, is a statue on the pedestal. Forcing her to renounce the first will have us conclude that the *second* cannot amount to more than a sexonomic heart filled with the promise of sexonomic utility—but void of sexonomic delivery.

What kind of strategy should a woman pursue when faced with those men who seem unable to recognize women as *women* and who treat them instead as china dolls? Her strategy will depend entirely on the mix of composite qualities that she will discover in each of these men but with the recognition that even most of these men can be induced to assign to the Lady LUSSEY her original natural rights in her prehistoric biological state unspoiled by civilization. If a man wishes to continue regarding a woman as his own personal pedestal, she should let him do it and should collect the respective sexonomic price, but she could add to her sexonomic valuation if she could convince him that she would not lose her (presumed) porcelain-like frailty if he "gave it to her good" and demonstrated to him that she would neither experience undue suffering nor would break apart over *it*. In so doing (and demonstrating), the quality of their sexual togetherness would significantly increase and would raise her sexonomic valuation. As we have already seen, a bit of occasional kinkiness can create extra delight even for Lady LUSSEYs that belong to the most exquisite owners in the order of Lotus-women. These ladies will have realized that men will devalue those LUSSEYs that seem uncontrollably desirous of "getting it good" all the time, a syndrome from which even the china doll types of women of the higher orders will definitively suffer less than would the less delicate-looking women of the lower orders.

Bedding with Women

Only a handful of the men in the sample claimed that they would not engage in sexual intercourse with a woman unless they loved her. Of the others, both the unmarried and the married ones professed that it did not take much more than an arousal and the desire to follow through with the respective (and willing) female. All men declared that all women were interested in short-term relations, even though many of these women would consent to a short-term relationship as a first step toward investing in long-term togetherness. None of the younger men admitted to ever having been too much in love (in the eyes of a few, the "market" was simply too good to entail such a "self-sacrifice"), but most admitted that most of their women partners (had) wished for much more than just fornication but would use fornication in order to achieve some of their other goals in particular relationships. It was not difficult to "get" women, usually at the cost of only one or two suppers out. Neither was it difficult to reject women in seeking to terminate a particular short-term relationship since most women, by far, had had numerous other sexual encounters and would easily shift from one man to another.

On the whole, most of the interviewed men thought they lived in a "man's world," and quite a few were brutally frank in their observations concerning women in general (presumably also including "their own")—women are easy to get into bed and are easy to discard once a man seeks to end a relationship because of the availability (especially among the younger set) of large numbers of competing and willing women. Women did not insist any more on being "loved" prior to consenting to engage in intercourse. In offering or consenting to make love, most women had a specific set of goals on their minds; most women did not need to love in order to make love and, in order to realize their goals, would even make love without having an emotional desire to do so. Most women were convinced that most men cannot resist a pleasing offer to engage in intercourse; more and more women insisted upon a total and effective sexual performance; finally, it was very difficult for a man to distinguish between a woman's passionate love (no strings attached) and a woman's loving with a purpose in mind. Women would often apply vaginal cream not for protection but as a lubricant, possibly to hide the fact that their fornication was neither for loving or lust but for material reasons; and most women had developed reasonable expertise in voluntarily masturbating their male partners and even happily engaging with them in oral sex and greedily swallowing the ejaculated mass—not as a protective device against unwanted intercourse, but as a proof of equal status and total sexual liberation.

Interestingly, not many of the nonloving women found that penises were really "beautiful," but even those few admitted watching with fascination the transformation of a limp penis into a fully and potently erect instrument of pleasure. A surprising number of the interviewed men expressed serious concern about their ability to "give *it* to their women really good" for self-explanatory reasons; these men feared that their women would leave them if their lovemaking was not satisfactorily performed.

While quite a few of the interviewed men claimed that they had "never" coerced their women into making love against their own wishes, an even more significant number of men (48 percent) claimed that lovemaking was their "natural right" and that they would do it elsewhere if they could not "get it" at home. We have found that most men would seek "relief" outside of marriage, whether their own women were beautiful and inviting but unwilling or had become unsightly and repulsive. But most men emphasized that just any LUSSEY would definitely not do; her owner had to be passionate and had to have style, grace, scent, and spirit if she was to deserve high sexonomic valuation. Ostentatious greed, putrid smell, and lack of hygiene make up the most objectionable set of discounting factors.

Bedding with women was also negatively influenced by the following traits or situations: loud yelling and shrieking during intercourse; a fly-catching attitude toward lovemaking; pretending that orgasm is being experienced; a condescending attitude with respect to "letting him do it"; making the sign of the cross before or after; absolute refusal to experiment with different positions; deprecating the looks, the size, and the performance of his genitals; and viewing her own vagina as nothing more than a viscous muscle with two uses, pissing and copulating. Not one of the interviewed men would think of *marrying* such a "base" woman, and only three of the interviewed Mob-men appeared to become horny when reminiscing about their unpleasant experiences.

The higher-quality men in the sample expressed strong romantic inclinations concerning the much higher state of being of a true Lady LUSSEY. But to our amusement, we did discover that the concern about these negative factors was not exclusive to Quintessential-men and Lace-men, as if all of the sampled men in all orders had experienced similar problems and had developed similar fears.

Are the Natural Liberties of Women
Equally Applicable to Men?

Sexonomic rationality suggests that they must be except that, unlike women, men have developed historical patterns of alternate forms of behavior in seeking to hedge against unhappiness in their personal experiences with women. Such forms of behavior have lately expressed themselves in surprisingly large numbers in public. Homosexuality has become the most manifest example of groupings of men who appear unable to cope with the inner contradictions of the dialectic duality in their relation to women.

Homosexuality and its major consequence, life-threatening HIV, must be accorded a sexonomic assessment, even though Sexonomics deals exclusively with phenomena arising out of the interaction between "normal" women and men in their ordinary business of life. Homosexuality ties in directly because, as we have seen, the ratio of men to women tends to diminish when the number of men who prefer togetherness and "sexual" intercourse with other men gets larger compared to those who prefer association and cohabitation with women. It is logical to argue that women's SEVACs relative to men's will devalue, the larger the percentage of men who join up and engage in homosexual activities gets. In fact, except for the order of Quintessential-men, the absolute SEVACs of all other orders of men will rise beyond their true sexonomic values. A forever increase in the number of homosexuals are even more likely to unbalance and eventually undermine the existing but precarious social sexonomic equilibrium by diminishing the numbers of men available in sexonomic markets and thereby exerting enormous pressure on individual women as well as organized groups of women to conform to homosexuality as a fact of life, which involves millions of men the world over. The sexonomic significance of homosexuality derives from two causes: an increasingly more unfavorable ratio between women and men and the socioeconomic consequences of AIDS in its specific application to the afflicted males (and females) as income-earning factors will increase dependence on government assistance. AIDS itself has a serious sexonomic significance since it involves three terribly detrimental aspects, each of which represents both an absolute as well as a relative concern. First, homosexually induced AIDS is most likely to forever keep the afflicted male (or female) from any of the sexonomic markets, whereby the terms of trade improve for men and deteriorate for women. Second, AIDS also leads to a vast increase in the use of condoms at the cost of diminishing a male person's enticement-and-control quality (instead of using one's "head" in order to minimize the possibility of contracting AIDS, we follow through on the easier way out—the use of condoms, which inhibits sexual pleasure). Third, AIDS also implies a vast misallocation of social resources away from combating epidemics or the historical diseases in their universal manifestation to catering to the needs of those most of whom could have prevented contacting this deadly disease by deciding to "act normal" or, at least, to refrain from engaging in what Sexonomics must consider an unusual course of sexual interaction.

The existence of these aberrations from normal human sexual interaction raises the question of whether homosexuality can possibly be the consequence, not of inherited or acquired inclinations, but of many a man's belief that he cannot be free unless he rejects women as his own subject of sexual interaction. Sexonomics will postulate that homosexuals are, in fact, men who live by the code that asserts that needing to have a woman robs a man of his natural liberty. Referring back to the umbilical cord syndrome, Sexonomics recognizes that oppressive mothers or other women in a man's boyhood and adolescence may well have played a significant role in his "turning toward men" for love, sex, and companionship. But Sexonomics also suggests that this condition may not be irreversible, especially if it was psychologically induced.

In concluding our deliberations concerning women as sexonomic subjects and having discovered that men's relations with women will also range from "pure loving" to "pure material self-interest," we are left with the question of whether men, like women, can also be "sexonomic losers," "sexonomic hopefuls," or "sexonomic winners."

Men as sexonomic losers: A man who is engaged in the "pure but unreciprocated loving" of a woman is a man who demands nothing in exchange for what he gives. He will have abdicated from every one of his natural liberties while allowing the woman maximum freedom in each. Such a man has no expectation of sexonomic gain and will find himself forevermore enslaved by her whims, eccentricities, moods, commands, angers, and tempers. Even in their lovemaking, he will depend totally on her snapping of fingers, commanding role, and outpouring of pure unmitigated lust while still considering himself the luckiest man alive. This kind of man's sexonomic valuation is very low (even though he may be of socially ranking origin and even well-to-do or even better educated) because, over the course of time, he is not perceived of as a man. The Quintessential-man will never find himself in this predicament, but the odd Lace-man might if he gets caught in the web of a very intelligent and thoroughly materialistic Conch-woman who will know how to satisfy every one of his sexual needs. The occasional Vulpine-man who might see himself trapped in this type of situation by one of the adventurous but silky-smooth Art-women (remember Lady Chatterley!) will need much character to handle this rare occurrence in their order; while Mob-men, in their crude and vulgar but physically powerful ways, will never even be aware of this possibility because they will, if necessary, beat their way on to the top of their women. The Girandole-man, the professional exploiter of the psyche of women who need sexual relief at his hands but are incapable of any feelings of love or self-sacrifice, is definitionally exempt from this category of hopeless men. But he is a loser in a much broader sense in that he cannot ever generate love in himself or in any of the women who are his clients in sex.

Men as sexonomic hopefuls: A "sexonomic hopeful" is typically a member of the order of Lace-men or an exceptionally gifted Vulpine-man whose main aspiration is to make it to the order of Lace-men, if necessary, by way of interacting with or even marrying an Art-woman. A sexonomically hopeful male has the capacity to enjoy in full the sexuality of his lady partner, but he will be very aware of the need to be giving love and receiving love equally, or else an unequal sexonomic relationship will likely develop. His other main interest has to do with his quest to arrive at perfect harmony between his desire to be free and his need to have a woman who will command his fealty, the latter evidently involving restrictions on his movements and associations. Essentially a liberal, he will swap liberties with his woman, the personal freedoms being granted by him becoming more numerous with the rise in order status of his woman. Naturally, his woman will have the capacity and the maturity to do exactly the same; she would neither tie him down nor seek to dominate him. His woman will view their relationship as a family partnership and will assign to him the dual role of high-quality lover and trustworthy and creative professional. She will expect her man to grow with her and to fulfill his sexonomic promise. If she is contented with their duality, when older, she might even understand his occasional but rare coveting of some other women who may have caught his attention for being very much like his own woman but younger. But above all, they both will be convinced that, in their togetherness, the self-imposed restrictions will be worth the price, a deal which he will attempt to bear out by keeping himself in top shape—a requisite whenever she calls upon him to respond to her multidimensional needs.

Men as sexonomic winners: A man is a sexonomic winner whenever he succeeds in sharing his lifetime with his ultimate woman. Being with such a woman helps him reach the highest sexonomic utility level while also retaining the liberty to be himself. A wise woman will recognize "her" man's potential and will naturally and without conditions consent to sharing her life with him. As already mentioned, the Lotus-woman and the Quintessential-man are naturally destined to make up such a unique complete union. Exceptionally gifted and foresighted Art-women and Lace-men will also qualify because they usually manage to keep in check their enticement-and-control functions and their passion quality.

Needing to Have a Woman—but Also Wishing to Be Free

Many or perhaps even most men suffer with what Sexonomics would call the "umbilical cord syndrome" (UCS). Unique to men, this affliction is not a physical sickness but rather a state of mind that sometimes takes on the acute form of psychosis vis-à-vis all women. All men who suffer with UCS will express forms of behavior typical of this syndrome when faced with or accompanied by women—in mild cases, visible nervousness, blushing, restlessness, anxiety, slightly shaking hands, perspiration, voice modulation and hoarseness, and inability to conduct conversation; in serious cases, nervousness bordering on agitation, breathlessness, jumpiness, antagonism, spasms, profuse sweating, croaking, speechlessness, unpleasant body odor, and angst. Which man does not recall any and all of these moments when, for the first time in his life (and evidently still a virgin), he sees himself face-to-face with a lustful woman (inevitably older and with lots of sexual experience) who suddenly strips off her bra and panties and firmly, lacking any finesse or patience, puts his hand on *her*, demanding that her LUSSEY be stroked, possibly from the inside. Defenseless and needing to prove his manhood, the young fellow will recall, in a flash, the years of trepidation about what to do exactly in this kind of first-time situation. Thoroughly ashamed at first (for, after all, he does not love the woman), he will feel the heat surge through his loins and will, almost inevitably, prematurely ejaculate when his fingers finally get to touch the hot oozing rim of her LUSSEY.

Carried and born by his mother, the boy will never forget the heat and the cuddling humidity of her womb and will often relive the crushing tightness of the passageway through which he is forced to pass until the mother's body finally liberates itself from him by throwing him from the safety and succor in her intimate protective darkness into the claws of a world in whose rampant sexuality only the fittest men are destined to hold their own. But whether enduring privation and the fear of death during war, while desperately hoping for an enduring peace (especially between the two genders), many men appear unable to shed this feeling of prenatal belonging because they always remember how totally protected they were in their most vulnerable state, a feeling that carries over into their adolescence and eventually into their manhood. The umbilical cord relationship that is unique to boys and their mothers wields its influence over a significant number of males, even to the extent of their shunning the world of women and, quite often, not ever wishing to get married. But also significant is the number of women who do get married to men with a milder version of UCS and are, in consequence, forced to suffer a marriage that seems like a never-ending ménage à trois.

The umbilical cord syndrome has a dialectic duality which, through its inner contradiction, propels most men through life while permitting only a very few of them to achieve that sexonomic harmony and inner peace that are exclusive to the men of the Quintessential order. In their deepest memory cells, all men retain the feeling of cognition concerning their prenatal protective environment and will, when engaged in choosing "their own woman," look for a female person who exudes that warmth. He will naturally wish to explore her personal source of giving life and may at times wish to experiment numerous times with different women in his quest to rediscover his very own source of life. If he is lucky, he will find her on his first attempt. If he is not, he may remain a searcher all his life, even destined to die unfulfilled. Since only very few men can ever become totally free of their own UCS, they will willingly offer high sexonomic prices to women who are able to offer them lifelong replacement for what his embryonic memory cells will carry right into his grave. Those men who suffer with the strongest Oedipus complex are convinced that there is no substitute for the perfection of their mother's Lady LUSSEY. Such men will not likely ever get married for, convinced that there is no substitute for "mother," they will never start looking for another one.

A man's dream woman is a woman who can confirm to a man that his illusion is a reality that will keep him going all his life. A wise woman, seeking to approach and eventually wed a particular man, will always inquire into his relation to his mother. A wise woman will know that she must be much more than just a substitute; she must grow with her man if she is ever to become more than a replacement for his mother. A wise woman's sexonomic valuation is very high because she takes time to discover what she must do. She will work with full devotion and intensity on their loving and lovemaking because, in so doing, she will build with him her own umbilical cord, one whose strength will eventually prevail over that of his mother's. A wise woman will let her man be free to be himself in all walks of life, including with his friends, in his profession, and in his games and hobbies. She will do so with a great deal of success because she will have learned how to build this inseparable and forever lasting linkage between herself and her man.

Most quality men desire being with a woman in a union that will involve much more than just her body. Even the Quintessential-man must first learn how to cope with his own umbilical cord syndrome before he can aspire to achieve that harmony in his relations with the women of his life that will assure him of a perfect balance between his needing to be with his woman but also wishing to be free of the influence of his mother's womb upon his life. Once achieved, this harmony will endure well beyond the moment when the sexual craving for another's body will have disappeared.

With this dialectic attachment to women, men will spend an inordinate share of their lifetime dreaming, thinking, and speaking of women. Body-oriented in their late adolescence, men will seek to "conquer" and will feel the urge to "tell about it." But unlike women, men will only rarely discuss with their friends the details of their intimate experiences with a woman they "love." The main reason for not telling is linked to his innate tendency to secure his "territoriality" against other competing males (which also includes his "best friends"). But as he grows older, the man's primary urge to keep his body's needs secure and satiated will be replaced with the discovery that his ultimate woman can give him so much more than either the care by his mother during his infancy or the raw sexuality of the girlfriends during his wild-oats years. From his mother to his ultimate woman in life, a normal male person will never seek to be completely free of women because being with his own woman gives his life a deeper meaning. Since finding "his own ideal woman" will help him achieve deeper personal harmony, he will invest much of his time and his means in the pursuit of a "successful" sexonomic strategy. In this quest, he will not worry about "losing his freedom" but will proceed to ruffle his feathers (develop his natural endowments), demonstrate the colors and dimensions of his plume (test the competitive nature of his masculinity), and perform the appropriate—and hopefully superbly competitive—ritual of his own song and dance (in competition with other suitors, move through the stages of an initial date to the moment of consummation). In the eyes of an intelligent male person, these actions have nothing to do with loss of freedom; rather, they are the natural expression of his liberty to act as a man. If he succeeds, his freedom to act will have borne him the desired fruit. In this sense, a man's personal success in life provides the best proof that his "needing to have a woman" is totally compatible with his desire "to be free."

Sexonomic reasoning suggests that men who have achieved this harmony are men whose sexonomic valuations are very high, but they are also men who will always bid full value to the woman with whom this unique duality must be realized. The ultimate relationship is that with a woman who is not afraid—that loving a man who has achieved this sense of harmony will rob her of freedom to be herself—a situation that is typical of the linkage between the Lotus-woman and the Quintessential-man. Perfectly balanced with their sexuality and their material needs and dispositions, the woman and the man in this union know that they have succeeded and know that they need not continue looking and searching for they have found their ideal partner. Their union represents highest level sexonomic utility and is illustrated by the perfect merger of their full sexonomic hearts.

CHAPTER SIX

Sexonomic Marketing Strategies I: The Fascinating World of Sexonomic Marketing and Success

In chapter 6, our reflections will treat two themes, each of which constitutes an essential tier in a woman's or man's drive toward personally fulfilling sexuality and the appropriately sufficient material base:

Sexonomic conventions: a set of principles and codes of conduct, the knowledge of which forms an essential part in women's and men's quest to succeed in marketing their sexuality.

Sexonomic rules of the game: a set of rules that reflects the pattern of interaction between women and men and by which participating women and men are presumed to abide. Specifically, this theme elaborates on the following three situations:

> *the rules that apply equally to women and men,*
> *the rules that apply exclusively to women,* and
> *the rules that apply exclusively to men.*

Sexonomic Conventions

In our assessment of the rules of the sexonomic strategies and games, we are faced with the initial recognition that some of these conventions must be identical for both women and men, while others are dissimilar. This total lack of parallel (an important issue since Sexonomics considers women and men totally equal in all respects except the physical manifestation of their respective reproductive systems) derives from history and may be explained as follows:

Up until the recent past, the rules of social conduct concerning sexual relations between women and men have rested on the premise that women were chattels and that their sexuality was officially monopolized by their de jure or de facto male partners. Reminiscent of feudalism and its institutions, especially serfdom, and under the spiritual tutelage of the various religions and churches, women were either the legal wards of their men (kaisers, kings, patriarchs, tribal chiefs, fathers, husbands) or they were considered free goods, of whom some would be guaranteed.

Yet even during those sinister times, women were granted compensating allowances, of which protection (from all men except the "protector" himself), livelihood, and guaranteed burial in properly consecrated grounds were the most significant. Many wars were fought and won or lost because of women. The reasons varied from exercising men's territorial rights over women to defending the virtues of the women belonging to a tribe or to another nation from trespassing men. Throughout this period, men legislated and enforced the rules concerning women's behavior—in the Ten Commandments, through censuses (only men were counted as souls) and by withholding their voting rights. Even though they were lovers, wives, and mothers, women were not only denied the right to communicate directly with God (or gods) but "proper submissive behavior" demanded that chaste, virtuous, and God-fearing women would never look straight into their men's eyes when talking with them or making love to them (except for Gypsies, women of the arts, courtesans, and whores).

Women were not expected to marry out of love, and they were literally risking their lives when seeking to engage in illicit amorous relations. No wonder, then, that women developed in the greatest secrecy an invisible network of linkages which they incorporated into their very personal mystiques and which would enable them to break through some of these constraints and to undo some of these prohibitions. This network had at its base the enticement and manipulation of individual sexuality and the recognition that money means and buys power. In spite of Vatican-sanctioned burnings at the stake and the executions ordered by Henry VIII, chastity and faithfulness, especially among the women at the top, could never be fully enforced, a situation which even lower-order women were beginning to enjoy in forever larger numbers. However, in most societies, virginity was to remain a requisite well into the twentieth century, as if even nature had conspired against women in rendering unto the hymen such an exquisitely delicate membrane, irreplaceable once subjected to the momentous act of its—usually wanton—destruction.

At present, the status of Western women has changed, possibly because the many wars had decimated the numbers of men and had left the industrial Moloch of capitalism without adequate manpower. Women were drafted into the labor force in increasing numbers the fastest, where, in comparison with men, their earnings were absolutely and relatively the lowest. But this sudden massive and broadly based augmentation in their purchasing power elevated working women to a major economic factor whose rising visibility was soon to find its extension as a potentially explosive clout in the body politic. First followed their emancipation; then they gained the right to private contract, personal financial responsibility, and membership in previously all-male clubs; and finally, the acceptance of women in all markets for goods and services and their open participation in the five sexonomic markets. No more condemnations, stonings, and burnings at the stake—but neither are there any more virgins or women saints. Protection, succor, and sanctity had become casualties in battles for the equality of the sexes. The traditional pillars of devotion and motherhood were replaced by women's self-interests that included abortion on demand. The moral and legal compacts to abide by the code of respect for a woman's personal right to being loved and cared for by her own man was rendered obsolete by the emerging free-for-all among all women for the men of their own choosing—the vicious infighting of younger woman against older woman, daughter against mother, single girl against wife.

In traditional society, women had suffered a lot, but most of them never faltered in their desire to give and to love (or to provide a bridge between the one God and humankind). In modern times, women have become free and have proceeded to emulate the historical pattern of men hunting down women; the chase was on for the good men as well as for the bad, a moblike form of behavior in which no holds are barred, and women appear to have become their own worst enemies.

The fundamental reason for this change in attitudes on the part of women and their game plan is found in the linkage between individual sexuality and personal material self-interest, the rationale being the calculated disposition of the three qualities of the Lady LUSSEY and LUSSEY in exchange for material advantages. The Lady LUSSEYs (in the highest order) and LUSSEYs (in the lower orders) had always been viewed as pure honey by the bidding men in their respective orders. In the modern setting, in which men of the highest sexonomic quality have become the exception, the rationality of contemporary women that was seeking to undo the evils of the past necessitated a sexonomic strategy in which a human female had to seek ways of how to outdo the other competing women. The period of women consciously marketing their bodies ensued—sex in return for personal material gain rather than for finding shelter, solace, and sanctity.

Obviously, comparing the past with the present and reflecting upon the causes and effects of this transition should enable us better to understand why Sexonomics prescribes a number of *conventions* for women that are different from the codes of conduct for men (as we shall see below), even though women and men are now deemed not only to have equal rights but also to have access to more equal opportunities of personal development. The existence of a set of different conventions is also explained by the following two facts as revealed by contemporary reality: (1) the increase in the number of women relative to men, especially in urban areas, and (2) the continuing rapid increase in the unequal distribution of wealth. The former has resulted in increasingly embittered and vicious infighting among women for the top-quality men of their choice—which is, in fact, causing a significant devaluation of the involved women's sexonomic valuation coefficients. The latter still remains heavily weighted in favor of men, with the effect that women—in anticipation of the material and career advantages which "cash-and-carry sex" always implies—will offer their bodies at a much faster pace and with far fewer conditions than had their mothers barely one generation ago.

Before we take up the discussion regarding sexonomic conventions, we shall first elaborate on the real-life backdrop against which human sexonomic interaction (at all levels) will be expected to take place. This backdrop is made up of a number of societal structures, customs, and conditions, of which we shall list the seven most important "couplings":

- honesty and integrity
- cleanliness and hygiene
- trust and confidence
- money and pecuniary values
- vertiginousness
- territoriality
- law and order

Honesty and integrity: Sexonomics views honesty and integrity as fundamental requisites in the building of both short-run and (in particular) long-term linkages. However, historical fact appears to contradict this particular requisite in the pursuit of sexonomic strategies and games; sexual urges and the monetary calculus have shown themselves to be much stronger motives in the sexonomic partners' propensity to maximize their lifetime sexonomic utilities with more than just one partner than the aptitude for honesty and integrity. Only in the exceptional cases of women's and men's "ideal loving" (loving totally devoid of self-love, of material self-interest, and of the desire for outside sexual partners) have honesty and integrity prevailed.

Cleanliness and hygiene: The sexonomic valuation of women and men presumes that they are healthy and that their body care involves modern standards of bathing and dieting. It also recognizes the existence of selfless love and its devotion to seek a cure for the handicapped, the ill, and the infirm, even though it considers these cases as an exception and, therefore, as belonging outside of the framework of competition in the sexonomic markets. A normal state of health accords the individual no valuation bonus and commands no special price premium. But it is a basic requisite because sexonomic games can be terribly exhausting and the winners are usually those who are the fittest. Sexonomics also views personal hygiene as an attempt to enhance one's own body boutique (and not to subject one's being to the dictates of the makeup cult), which includes the enjoyment of the naturally induced scents during lovemaking.

Trust and confidence. Even though many social philosophers claim that sympathy, approbation, and a sense of fair play form the bases for viable social compacts, sexonomic markets demonstrate that human sexuality on the hunt amounts to a no-holds-barred free-for-all, albeit in an outwardly much more civilized form in the top-ranking orders. Sexonomics is only too aware that cheating and betrayal are but two of the widely practiced aspects of sexonomic games. But it wishes to submit that, for a relationship to endure in the long run, trust and confidence are essential elements in which both partners must share if they are to get together and to stay together. In the sexonomic valuation of women and men, these two characteristics not only provide for a hefty increment but also constitute a powerful bargaining chip. While men, especially older men with substantial means, are viewed by women—particularly by the younger set—as belonging to the "trustworthy" category, there is widespread evidence proving that women are much more likely to be trusting than men and that young uneducated women fall easy prey to predatory men.

Money and pecuniary values. Sexonomics is only too aware that money buys not only sex but also power. It assumes that women and men will use money as a medium toward securing for themselves the highest sexonomic happiness. It will never consider money as the ultimate end of the sexonomic partners' aspirations in life; human reason will always prevail over greed and avarice. This is so because money, like sex, is valued the less the more that it is available and consumed; extra dollars will always be valued less than the previous increment—just like the enjoyment of extra sex partners. With an excessive consumption of each, the valuation of both will tend to decrease toward zero—leading to the total depreciation of the individual sexonomic happiness heart line.

Vertiginousness. This term involves the uncertainty that arises from our attempts to reach the highest level of sexonomic happiness. The attainment of this quality dimension depends on the size of risk that is involved in an sexonomic bidder's quest to develop and to market successfully her/his complete set of sexonomic endowments, especially irresistible sex appeal, adaptable ability to reason, and competitive spirit. The pursuit of a successful sexonomic strategy is only possible in a society that has evolved from the initial era of superstition and prehistoric ignorance, followed by the long period of rule by the Ten Commandments and prohibitions—as enforced by the various religions and churches—onto the period of Enlightenment and utilitarianism to its contemporary cultural status of respect for individual freedom, accountability, and the Charter of Human Rights. Only in this mature society are women entitled to equal opportunity in the development of their sexonomic endowments and to full control of their sexuality.

However, in spite of this advancement of women's rights, female vertiginousness remains a serious problem. This is so because only very few women have been able to ascend to their own personal sexonomic apex, while most women have remained unable to extricate themselves from the quagmire of double standards and discriminations. As a result, they may be said to be subject to the vertigo complex. Except for Lotus-women and Quintessential-men, most other human beings have great difficulties coping with the following three vertigos in their quest to raise their sexonomic utility functions and to ascend to the next higher order: the *lateral*, the *objective*, and the *subjective*.

The disorder of the *lateral vertigo* is marked by a lower-order member seeking to improve her/his sexonomic valuation but by being held back by the other members of her/his order; the more a person tries, the more drag the other persons exert. These chains cannot be broken unless an enormous acceleration effort is undertaken, an effort that burns up an immense amount of energy and often leaves this kind of order person in a state of prolonged exhaustion and dizziness.

The state of *objective vertigo* is encountered by a lower-order person who was able to move up to the next higher order but then discovers that she/he is confronted with a much more competitive sexonomic milieu, one in which the members of the higher order appear to be engaged in a relentless pursuit of the "newcomer" as if determined to force him back down. Exposed to terms like *parvenu* or *social climber* and continuously and often mercilessly tested, the newcomer experiences symptoms typically caused by stress and insecurity—a whirling which intensifies as his new order members who surround him increase in numbers and threaten to contract his personal energy field. Since higher-order humans claim more breathing space for themselves and are quite unwilling to share or give up some of this space voluntarily, the newcomers often find themselves squeezed out, and many of them will have no choice but to descend to their previous lower order.

Subjective vertigo is experienced mainly by Art-women and Lace-men, Conch-women and Vulpine-men, and Vampire-women and Girandole-men. It is caused by the often immense vertical distance between their biological urge to find sexual fulfillment versus the use of their reason in the pursuit of increasing material welfare. Sexonomics recognizes that the scarcest of all qualities in the human existence is a perfectly compatible partner for life. In consequence, sexonomic strategy demands that we engage in the search for exactly such a partner and that we do our best to retain that partner for ourselves once we have found him/her. Being what we are, we are often tempted to look for a higher-order partner. In so doing, we will, as has been well documented in studies reflecting upon our patterns of behavior, often disregard the rules concerning the acquired rights of others and will fight with vicious determination in order to secure for ourselves what would appear to be our "ideal" companion. It is against this backdrop of "no holds barred" that the marketing of our sexuality in exchange for someone else's will result in subjective vertigo—a situation in which we feel caught in the cauldron of two contradictory pressures within ourselves, the introitive and the extroitive. These pressures must be balanced if we are not to get enmeshed in faster and faster and eventually uncontrollable rotary movements of our bodies and spirits. Vertiginousness can be diminished and eventually neutralized if our sexonomic strategy finds the proper equilibrium between the primacy of human reason and the biological urge to reach sexual fulfillment.

Territoriality: The horizontal extension of the explosive linkage between reason and sexuality, this aspect of human behavior has to do with human possessiveness; once we have secured for ourselves the presumed ideal partner, we will proceed to protect our investment (our proprietary rights?) against possible intruders. Unlike in our own prehistoric phase of the "hunt" when we disregarded codes of behavior and unwritten conventions, in this stage, we are only too willing to invoke the letter of the law and its manifest interest in maintaining the social balance by securing and upholding a personal monopoly. Marriage had always been viewed as the chartered enjoyment of a monopoly patent of husband over wife and of the parents over their children—an essential requisite for the social fabric to survive. Sexonomics views territoriality not only as an inherent naturally equal propensity in women and men but also as an inherent explosive force, the "beast" in each one of us. The so-called murders of passion have territoriality as their emotional trigger. Territoriality can neither be fully contained by nor dependably subjected to the power of human reason. No wonder, then, that in sexonomic strategy and games, this inherently and enormously powerful drive is considered to be a potentially most destabilizing force, one that will often test the limits of the rationality of the sexonomically competing women and men.

Law and order: The readers must have noticed by now that the sexonomic behavior of women and men does not bear out full compliance with the existing systems of law and order, meaning respect for the letter of the law and an adherence to the set of moral standards on which all legal systems claim to be based. In our own society, law and order reflect a mix of Judeo-Christian values (presently in a state of transition even more pronounced than ever in the past, albeit a much more peaceful transition as a whole), of oligarchic pressure-group tactics, and of the enfranchisement of the masses (women included). In this setup, family has always been—and still is—regarded as the microcosm of social stability, the founding stable cell of society which our legal system is designed to protect. In the past (up to about forty years ago), the ties within the family were considered viable as well as strong enough to sustain the family through the pressures of industrialization, wars, and economic cycles, perhaps because the wives provided the moral fiber and commitment, while the husbands brought in the wherewithal. Cheating and infidelity had always been going on but heeded to the basic premise that the family had to be sustained and borne out by the fact that most of the unhappy wives simply had nowhere else to turn. However, during and since the Second World War, the Sexonomics of human interaction began to take on increasingly predatory forms; sexual intercourse as a business proposition was being brought into the open as a mass phenomenon and made to apply equally to women and men. Women, seeking equal rights (including that of premarital sexual activity as the new standard for the many), entered the labor market in the quest to seek their own material independence and thereby to secure the means with which to buy themselves sexual freedom (as the presumed rational alternative to the distasteful and dehumanizing experience in marriage of having to make love without consent). However, out of this yearning to be equally free and, therefore, able to pursue the pleasures of intimacy on one's own very personal terms has since arisen a no-holds-barred free-for-all for all men, a brutally competitive situation in which each participating woman seeks to realize her own particular sexonomic priorities.

Thus began the open season on all men. It soon resulted in an increasing disregard for the values that had been the foundation of the established system of law and order. How did the men respond? Did they, who had been the creators of the traditional system, fall into step and openly express their support on behalf of the total freedom and independence of women? Overall, most of them did, which includes most of the male lawmakers—for they had become the net beneficiaries of this powerful process of the self-liberation of women. Never before throughout history—and, in particular, since the 1950s—had men in such large numbers and so openly been able to engage in fornication with such a vast outpouring of women willing to market their sexuality so freely—with the consequence of a rapid decrease toward zero of the sexonomic valuation of their LUSSEYs, however. This massive public offering of female sexuality (even though understandable and even justified in the wake of the centuries of repression) cut across all class barriers and levels of education. Not only did it result in bringing into the sexonomic market forever younger girls right down to the early teens, but it was also extended well into the postmenstrual stage of mature women, thereby tarnishing the traditional image of the white-haired and saintly-looking grandmother to whom menopause had been God's personal signal to stop her "sinful" ways if she was to qualify for direct promotion into "heaven" without first having to pay substantial penance while in the "purgatory."

Even though Sexonomics admits that "pure love" may have been one of the motivations for this outpouring of mass sexuality (see page 1), it submits that a rapidly increasing share of the women's desire to engage in intercourse may be linked to their teleological strategy of either pulling even with the men ("loin heat–induced fornication," see page 1) or of assuring themselves of those net material gains which would enable them to purchase and enjoy unmitigated sexual freedom. In this evolution, the traditional view of men as the providers of women's lifetime material safety nets in exchange for treating men as subjects deserving devotion and care, if not also love, was being turned into the rational orientation toward exploiting men as material objects. The process of transforming men into "sexonomic objects" had not been the intention of those women who were the original prophetesses and standard bearers of the liberation of women. Their intention had been to succeed in freeing women from ever again having to make love without personal desire or consent, whereby women's dignity as human beings would be fully restored and respected. Yet unexpectedly, a situation arose in which the women found themselves "free to choose" the men of their liking, either just for sex or still as long-term partners. Counting especially on the men's weakness for the "honey" or their biologically induced desire to avail themselves of the Lady LUSSEYs conception-and-delivery quality, many of the participating women proceeded to extort from men the highest possible material benefits in the expectation that the sexonomic valuation of the massively marketed LUSSEYs would remain high. However (and after the initial period of enthusiasm over all that free sex), the opposite happened; the men, their bodies and psyches increasingly tired, began resenting the openly manifested materialistic attitude of women. In consequence, soon, a "seller's market" emerged; the men's sexonomic valuation was going up, while that of the women was falling. Instead of bearing out the yearning for the full equality of women by undoing past disparities by a process of legal change in the traditional framework of law and order, the world of women was faced with a rising critique of the sexual "free-for-all" as it was viewed as endangering the structure of our institutions and their most precious microcosm, the family. The hunt for men had been conducted with increasing disregard for "pure love," especially in the lower-order sexonomic markets; acutely private sexual pleasure in exchange for increasing material benefits was replacing the stable—even though far from perfect—social institution of marriage; instantaneous satiation of sexual appetites, rampant infidelity, and high rates of divorce were replacing the sense of long-term commitment; and family structure was being replaced by sexual anarchy, endangering the traditional moral imperatives of the old social order (as we shall reveal below in sexonomic conventions).

Sexonomic Rules of the Game

Compared with the existing backdrop of societal structures and customs, Sexonomics envisages three distinct sets of the "rules of the game":

1. THE RULES THAT APPLY EQUALLY TO WOMEN AND MEN

Rule of reason: Having achieved fairly high standards of education, women and men engaged in sexonomic strategy and games are expected to have their minds prevail over their loin heat. This rule follows from the premise that sexuality and material self-interest are inseparable. The dignity of being human requires that human rationality shall not permit the sexual urge to become the dominating force in interactions among women and men. We are speaking here not of the stifling of sexual impulses but of a system of guidance which will know how to make the expectation of sexual pleasure a function of the appropriate material setting. A standard example of the application of this rule may be found in a situation which is typical of human sexonomic interaction and which was mentioned earlier in this book—women and men will be expected to choose a better-to-do partner over a less well-to-do one if all other qualifications and personal characteristics are deemed to be the same. Not adhering to this rule will imply that an individual is unable to handle his own sexual urges, as a consequence of which she/he will experience a diminishing personal lifetime sexonomic utility function.

Rule of sexuality: Since human sexuality is one of our three basic natural propensities (from which we derive the natural right to seek to maximize our sexual pleasure), Sexonomics declares itself in favor of a program by which, starting in early adolescence, women and men will have the opportunity to learn about their sexuality, to study its fulfilling aspects as well as its pitfalls, and to engage in sessions in which the attainability of maximal sexual pleasure will be demonstrated. As a natural urge and guided by reason toward its refined and skillful management, human sexuality is viewed as an eternally creative force. Its suppression (as we know from historical experience) will not only reinforce the malaise of degenerate behavior but will also continue imposing upon individuals and society a diminution of welfare and happiness.

Rules of civility: In our discussion so far, the sexonomic drive of women and men has been portrayed as being a primeval force and that sexual liberation since the 1940s has taken on an increasingly vicarious and even predatory expression. Nevertheless, human experience has manifested the existence of, even in worst forms of competition, certain rules of the game and patterns of behavior in all markets—patterns which Sexonomics wishes to call "the rules of civility." Sexonomics considers that all parties involved in particular sexonomic strategies will adhere to the rules of civility, whereby the intensity of the suffering of those who find themselves the "losers" will be more than offset by the greater happiness of the "winners." These practices are as follows:

Attitude of chivalry: Once you have won out over another competing individual, do not proceed to destroy her/his dignity as a human being.

Commitment to equality: Once you have succeeded in finding your ideal sexonomic mate, you will abide by the commitment to equality as a natural course of events, or else your togetherness will suffer and you will fail to maximize your joint sexonomic happiness (utility functions). This rule applies naturally to all partners and allows for some flexibility since even the most ideal partners in orders below the Lotus-woman and the Quintessential-man manifest imperfections over time. Should a partnership be dissolved, this rule will quickly enable each party to resume her/his sexonomic search and to rebound with a much greater chance of success.

Practice of generosity: Winners or losers, most of us suffer ups and downs throughout our lifetime. In consequence, it makes a lot of sense to attempt to diminish possible private suffering and discomfort by demonstrating in public an attitude of noblesse oblige vis-à-vis those who are down but not quite out (which may at times include ourselves).

Sense of devotion: To excel in our strategies, we must commit ourselves to their successful implementation. In sexonomic games, success means not only to have found our ideal partner but also to seek to make this relationship of equal long-term benefit to both of us. The sense of devotion means that we are willing to give as well as to receive but that we are mainly and foremost willing to give more than we expect to receive. Obviously, this attitude applies only to our partner and not to those against whom we have to compete in seeking to secure our preferred partners for ourselves.

Passion for freedom: Since liberty is the essential message of Sexonomics, in our sexonomic strategies and games, we must ensure our partners of the attainment of that quality of freedom which we will seek to secure for ourselves from her/him. While we will not likely wish to be as generous in our dealings with our competitors, we must realize that annulling the freedom of others will eventually result in the enslavement of everyone. We must also remember that nothing makes competition as mind-arousing (and sexonomic competition as fascinating) as granting upon others the same liberties which we would wish to enjoy if we are to devote ourselves successfully to the attainment of maximum personal sexonomic success. All freedom has its price, but the cost of robbing others of their due share of their freedom to act out their sexonomic rationality is guaranteed to be even higher.

Calculus of pecuniary preference. Sexonomics postulates that the primary function of money (cash, assets with different degrees of liquidity) is to satisfy the whole range of human wants; the primary purpose of money earned is to spend it intelligently on increasing material welfare as well as on securing long-term returns on our investments. Sexonomics does not consider money as a goal but only as a medium of exchange, a liquid means which acts as a lubricant in our personal striving for happiness. In Sexonomics, money as purchasing power is linked with sexuality because it serves as an instant means for the cash-and-carry satiation of loin heat, whereas money as sexonomic capital funds serves as the basis for our long-term investment into a lifelong fulfilling relationship. Investment into perfecting one's sexuality is imbedded in human reason. Sexonomics submits that it is rational to recognize opportunities and weigh their alternative significance, to estimate their cost-benefit ratios and calculate the probabilities of success (or failure). Human loving may provide an intrinsic motive, but it is presumed that normal loving (versus the women or the men who "love too much") is fully compatible with the rational process of developing our sexuality and that, in this process, our innate loving capacity will even be enhanced. As a matter of fact, it would appear logically consistent to expect that the loving in its historical and poetic manifestation (including the appropriate chemistry) will be rendered still more spiritually fulfilling if both partners view the material environment as satisfactory, promising, and rewarding. The convention of pecuniary preferences means that the players in the sexonomic markets know money, its value, and how to handle both. Irrational lust for money is as useless to Sexonomics as irrational loving (the totally pure selfless love, the love totally devoid of reason) of humans.

Dictates of time preference. Since humans are mortal, Sexonomics places special emphasis on the time dimension in human loving. This is so because our sexonomic happiness functions cannot be maximized if we have no awareness of the passing—and of the cost—of time. This rule combines a sense of urgency, an awareness of sacrifice, as well as the calculus of pleasure. The sense of urgency arises from instant loin heat (we absolutely need to fornicate, even though it may turn out to be very costly), but it is also an expression of impatience and disquiet (if, once in our forties, we still haven't secured for ourselves the "right" partner). The time dimension of the awareness of sacrifice manifests itself in two ways: the first concerns our quest for a permanent and enduring linkage with one partner (which excludes having another permanent partner at the same time); the second has to do with the time element involved in our life cycle. As we grow older, we reflect upon our past relationships and are only too aware that "our time" will soon run out, with the result that both women and men may engage in last-minute relationships of a very unsatisfactory and costly kind.

The greater the urgency for such instantaneous gratification, the less satisfactorily will we live up to our calculus of pleasure—the instrument which records how we are doing in the sexonomic sense and directs the individual to improve on her/his performance (if there is discontentment). Sexonomics presumes that most older women and men, especially those whose sexuality had remained dormant or underexploited, will seek to make up for this loss by spending much energy and significant assets in order to "catch up," usually by both turning to the younger set of men and women.

2. THE RULES WHICH APPLY ONLY TO WOMEN

As we have already outlined the basic sexonomic problems which modern women are facing (pages 15–18), let us accentuate another very important observation—women age physically more quickly than men, which in fact, in spite of the great advances in hygiene and medicine, represents an increasing handicap in sexonomic strategies and games (as we shall see below). And we must again emphasize that older women are much more threatened by the competitiveness of younger women than are older men by the combativeness of younger men. Adding to this recognition the fact of the high ratio of women to men and the relative impoverishment of women, we deduce the following conventions—that is, rules of the game to which most women are instinctively bound and which they will attempt to enforce by the sheer power of their natural intelligence.

Rule of the honey: Higher-order women know that in their Lady LUSSEYs, they have not only something intrinsically most precious but also a commodity which will fetch the highest price if she is marketed with care and exclusivity. The Lady LUSSEY is a honey that normal men absolutely cannot resist, especially if offered within the appropriately pleasing and stimulating total environment. If all women would only recognize that, at the appropriate level of sophistication, most men prefer the superior quality of the Lady LUSSEY to a vagina in her primitive state and that they would, with proper enticement, offer much higher value in exchange! Even though the men's overall valuation of the Lady LUSSEYs' enticement quality and conception-and-delivery function may change relative to their appreciation of her pleasure quality, the total valuation of Lady LUSSEYs (Lotus-women's and the outstanding Art-women's) will always be high provided that they are marketed with infinite prudence and consistent exclusivity. In this sense, "the rule of the honey" simply means that all women can increase the valuation of their sexuality if they recognize that the quality of this honey must be kept the highest possible, reflecting the fact that every women's vagina is not only her scarcest commodity but also uniquely the property of her natural owner. Even if the number of men is smaller than that of women, sexonomic rationality demands that the competing women never underbid one another, or else they all will cause losses in their valuations and will suffer the consequence of falling sexonomic utility functions, of discredit, and possibly even of sexploitation.

Rule of the cat: Most women know that running after men is detrimental to their self-interest in that it will lead to a demeaning situation. A certain air of aloofness, an exquisite flair for quality, and a visible portrayal of exclusiveness are characteristics that render "the rule of the cat" the other convention of key importance in women's marketing their sexuality. After all, catching mice at random as they come running may well be a cat's naturally conditioned pastime. But catching men, especially the scarce and select ones, takes so much more than an inborn propensity; since it involves sexuality, it is meant to be a creative enterprise, one which will lead to a rewarding feeding and nesting process over a long time period. The fangs and the claws should be used uniquely to ward off the advances of the more predatory competing females.

Rule of Hebe: Younger women have two natural advantages over their older sisters, both of which are of enormous sexonomic significance: their instinct for predatory behavior that emanates from their physical attractiveness and their conception-and-delivery quality within their enchantingly aromatic and youthfully lubricated Lady LUSSEYs. Men of all orders are forever vulnerable to these traits of the younger set of women relative to older ones and are willing to incur and to bear the additional acquisition cost, especially when they absolutely insist on offspring. The older women's possibly greater wealth; profound experience in life, including wisdom and patience concerning the ways and the manifestly brutalizing attitudes of men; and infinitely greater patience are usually not strong enough to overcome these natural advantages of their younger sisters. But though they may, by using their cumulative experience in catering to men's needs, slow down or even neutralize for a while the trespassing attempts on the part of the younger women, they will succeed only in part and must, therefore, learn how to ward off or diminish pain.

The rule of Hebe simply indicates to women that the younger set, in their reaching out for men, will not directly try to hurt the older set of women but will wish to assert their perceived natural right to decide what they deem to be the best for themselves. The faster the set of older women realizes that only the exceptionally gifted and creative few among them will really be able to keep their men all for "themselves," the more quickly will the competition of women of all orders and all age-groups for the men of all orders cease being a predatory free-for-all and the more effectively will all women go on to retain their men while also sharing them, for a limited time and only from one amorous occasion to another, with their sisters. Against the rule of Hebe speak two uncompromising propensities of women with respect to property relations concerning men: territoriality and material security.

In fact, however, most older women will react forcefully—and even viciously, if necessary—against the attempts of younger women to "steal their men" and will not wish to compromise themselves in seeking to find the proper balance between their need to assert the latter while also learning how to live with the former. The rule of Hebe, as viewed by Sexonomics, does not apply to those women who have never loved a man and have therefore learned to live all by themselves, possibly because many of them are not only superintelligent but also experienced enough to recognize that men are not worth it because of the low valuation of their sexuality. Going against the rule of Hebe is likely to attain an ever greater social significance as women in increasing numbers become university graduates and will consequently proceed to rationalize with clearer foresight—and higher expectations—about the role and the sexuality of "their" men—a process that will expectedly lead to a reassessment of the sexonomic valuation of men in general. But it could also result in a steep decline of the men's average valuation and, in consequence, cause a downward shift of their personal sexonomic happiness functions.

Rule of Aphrodite: In the eyes of all selective higher-order men, a woman's personal bouquet must mirror itself in an exquisite body, with well-nigh perfect forms and the appropriate feminine accents from the delicate cleft in her chin, touching her firm and rising breasts and descending across the pulsating contour lines of the navel right down to the silky whiff of her pubic area, which, if the woman is to be anything close to the perfection of a Greek goddess, must absolutely discreetly hide between two fully and gently rounded thighs the access to her honey-containing and child-carrying receptacle. The razor's edge between *belladonna*, the fair and kind queen of women, and *belladonna*, the deadly nightshade plant, is more often than not a matter of delicacy, of fragrance, and of the ability to arouse in the perceptive male the appreciation of esthetics and the promise of ambrosia rather than instilling in him the angst from suddenly finding himself face-to-face with a fully exposed gluttonously varicated and lustfully oozing abyss that threatens to swallow him up. The rule of Aphrodite seems like nature's injustice on unsightly, homely women and a tragedy on women who let themselves go because they cease believing in themselves as women. But the rule of Aphrodite is also the very promise that exactly such women can learn how to portray themselves in the most exquisite, most feminine being of a goddess. Sexonomics undertakes to help nature along—and even to challenge nature—because it postulates that, deeply hidden in the very inner self of all such women, beauty, poise, and the promise of ambrosia are just waiting for the right occasion to reveal themselves.

In its basic essence, we are speaking of a love-hate relationship. How else can we explain men's frequent use of the foulest language imaginable in cursing those parts of a woman's body for which they otherwise demonstrate painfully intensive longing? How else can we view a man who, while using an endless stream of bouquets of flowers in seeking to convince a particular woman of his eternal love, turns to another man and curses the doglike nature of his mother? How else can we comprehend an older man's genuine testamentary concern for his wife's welfare while, at the same time, he proceeds to arrange (on his deathbed) for payoffs to those younger women with whom he had been cheating on his (presumably older) wife—only to hate it all and curse himself for his uncontrollable weakness for some extra "honey"? Will we ever understand the actions of men who, while expressing undying love and fealty to "their own" women, go about brutalizing, beating, and raping them and even causing the same agony to many other women? And finally, how do we interpret men's desire for war (other than wars for the "surplus women" from other tribes) but as an organized attempt to remove themselves from women, to demonstrate their ability to function in purely male company, and to recreate the environment of prehistoric times with their custom of a free season on all women—not as partners for life but as lower-order reproductive animals—while at the same time continuing to dream about the ideal woman and of sharing with her the ultimately meaningful and rewarding life?

Intrigued by these real-life observations and reflections, Sexonomics deduces the following conventions which are germane only to men:

Rule of the silken rope trick: The essence of this rule arises from the following practical considerations with which men are faced in their wont of women:

- How do men reach out once they perceive the whiff of an interesting woman's being and feel the urge to submerge themselves into her "honey"?

- Hoping that this woman would turn out to be his "ideal" woman, which of the existing alternative sexonomic strategies must he choose and pursue in order to secure his acceptance and obtain permission to proceed with this union?

- How does he, at the same time, prevent competing males from attempting to muscle in on and possibly climb upon his own envisaged "honeycomb" tree?

- Needing this particular woman, the "perceived woman of his dreams" yet also wishing to reassert his own freedom, how will he arrange to detach himself from her, should he discover in reality that she is far from perfect—recalling the worst moments of regimentation at the hands of his own mother?

Obviously, the sexonomic answer to these fundamental questions lies in every intelligent man's innate ability to perform one of the originally prehistoric and forever tantalizingly male Gnostic revelations of the male psyche—the silken rope trick. Why a rope? Because it reminds men and women of Oriental magic. In a situation of precarious sexonomic intimacy, a perceptive man will wish to rise to the very tip of his magic rope and seek to be truly and fully *her* man, the sole beneficiary of her beloved ambrosia; however, concerned that he might get caught in the very delicate trade-off between wanting to ascend to the highest acme ever but at the risk of finding himself tied down before his proper time, he would be looking for a magic trick that will help him get away and will thereby enable him to secure his freedom—an instantaneously adaptable and flexible means of Gnosticist quality. But why a *silken* rope? Because pure silk is pliable as well as resilient, soft as well as firm, smooth as well as volute, and because women, like cardinals, prefer silk underwear—all of which are intricacies that make for quick climb-ups, pukkacious touching of all crevices, and possibly an even faster slide down and out if an expeditious getaway—along the slippery silken rope, of course—should have to be called for in the face of the unexpected.

The silken rope also has the sentimental advantage of tying down the woman of one's dreams without making her feel caught and, expertly handled by the higher-order men, of making a woman feel the difference between the finest sense of touch of a top-order man and the coarse, rough hemplike entrapment, which is the exclusive trademark of lower-order men. Finally, the silken rope is also the perfect means for ridding yourself of your most persistent competitors; its cobralike smoothness works like a charm and leaves no traces.

Rule of the whip: Since pukkacity is one of the four most coveted qualities of the Sir MOJJ and MOJJ, Sexonomics can easily construe a generalized situation in which the men whose performance in this respect is ranked by women as being well below par will face increasing problems in enticing and retaining a female partner. Obviously, in the naturally joyful experience of "now you see him out and then he goes back in," the Sir MOJJ's potency commands key attention. Manifest potency will not only rank his sexonomic valuation among the highest but will also secure for his Sir MOJJ (and others of similar stature) the sensuously totally fulfilling togetherness with his chosen Lady LUSSEY. Age-old is the adage that a man who "does it well" will retain "his" woman, even though Sexonomics would wish to add that, in modern times, the most important of the other attributes (including a propitious material environment) must also be selectively present.

It follows from *the rule of the whip* that men will not only be personally committed to devote exclusive attention to the sexual needs of their lady partners but that they will also prove the more competitive against other men the more they are able to convince their lady partners that it is they who are indeed "the best at it." This rule pervades all orders of women and men and all five sexonomic markets and forms, perhaps even more than the men's material status, the basis for a fulfilling long-term relationship between a man and his ultimate female companion. In a parallel sense concerning human biology, the women's *rule of the honey* and the men's *rule of the whip* are complements; the existence of both appears as the prime requisite in rendering the overall—physical as well as spiritual—linkage between women and men—a strong and enduring one. They also balance out in the sexonomic marketing sense in that the "exquisite honey" commands as high a valuation on the part of men as does their "ultimate potency" as viewed by women.

Rule of Midas: We have already emphasized several times that women, much more than men, view the marketing of their sexuality as having a material (monetary) base, not because this disposition is inborn in women but as a consequence of the historical distribution of wealth and income that favored men. In this sense, the honey of the Lady LUSSEY has performed the function of an implicit (and underresearched) but all-important "great equalizer" (on the assumption that most men's valuation of her "honey" is deemed higher than most men's valuation of the pukkacity of their own Sir MOJJs or MOJJs). Since, in the past, most women saw nothing wrong with being funded by men (even outside of marriage), Sexonomics will suggest that, even in the era of women's movements, "tapping" wealthier men constitutes a thoroughly rational undertaking because educated women know that the rich men's marginal valuation of the extra wealth dollar is quite a bit lower than that of a poorer man and that the feelings of guilt are correspondingly lower once the relationship ends. Viewed in this sense, the practice of women preferring wealthy men to men who are known to be paupers is easily understood; on the assumption of a lovemaking session of equal intensity, the LUSSEYs of Conch-women will command a much higher quantity of sex-consumption dollars from a wealthy male than from a less well-to-do one, if only since high-income males appreciate their extra income dollar much less than men with lesser levels of income do. As a matter of fact, this observation has been multiply confirmed by the recent sampling of the women who make up the sexonomic market for male millionaires and other men of success; unlike in traditional times, when "eligible" men were reserved for the daughters of "good" or even "noble" families, contemporary bidding practices have seen the emergence of large numbers of "professional" women who have absolutely no qualms about their preference for such men and whose networking practices have been very successful in keeping their poorer and less competitive sisters off this particularly lucrative market.

Obviously, the Midas rule is a very important determinant of women's and men's behavior in sexonomic marketing. First, it leads to a redistribution of income and wealth from men to women. Second, it also induces those men whose nonpecuniary characteristics are less than competitive to try to compensate for these shortcomings by becoming "competitive up front." Accumulating sizable assets in order to make up for their nonmaterial shortcomings, they will hope to secure for themselves the females of their choice. However, and much to our regret, most wealthy males tend to believe that their money will do all the talking and that very little personal effort is required in order to cultivate a relationship in seeking to make it long-term. Many such men not only take their ladies for granted but also often manifest outright rudeness, possibly because of their reaction to the sheer weight of numbers on the part of the competing women. In this sense, Sexonomics does not approve of the Midas rule, but it does recognize this rule as one of the most interesting (albeit usually very painful spiritually) determinants of value and price in the sexonomic relations between women and men.

CHAPTER SEVEN

Sexonomic Marketing Strategies II: Action Flowchart

Sexonomic strategy is both like and unlike strategy as in the "art or war." It is like the art of war in that it must command an abundant resource capacity (i.e., personal qualities), up-to-date technology (training and experience), mobility (spiritual and physical flexibility), a goal (coupling with an ideal partner), and a battle plan (comprising the following considerations: having in sight a sexonomic partner and designing the appropriate game plan to "land" him/her; the desire to succeed—losers do not count, only winners; peak efficiency and highest morale in order to make the strategy work; and an awareness of time—it makes for hope, but it also heals wounds).

But sexonomic strategy is also unlike the art of war because sexonomic behavior is not out to destroy but to create (love, partnership, linkage for life, material welfare, maximization of sexonomic happiness over time). It is individualistic since it is not subjected to corporate hierarchical decisions or to the military structures of command and obey. In fact, in sexonomic strategy, every participating player is at the same time her/his corporal and her/his general. Sexonomic behavior does not lead to the shedding of blood but results in blood mixing and therefore in children, families, happiness, and material welfare—and all of these while seeking to minimize government control over our private lives.

Sexonomic strategies are a very profoundly personal experience that involves a woman's or a man's whole life and renders her/him accountable to herself/himself and, through the self, usually to only one other person at any one time. Sexonomic strategies are also unlike the art of war because they involve private (sexonomic) costs in the expectation of private and personalized benefits. There are no medals or heroes, public accountability or traitors, and the losers do not normally suffer loss of life.

However, unlike the rules of conduct of modern warfare and nationally and internationally accepted rules of the game, sexonomic strategies by individuals often seem like a miniature replica of the law of the jungle and of the power plays of nation-states. They reveal themselves as possibly the strongest influencing factor in relations between individuals in spite of the continuous evolution of our legal institutions and of the updating of contracts concerning marriage and other less official forms of sexonomic togetherness between women and men.

In the quest to design the most effective winning strategy, the competing individual woman or man needs to possess the following up-to-date information:

- the makeup of the particular sexonomic market and its rules of the game;

- the characteristics of the targeted sexonomic subject as well as of the other competitors;

- the history of her/his previous successes or failures;

- the history of the targeted individual, including her/his successes or failures; and

- the sexonomic market–determined conditions of reward (for success) or punishment (for failure).

Evidently, designing the strategy that will make for the greatest certainty of success will require not only that the player possess a top-quality mind as the source of ideas and the tool of rational objective thought but that she/he also muster a well-trained, well-exercised, and resilient body, primed through continuous exposure to competition and able to weather excruciating physical pains and seemingly unbearable psychic pressures. The competitors' reactions will also have to be taken into account by her/his activated and incessantly engaged information—and impulse-gathering nerve center as yet another principal requisite toward the greatest possible personal sexonomic success. In initiating the strategy, the bidder will seek to reverify her/his understanding of the scope or dimension of the strategic master plan and will bring up to date her/his knowledge of the sexonomic characteristics of the particular market for which the strategic blueprint is being designed. During the former years of participation as a sexonomic competitor, she/he will presumably have become thoroughly experienced—if not an expert—in the functioning of that particular market, its structures, linkages, and sexonomic valuation conditions. An intelligent and experienced sexonomic competitor will, in fact, always picture in her/his mind the complete layout of the strategy plan, a chart which is a composite of the five orders of women and the five orders of men of the five sexonomic markets, of the whole network of overt or covert horizontal (within each of the orders) and vertical (between the orders) linkages, and of the pertinent social institutions. Unlike an architectural blueprint, this chart is live; it pulsates with the doings of millions of individual women and men who seek to maximize their sexonomic utilities.

As outlined earlier (pages 5, 84–86), sexonomic strategies are conducted on the premise that the participants have freedom of entry (to interact in the market pertinent to their particular order) and exit and that they are well informed about the existing conditions that they seek to maximize, but also that moving up into a higher-order market will be rendered difficult by the existence of institutionalized restrictions on free entry from lower-order markets to higher-order markets. The pulsation never ceases because, by their natures, women and men will expend a lot of energy in the quest to "improve" on their situation, an attitude that will imprint onto this strategic flowchart the incessant dynamics of the goings-on in a beehive.

Just imagine—hundreds of millions of women and men interacting in their respective orders in scenarios in which the ultimate goal may range from the raw enjoyment of loin heat–induced instantaneous fornication with a prostitute or a pickup to the commitment to find long-term harmony and happiness by getting hitched to the ultimate sexonomic partner. The pulsation not only never ends—because only the few Lotus-women and Quintessential-men in their top-level orders will ever find themselves in sexonomic balance—but it also takes on, at times, the frantic pace of a massive rat race that threatens even the most accepted and revered institutionalized constraints. In especially turbulent times (after major wars with their higher numbers of dead men than dead women), massive horizontal shifts and vertical transfers will take place because each of the sexonomic markets will tend to self-adjust over time. These shifts reveal long-term trends and must be studied by those participants who insist on maximizing their chances of success.

Let us now study the sexonomic strategy chart and its composition and then proceed to describe its essential characteristics.

Sexonomic Strategies and Games: Action Flowchart

Orders of Men:		Orders of Women:		Name of the Market:
Quintessential	+	Lotus	=	Queentessence
↓ ↑		↓ ↑		
Lace	+	Art	=	Artlace
↓ ↑		↓ ↑		
Vulpine	+	Conch	=	Conpine
↓ ↑		↓ ↑		
Mob	+	Elephant	=	Mophant
↓ ↑		↓ ↑		
Girandole	+	Vampire	=	Vampdole

Note. The arrows indicate the following:

- an up arrow points to a movement from a lower order to the next higher order but only during the life cycle of an individual;

- a down arrow points to a relegation from a higher order to the next lower order; this movement could be multilevel during the life cycle of an individual; and

- the down arrows from Vulpine-men to Girandole-men indicate that most of the Girandole-men come from the group of unusually gifted men of the Vulpine order.

As we have already learned, all these markets are interconnected with stronger linkages between two contiguous markets but with hardly ever a chance that someone might move up (or fall down) by more than one market during her/his lifetime. In planning our strategy, we should also bear in mind the rapidly decreasing numbers of order members as we seek to move toward the top. For example, if we sought to move, say, from the Mophant market up to the level of the Conpine market, which is by no means an easy jump to make, we would still have a much easier task than if we wished to move, say, from the Conpine level to that of the Artlace.

In fact, the sexonomic strategy chart reveals the typical social pyramid, with the small and exclusive elite at the top and the broadly based population at the bottom (except for a substantive difference: in Sexonomics, you may be, but need not be, wealthy to belong to the Queentessence market; this is so because priority significance is assigned to the other higher qualities). What this means is that if, in your estimation, your characteristics qualify you as member of the order of Art-women or the order of Lace-men and if you wish to ascend into the Queentessence market, you will be competing for one of the very few "openings" in that, the highest order, which may take you a long number of years to achieve (which may include your successful marriage to one of the members of the higher order) and then a lifetime to secure.

But looking at this chart, our readers should also note that advancement into the next higher order will be made the more problematic the more inadequate are the lower-order members' personal endowments. In modern capitalism, disposition over substantive material means will also be required in order to enable anyone wishing to move up to the order of Art-women and the order of Lace-men, with the appropriate advanced-level education as well as the ability and the time that are necessary to learn about the "rules of behavior" that are typical of those higher orders. Our readers may also wish to note that, in the social pyramid of Sexonomics, the children will not be viewed as having an assured lifetime place in the order of their parents. This is so because, in the worldwide system of open globalization, many past barriers to local horizontal and vertical mobility are expected to vanish. This leaves the children of each new generation with the challenge of competing for the sexonomic valuation that is appropriate for the higher orders to which they might aspire and which they will have to work for with an extra sense of commitment in order to maintain their standing once having become new members of that order.

Visualizing this complete structure of the sexonomic market and reaffirming her/his understanding of the "rules of the game" (including the conditions of exit and entry) in each of these markets, the competing participant will next seek to ascertain with which of the particular sexonomic markets she/he would wish to affiliate, a process that would involve the following steps:

- reconfirmation of her/his sexonomic valuation coefficient;

- reassessment of her/his up-to-date sexonomic qualities (a continuous sampling of her/his sexonomic evolution pattern);

- proceeding to analyze the characteristics of her/his would-be (targeted) sexonomic partner in the order she/he is seeking to enter; and

- entering the appropriate sexonomic market by accepting the challenge of applied sexonomic strategy.

It is only upon the completion of every one of these preparatory steps that the competing individual will know the scope of the task with which she/he is faced and will then proceed to design and to implement the appropriate game-winning final strategy.

Evidently, each of these steps and the reflections embodied in them are functions of the rational pulsation of reason that is presumed to be fully triggered at the beginning of the "arousal" stage. Clearly, for higher-order women and men who are already safely ensconced in their order and are contented to remain therein, the implementation of these strategic moves will have a greater chance of success than will the strategy of those lower-order women or men who are wishing to move up to the next higher order.

The sexonomic players have one single primary goal in mind: to maximize their sexonomic utilities during the course of their life cycle. By now, our readers will have learned that the maximization of their sexonomic utility does, in fact, require that the enjoyment of each of the two major building blocks of their sexonomic happiness, of their personal sexuality and their material benefit environment, must also be maximized.

From what we have seen, our readers will be able to anticipate the maximization of their happiness from fulfilling sexuality by studying carefully the description of the functions and qualities of the Lady LUSSEY (and the Sir MOJJ, respectively), by reflecting upon the question of the linkage between the enticement quality of the Lady LUSSEY (and the Sir MOJJ) and her control quality (with reason as her control center), and, if needed, by taking respective theoretical courses and applied seminars in one of our Sexonomic Institutes. Finally, they will also proceed to gain the appropriate practical experience from getting involved in marketing their improved sexonomic skills—the sexual as well as the creatively developed materialistic—which will enable them to secure for themselves—and to their sexonomic partners—maximum possible benefit.

Evidently, since this study and preparation will reveal to our readers their "strengths" and "weaknesses," they will wish to act wisely to make the best of trying to diminish their (visible) deficiencies while still in the learning stage. Subsequently, and over the course of their sexonomically competitive life cycles, they will then be expected to do their best in the quest to replace their inadequately competitive characteristics with that set of more superior qualifications that will guarantee them sexonomic happiness.

Taking upon themselves the challenges of this transformation, they will be motivated by the following very simple truth: the image and presence of a person of "character" reveals to the observer the creative glow of the many complex goings-on within the being of that person who is the owner of the face. No surgical face-lift—which is only a transitional palliative—can ever achieve such a glow since it cannot ever remove or cure the causes that necessitated the face-lift in the first place.

Before our readers decide whether they will participate in sexonomic strategies and games, they are advised first to take out time in order to reflect upon the following six considerations that are at the core of sexonomic reasoning, each of which is essential in the selection of those combinations of steps and stages that will crown with success the pursuit of their own particular strategies:

1. *The time factor:* the longer the number of years of sexonomic neglect, the more years will it take to make up for the deficiency in a player's sexonomic valuation, an absolute necessity for the creation of a more promising path toward a net gain in sexonomic happiness.

2. *The intensity factor:* the more time a player can count upon in seeking to make up past deficiencies and the more she/he desires to realize an increase in such happiness within the shortest period of time, the more intensively she/he will have to work at implementing her/his particular strategy, all of which will involve a special effort—at times usually by sacrificing lesser priorities or commitments.

3. *The stamina factor:* An intensive engagement to achieve a satisfactory breakthrough in a bidder's sexonomic standing absolutely demands the devotion of a true disciple who will need to have endured a top-level physical preparedness and to have acquired a spiritual toughness that resembles the endurance of the stoics. Both of these primary requisites will require enormous self-discipline in order enable the bidder to enhance his competitive sexonomic qualities. Evidently, the stamina factor must be uniquely linked to a strict bodily regimen, to vigorous spiritual exercises, and to exemplary dietary habits.

4. *The follow-through factor:* Once a bidder has decided on her/his sexonomic strategy and is about to commence with the game plan, she/he must muster all of her/his unremitting sense of commitment in order to achieve unmitigated success. Since all aspects of sexonomic reasoning and interaction are viewed as educational and progressive—within our societal framework of fundamental liberties and individual freedom—the chances of eventual failure are diminished. However, there always remains the possibility of premature breakings-off because, at some point and in spite of trying their "very best," the challenge may become unexpectedly too difficult and is likely to place the participant in a situation of returning

to the situation from which she/he had been trying to get away from. Several such backings-out will inevitably impose upon the participant the mentality of a "loser"—a situation that looks very similar to some men's repeated premature ejaculation and its destructive effect on their qualities of potency and prolificity. In situations in which, even after a lengthy and tedious effort, a participant's particular sexonomic target (preferred partner) is not responding quickly enough, the originally anticipated time horizons will have to be extended. Quick pessimistic conclusions about "one's own sexonomic inadequacy" should be replaced by rationalizations that the "preferred partner" may have been unable to recognize the player's full range of sexonomic caliber. It may even be necessary to shift one's attention to another "preferred partner" (for example, since about 15 percent of our population is made up of Lace-men, if one particular Lace-man does not "bite," a switch to another chosen one may be quickly and expeditiously arranged—perhaps getting even better value for one's efforts).

5. *The confidence factor.* Once a player has decided to engage in a particular sexonomic game, she/he must maintain her/his enthusiasm and must remain in a winning frame of mind. It will be absolutely essential not to ever let up on the basic principles of sexonomic rationality, viz. never to try to arouse the sexonomic interest of the "preferred partner" by offering money. This is so (in the higher orders) because money itself cannot ever compensate for a sexonomic player's personal lack of perceived sexonomic quality; neither will "only" money ever secure for a player a preferred partner of equal sexonomic quality and valuation. Studying the message concerning the qualities of women/men in their respective orders, being honest about the need to discover a player's real needs concerning an "ideal" partner, and mustering the appropriate degree of self-confidence are uniquely more effective ways of putting the participant onto the road to success in sexonomic strategies and games. Any and all of these reflect the players' personal development capacity and the willingness to bring it to full bloom; the more incessantly a player will work on perfecting her/his inborn talents and endowments, the more securely will she/he be able to reach up to the desired man/woman in the next higher order.

6. *The liberty factor.* As announced in the definition, Sexonomics views human sexual and material interaction as one of our fundamental liberties, which are founded in natural law. We are born with different endowments but are deemed free to choose between doing the best with our given innate capacity or to improve on it through the process of learning and training. The liberty factor comprises three dimensions: freedom to choose our

sexonomic partner, freedom to improve on our sexonomic standing, and freedom to maximize our sexonomic happiness.

The liberty factor is considered equally binding on every participant in sexonomic strategies and games. Manipulation is viewed as an attempt to abrogate these freedoms. As outlined earlier, societal sexonomic equilibrium cannot be achieved unless all members of society are assured of their freedom to choose their sexonomic lifestyles and to maximize their sexonomic utilities.

CHAPTER EIGHT

Sexonomic Marketing Strategies III

We shall now take up our discussion of the two initial phases of *sexonomic marketing and success*: "Cupid and the Moment of Truth" and "The Arousal: Awakening the Body but Alerting the Mind." This analysis will then be followed by a vivid portrayal of the highest quality genre of sexonomic games as played in the highest-order sexonomic market: Queentessence. The description of a lower-quality sexonomic game will then follow to demonstrate the strategic scenarios of game plans by the majority of populations in developed countries and developing countries in their own quest to achieve as much sexonomic happiness as their lesser qualities and endowments allow. Even though possessing vastly disparate sexonomic valuations and utilities, all players in all sexonomic markets are deemed to have in common two motivations: to find the appropriate sexonomic partner and thereby increase the quality of the players' sexonomic lifestyle. We should perhaps mention once again that we presume that the players from the lower orders are also driven by the intense desire to move up to the next higher order (e.g., the younger Art-woman who will attempt to marry up to a Quintessential-man; the younger [and exceptionally good-looking] Vulpine-man who will attempt to improve his sexonomic valuation by acting as an escort to and bedding with a dynamic Art-woman working as a senior executive; and the younger Conch-woman, unhappily married to a middle-level Vulpine-man, who will use her women's wiles to charm one of the married middle-aged Lace-men looking for an amorous encounter).

In line with our view that sexonomic strategy must involve both romance and rationality, we shall assume in our discussion that "Cupid's arrow" will have initially succeeded in generating an upsurge in romantic sentiment in each of our initial two players, a Lotus-woman and a Quintessential-man, thereby setting the stage for the "moment of truth," the second step toward playing the sexonomic game, the stage in which rationality and self-interest will be viewed as the determinants of the material base of sexonomic strategy, the course of involvement that follows Cupid. As the material self-interest stage, it involves considerations which had, in the past, taken diverse forms (e.g., marriage contracts) and have, in fact, applied to all sexonomic orders—a stage that is of particular significance to the sexonomic behavior of the sets of younger women and younger men of the lower sexonomic orders.

Sexonomic Phase I: Cupid and the Moment of Truth

Commencing our reflections concerning sexonomic strategy and games, we shall make the following assumptions about the experience, the state of mind, and the intentions of the readers of our website:

1. By now, you are thoroughly knowledgeable about sexonomic terminology and are presumed to be amused by and to accept the following propositions:

- Sexuality and material self-interest represent a unique human duality that can be a profoundly enjoyable experience;

- Marketing too generously one's LUSSEY will demean the sexonomic value of all LUSSEYs well below that of MOJJs; and

- Achieving one's own highest sexonomic valuation implies the existence, in women and men, of a basic driving force that constitutes the primary element in human striving.

2. You are intrigued by the description of the qualities of the Lady LUSSEY and the Sir MOJJ and their usefulness as marketing devices, and you are willing to experiment in the sexonomic market of your choosing with the hope of ameliorating the sexonomic quality of your life.

3. By this time, you will also have read the following books dealing mainly but not exclusively with women's views on lifestyles and sexuality (in addition to the basic "scientific" treatises on human sexuality): *Out on a Limb, Having It All, What Every Woman Should Know about Men, 79 Park Avenue, Lace, The G-Spot, The Naked Ape, Sons and Lovers, The Hindu Art of Love, The Ten Principal Upanishads*, and *Self-Reflections* (by Marcus Aurelius).

4. Taking off into the world of Cupid and the moment of truth, you will also have had several experiences of falling in love, of meditating on the implications arising from a particular relationship, of cohabitation, and of (usually a very painful) separation. You will personally have enjoyed to the fullest that immensely slowly spreading feeling of warmth within yourself that was triggered by the sudden appearance of a person whom you had always yearned for as the natural extension of your self and over whose presence every fiber in your being caught fire and started to glow until

you could not stand it any longer and absolutely had to reach out for that person's hand, wishing to hold on and never again let him/her go away. As a woman, you will have experienced that warmth permeate every pore and eventually radiate toward three areas of concentration, resulting in three intensively dissimilar but wonderfully merged feelings—a glow which you would have wanted to last forever after. The contentment of your reason to have found its dynamic equivalent with whom to share your creativity, your aspirations, and your belief that the ultimate meaning in life derives from the togetherness of the two of you—of this particular man and yourself. The rapid throbbing of your heart and its echo in your being as a woman—an immense heat wave which spreads itself out across your knees and down to your toes, making them burn, shiver, and itch at the same time until, fearful of the vertigo effect, you attempt to recover your balance—at the price of an enormously powerful surge of emotion which appears to take full aim at those intimate parts which you will normally have considered vulnerable and totally private to you but whose revelation and opening up to this particular man will have seemed to you as the most natural thing ever in your life. And finally, the calmness of your inner spirit, as a counterbalance to the racing of your mind and the frantic pulsation of your blood flow—we as individuals are children of the universe, but our deeper meaning derives from our sharing in the universal spirit through our merging with our true soul mate who appears so well-nigh perfect, the man with whom we are destined to procreate the children I, as a woman, really want.

Cupid and the moment of truth have to do with humans falling in love, possibly the ultimate human experience (how totally idealistic but also utterly defenseless we are when *it* hits us for the first time). However, the Romeo-Juliet type of falling in love is in contradiction to sexonomic reasoning because it involves ideal types to whom loving signifies a totally emotional state of being, one that is beyond human rational capacity to handle and is, therefore, doomed to suffer an unhappy ending. Most of us have gone through the agony of the first love, and most of us have learned how to cope and how to bounce back. After several rebounds, we are aware of the risks involved and have learned how to minimize the possibility of pain. "Cupid," whenever it happens, cannot be helped by sexonomic reasoning because biological laws are irrevocably binding upon humans, even though experience teaches us how to become more selective and, eventually, how to ward off misdirected arrows. But "the moment of truth" is eminently one of the composites of sexonomic reasoning, its primary tool. Since the men's sexonomic reasoning with respect to women accords greatest emphasis to sexuality and only secondarily, and on a vastly diminishing scale, to material means and power, the "moment of truth" of quality men is primarily aimed at the need to build up defenses against the forever present danger of engaging in purely loin heat generated sexual intercourse, which represents the lowest form of sexonomic interaction (do bear in mind that the Lady LUSSEY is "pure honey" and, therefore, quite impossible to resist if offered in an enticing and truly feminine setting). It is, therefore, during this crucial moment of intensive reflection that a man will decide what he wants of a woman; it is during this flash that he will perceive of her as being worthy only of fornication or that he will recognize her many other qualities and will preempt instant consummation in exchange for the desire to explore her many interesting dimensions of those presumed qualities and even to contemplate the possibility of a long-term relationship. Her own appearance and behavior will evidently serve as basic determinants in his momentous decision, for nothing is easier for a quality man to reject than a woman whose presence is cheapened by her shamelessly manifested lust and all too evident expectation of a material gain. In fact, a higher-order man will always be guided by his perception of the reflections going on in the mind of the woman, knowing that they will eventually reveal themselves as her own "moment of truth."

"Cupid" needs no classification as to the first four orders of women and the first four orders of men (remember: Cupid knows that Vampire-women and Girandole-men are incapable of loving, and he will not waste his precious time on seeking to cause mischief upon them!) since the biopsychic effect of his arrows is the same on all members of the top four orders. It is only in the immediate aftermath, the stage of the "moment of truth" that sexonomic rationality will be invoked and will become the instrument of control in directing the evolution of a particular relationship. Evidently, the quality and the duration of this evolution will be the expression of the primary purpose of a particular relationship (see page 1) as well as of the nature and the level of the sexonomic market. Realizing a high-utility long-term sexonomic relationship in a higher-order market will require a game plan that will call for the continuous application of the participating individuals' characteristics and endowments, especially their sexuality (the qualities of the Lady LUSSEY and Sir MOJJ), material means, and power. A thorough practical and theoretical knowledge of human sexuality and of the order of ranking of the qualities of the Lady LUSSEY (and Sir MOJJ) constitutes an absolute requisite since, as outlined in the section "Bedding with Men," the eventual sexual linkage will have to be exquisite for the relationship to endure (even though a lot of "hard work" may have to be involved in creating such precious and joyful long-lasting lovemaking).

The degree of success in the quest to generate the appropriate sexually enticing atmosphere will also depend on the would-be partners' awareness of the marketability of the qualities of their Lady LUSSEY (or Sir MOJJ) on their desire to market them and on their willingness to drive a hard sexonomic bargain in order to secure for themselves maximum value in exchange, in return for an equally maximum value given up. Nothing will kill off a promising sexonomic relationship as effectively as will unequal terms of exchange.

Whereas the sexonomic game plan is designed and initiated during the "moment of truth" stage, the overall strategy will be perceived of as an ideal blueprint that calls for the maximization of sexonomic happiness (the minimization of sexonomic unhappiness). In the blueprint and in playing the real game, the attempt to maximize will involve all sexonomic variables, but it will also necessitate a calculation of private and public sexonomic gains (losses).

Sexonomic Phase II: The Arousal
Awakening the Body but Alerting the Mind

In the second phase of sexonomic strategy, "the arousal," the players will seek to implement the game plan with the aim of achieving the desired end result in a particular relationship. During the second phase, both players will have increasingly more trouble keeping in check their sexual appetites for each other, and the length of this stage will depend on their ability to put this intensive desire on the back burner, while they proceed to reflect on the pros and cons of this particular relationship and its possible duration. At this stage, a wise game plan will also include a provision for an unproblematic discontinuation of a relationship, which is of special significance in instantaneous or short-range sexonomic get-togethers. This provision is implicit but essential in that it serves as a warning device, a rational means to cool off the initial heat wave that is triggered by Cupid. But overall, the game plan will manifest an essentially positive orientation in that it will aim at winning, not losing, whereby it will maximize the chances of sexonomic success.

Once the intensive eye-to-eye contact required for the "arousal" stage to be initiated has been established between the respective sexonomic players, both the female and the male are presumed to proceed to reflect upon the pros and cons, a process which will normally result in a number of questions and will necessarily call for answers if the game plan is to take its course. The nature and kind of questions will depend on the players' membership in a particular order; on their overall experience in life, including sexual activity; and on their material propensities and qualifications. One of the main undertakings by all players during this stage will be attempts to discover, whether the qualities of their counterplayers will place them into the higher, the middle, or the lower valuation range of their particular order. Evidently, the concerns of higher-order players are not only different from those of players who are members of lower orders but are also expected to reveal themselves over a longer time frame. Sexuality, wealth, and power being the principal considerations, we must once again point out that the effect of Cupid—even though biopsychically a similar experience for all humans—will express itself in a much more cultured and sophisticated manner with the higher orders than it would with the lower ones. The higher orders' sexuality takes on a much more reserved form than does their preoccupation with power.

Concerns typical of sexuality arise from the players' respective qualities of the Lady LUSSEY and Sir MOJJ. As we have already seen, "highly exquisite sexuality" has a totally different connotation in the Artlace market than it has in the Mophant market; accordingly, the game plan of two partners in the former market will express its sexuality in a manner different from that of two partners in the latter market. For instance, the lovemaking scenario of the Art-woman and the Lace-man will never involve vulgarity, brutalization, or crudeness; such will simply never form part of a typical Artlace game plan. Neither would partners in the Mophant market ever long for mind-arousing lovemaking that arises from the harmonious merger and unity of the virtuosity of a Stradivarius bow and the resonance of its own viol in creating a rhapsody of rapturous sounds. A prudent Art-woman will, in the sexuality part of her game plan, allow for the possibility of intercourse at a time earlier than what her control function might otherwise consider the "ideal" moment; but in seeking to marry a Lace-man, she will play up to the fullest her enticement function without allowing her passion to slip out from under her control quality (as we know, the odd Art-woman will, with passion blazing, go after the more eligible Vulpine-man, looking for a body-exhausting screw, but she would never marry that man). The Lace-man, in his prudence and foresight, will not jump upon his counterplayer before she gives him the appropriate signal. Even though only a man, his highly trained reason will not allow his sexuality to run wild before the proper time, for he knows that Art-women can be fickle and easily scared away by men who trespass or do not otherwise grant them equitable terms of exchange. Even though a typical Lace-man, he will hop into the sack with any of the physically enticing Conch-women in the expectation that she would do to him what his Art-woman wife would never allow herself to demand of her husband. A linkage between the Art-woman and the Quintessential-man also falling into the realm of possibility, the Art-woman may have to be even more prudent in her game plan follow-through because, if she gives in too quickly, she may forever have to forgo being courted by other Quintessential-men, the men of the latter order having the fortitude to resist advances before their "proper time" by the impatient types among Art-women.

The sexuality aspect of the Art-woman's game plan will know when to highlight, in the presence of the Lace-man counterplayer, her feminine "charms" (from the whiff of her personal bouquet to the twinkle in the specks of her retinas revealing that she does indeed enjoy feeling his masculine presence and coveting to pinch his firm-looking ass) for, after all, she wants to keep him interested and hanging on such that, at the proper time, he would find her simply impossible to resist and to live without. However, the Art-woman will prudently and with perseverance gather substantiated information on the other two principal aspects of her game plan—her counterplayer's wealth and power. But as the play unfolds, her game plan will have to prove flexible enough in order to permit revisions in case something unforeseen should occur. For instance, an immediate critical review of the whole situation might be called for if the control function proves too weak to keep in check the enticement quality and the pleasure function. Such changes in the game plan form an essential part in sexonomic marketing in order to ensure that, for the duration of the game, the relative sexonomic valuations of the two players remain at about the same level. When passion is let totally loose, this precarious balance will be endangered in that the sexonomic valuation of the bidding individual whose control function cannot keep passion in check will diminish, while that of the counterplayer will be enhanced. If a game plan fails to provide for instantaneous readjustment as the play unfolds, the terms of sexonomic exchange will shift increasingly more in favor of the flexible individual and against the rigid one. In no time, the whole play will then tend to take an unfavorable turn because increasing inequality in the bidding and counterbidding—a violation of the basic premise concerning sexonomic rationality—will make it impossible to bear out the first assumption in sexonomic strategies and games, viz. that of equality between any two bidding partners in their respective sexonomic markets. Clearly, sexonomic flexibility presumes the presence of human wisdom. Wisdom being the ultimate level of reason, women and men who are devoid of the latter cannot attain the state of the former; they are destined to be sexonomic losers.

A higher-order woman's typical game plan, in its two initial stages of conceptualization and implementation, will involve considerations with respect to the sexuality, the wealth, and the power of the counterplayer that will reveal a different order of ranking from that of a man's game plan. Such a woman will bring her sexuality into full portrayal and will make it bloom at the crucial moments during which she will expect the counterplayer to make his definitive move toward a longer-term committal. But in so doing, she will subject to control her own sexual impulses (even *intensive* control) whenever necessary. This attitude is explained by the fact that sexuality is ranked much higher by men than by women, which, tendency-wise, women seek to exploit by limiting their sexual availability in order to secure themselves greater long-term material benefits than sex on demand ever would. Owners of high-quality bordellos, many of whom are Art-women, know only too well that their success is linked not to the men's recourse to instant intercourse whenever the urge hits them but to developing, in the men, a perception that, in their particular establishment, they will obtain uniquely specialized and therefore extremely scarce accommodation, including the appropriate ambiance, for their sexual and spiritual needs. A higher-order woman will feel the same intensity of sexuality as does a lower-order woman, but the quality of her sexuality will obtain a much higher valuation because she will know how to keep her sexuality her own very private affair. Her sexuality is much more like the backdrop than the curtain on a stage, in that it accords to the play depth and directive for a particular setting. Her coplayer(s) is (are) high-quality actors in the world of power, of personal magnetism and charisma, and often also in the realm of wealth generation. Knowing that her sexuality will always find high-quality takers, she is contented to keep it in the background and to let the "whiff" sprout forth when she deems the moment right. Which means that she will devote most of her time to the quest of meeting and getting to know exactly those kinds of men. Most of her "preparatory" time is taken up with her wiles' plotting the appropriate power and wealth game plan. Unlike her lower-order sisters' coarseness, her sexuality is refined, which is why she will succeed in all three areas of sexonomic games and will earn a very high sexonomic happiness rating.

Unlike the sexonomic discreetness of their higher-order sisters, lower-order women see no shame in revealing, even in public, their sexuality. They will use their sexuality blatantly and frequently in the sincere belief that their bodies represent the best that they can offer. The game plan of these women will include an explicit material consideration because these women look at money and the accumulation of things not only as safety devices but mainly and foremost as their major purpose in life. To them, power is a means toward securing material succor through the government or via controlling the market forces. But these women rarely reach ranking societal power. Their primary strategy aims at the exchange of the body for improvement in material conditions when they are young; when older and successful in amassing wealth, they are noticed wearing expensive but flashy jewelry as if trying to hide behind the façade of gold their lack of other qualities. Lately, the younger women of the lower orders have added their own earning power to the material base of their sexonomic game, possibly because, influenced by the philosophy of women's liberation, they are seeking to diminish and eventually to remove the use of their bodies as the primary means of bargaining for a better material life in their respective sexonomic markets.

Sexonomic Games in the Highest Orders:
A True Love Story

In our first demonstration of sexonomic strategy, we are dealing with two individuals from the two highest orders, a Quintessential-man and a top-ranked Art-woman. Their personal data are as follows (updated as of February 2007):

- *Lundquist*, Goran Joachim, forty years old, widower, no children
- Swedish citizen living and working at his villa in Saint-Raphaël, France
- Ranking Swedish contemporary neo-postimpressionist
- World renowned for his exhibitions
- Permanent display of his seven major paintings in the postimpressionist wing of the Guggenheim
- Holder of the Légion d'Honneur and of the Royal Swedish Bernadotte medals

- Several honorary doctorates from top-level European and American universities
- Two of his most recent paintings, *A Toast to the Toad* and *The Turquoise Frog Orchestra*, were recently sold in New York, each for more than six million dollars.

Lifelong member of the Swedish Socialist Party, even though multimillionaire by inheritance (paper and pulp, timber) and from selling about 150 of his paintings. Formerly expensive lifestyle, including a Piaggio amphibian and a forty-foot yacht, the *Lady Dagbar*. Silver medal for épée at the 1990 Olympics. Captain of the Saint-Raphaël polo team. In 1995, seriously injured in an avalanche off Kitzbühel, still slightly limping. Superb bearing, with the famous Lundquist nose.

One of Europe's most eligible bachelors in the world of the arts, he married Dagbar van Soencken, Miss Denmark 1988 and Givenchy's top model, in 1987. His wife perished in the same avalanche. For years, he suffered terribly from her death, kept aloof of women, gave up all of his wealth—except his villa and the yacht and 50 percent of his revenue from the sale of his paintings—to the Lundquist Foundation for Disadvantaged Children. Rumors concerning his alleged homosexuality seem unfounded. Is cared for by his domestic of many years, Magdalena Sophie. Business agent: Dagobert Elcken-Hubéry, Paris, 16e. Banks: Banque des Pays-Bas, Schweizer Kommerzbank.

The quintessentialness of Lundquist's person is revealed only in part in his personal data. The ability to forgo highly materialistic living standards, honoring the memory of his dead wife, and the strength of character that showed itself, especially in his continuing creativity, are attributes that many of the high-quality Lace-men were also deemed to possess. What, then, made Lundquist truly Quintessential? This was exactly what de Bellemaire would have to find out because Lundquist's ranking within the Quintessential order of men was of crucial significance in her own quest to fill her sexonomic heart.

- *De Bellemaire*, Francine Sharon, thirty years old, divorced, no children
- Canadian citizen, cultural attaché at the Canadian Embassy in Paris
- BA Honors Political Science; BCL, LLB, McGill University, Montreal
- Linguist
- Member of MENSA
- Top graduate of the class of 1997 of the Sexonomic Institute of America
- Art evaluation diploma from Sotheby's
- Only daughter of the Hon. Pierre de Bellemaire, senator, and Mary (born Harting, remarried Osborne, de Benedicti, Loxenfeld, Schoenheit)
- Former assistant editor of *Professional Woman's*

Only fifteen years old when her father committed suicide after wasting his family fortune drinking and womanizing, Sharon, a long-legged tomboy teenager who had loved skiing, boating, horses, and designing and hated her father's escapades, joined a commune after her mother remarried. Brutalized by the leader, she became pregnant, had an abortion, went through a six-month drug binge, and then recovered. Finished high school, maintained an A average throughout; at McGill, won two medals as a ranking law graduate but never again allowed a man to touch her until she decided to marry an intellectually remarkable but otherwise nondescript law professor. Applying for a divorce before the year was up, she enrolled in the one-year intensive program at the Sexonomics Institute in Montreal and obtained five A+'s in the most challenging courses (Biology of Human Sexuality, Human Ethics and Sexonomic Strategies and Games, Seminar on Sexuality and Power, Lab Session on Refined Sexual Practices, Theory of Finance and Sexonomic Behavior, Blue Chips: Stock and Men) in her quest to learn everything possible about high-quality men and their sexonomic needs.

Took time out to become the Canadian women's Laser sailing champion. Fluent in the two official languages as well as in Spanish and German, the posting to Paris followed a junior assignment at the embassy in London, during which time she earned the art evaluation diploma. Still an avid rider, the formerly unruly and undisciplined teen had, since her posting in Paris, become one of the remarkably attractive personages with the youthful set at Deauville. Her responsibilities at the Canadian Embassy involve mainly cultural liaison and representation, art exchanges, and exhibitions.

Lives alone in Le Marais with a part-time domestic. Has season tickets for the Paris Opera and is member of the Riding Club of Paris. Banks: Banque Nationale de Paris, Royal Bank of Canada. Few savings. Favorite designers: Givenchy, Lagerfeld, de Shmorinsky.

The sexonomic issue at hand? Lundquist had no intention of even looking for a woman, even though lately, after his frequent agonizing hours about the death of his beloved wife, he started noticing an increasing disquiet, not so much about the void in which his wife left him but about the moments of general emptiness in his life. The arrival of new neighbors with their two lovely children would induce him, even during his most intensive painting sessions, to wonder what his own children might have looked like.

Paris. Stage One: Cupid and the Moment of Truth

De Bellemaire had first seen some of Lundquist's work at the Montreal Museum of Fine Arts about one year before her posting to Paris and experienced a very intense gripping moment—an instantaneous revelation which caused her great anxiety and descended right into her calves, making her shiver. As a lark, she then took the plane to New York, wishing to be present at the auction by the Silverstein Gallery of Lundquist's two most famous paintings. Once again, she experienced that inexplicable vertigo-like effect. Upon her arrival in Paris, she was given authority to promote Canadian art and to arrange for exhibitions, especially of French Canadian artists, to be held in France. Pondering upon how to get the semirecluse Lundquist to leave Saint-Raphaël for a matter other than his own private affairs, she hit upon the idea of staging a prize-winning exhibition of young French Canadian painters studying in Europe and inviting three renowned artists to be the judges, one of whom would be the Swede. His enticement: the said two paintings had been bought on behalf of a Vancouver multimillionaire.

Recalling one of the three most exclusive principles of schooling at the Sexonomic Institute, viz. to become perfectly well informed about the future partner's sexonomic valuation, which would consist of confirming Lundquist's character traits; checking out his sociopolitical priorities; updating the information concerning his assets and income expectations; and compiling a dossier on his views on and relationships with women, including their preferred gifts and personalized perfumes. If all this data were to her liking, she would then, about six months before the exhibition, use high-level intermediaries in order to extend the invitation with the maximum chance of success.

She would also have to think of her official role as well as of her being a woman. What were his likes, dislikes? His pleasures, displeasures? How could she attract his attention? What would the apparently very sensitive hands of this man holding the painter's brush and projecting such opaque images in their translucent pastel shades feel like touching her face and seeking to trace out every one of the throbbing azure blue speckles in her eyes? Will he appreciate her expertise in sailing and invite her to his yacht? Even if he did, she would never board the *Lady Dagbar*. Noticing that her passion quality was threatening to run away from her control function, de Bellemaire recalled the second of the most exclusive principles of sexonomic behavior: "Unlike a LUSSEY, a Lady LUSSEY will never emit even the faintest of her personal whiffs even at the most qualified and exciting suitor before her owner's reason signals the go-ahead. A go-ahead will be given only if this particular relationship is expected to result in an increase of total sexonomic happiness." Critical of her moment of weakness, de Bellemaire, true to her nature as a top-level Art-woman, snapped back into performing her highly rational professional tasks and went about staging the exhibition. But she decided to check out the favorite eau de cologne of the former Miss Denmark and, after a tantalizing moment of reflection, proceeded to spray the tiniest amount of Cacharel's Anaïs Anaïs right in the center of the invitation and written by her own hand.

His reply did not take long in coming. Bemused by the letterhead and the great seal of Canada and instantly perceptive of the woman's exquisite touch, Lundquist couldn't evade the scent and looked puzzled at his wife's portrait, framed in black and hanging on the wall right behind his favorite easel. Then he glanced back at the longhand note and traced the ups and downs of the letters as if attempting to discern the spirituality of the writer. He then raised the letter to his distinctly aquiline nose and, suddenly deeply pained, looked back at his wife. In his face, the reflection of the agony over her death transcended toward the scent that arose so enchantingly from that unknown woman's hand. Motionless for an impenetrably personal moment of lonesomeness, Lundquist moved to his easel, looked around among his many tubes of paint, and picked three tubes: French ultramarine, cadmium deep red, and gold ochre. Typical of postimpressionists, he then tried to match the scent and the color, which would give him an identifying clue of the nature of the Canadian woman who had signed the letter. De Bellemaire.

In an instant, his thoughts were racing—the New York sale! De Bellemaire—the tall, willowy, ever-so-slightly bowlegged chestnut brunette—bid twice—smilingly, challengingly, invitingly—only to turn abruptly and depart after catching his eyes and leaving behind the pulsating glow of millions of eternal royal blue speckles. For the briefest of instants, she seemed defenseless, then she was gone. Three years ago, almost to the day. Once again, Lundquist looked at his wife then proceeded to squeeze a drop of ultramarine and a tiny touch of the cadmium red. He stirred them ever so lightly, transferred a speck of the blue onto his left palm and of the red onto his right palm. Then he stood motionless, looked back at his wife, and merged his palms, almost as if begging for forgiveness. The pain vanished from his eyes, and his faced relaxed as he took the few steps toward the portrait and raised his ring finger toward his wife's face, stroking her lips ever so gently. "Thank you, my beloved, for giving me a sign." He then turned around and moved toward his desk, resolute in his desire to accept the invitation. He looked at his open palms; the two colors had blended perfectly into millions of royal blue speckles.

Paris. Stage Two: The Arousal— Awakening the Body but Alerting the Mind

The third specific principle of sexonomic behavior is, in its long tradition, of special significance to quality women; a woman of the two top orders of women will never agree to a first date unless the suitor has been granted three opportunities to be officially introduced, the time Cupid needed to act or to refuse to act. If Cupid refuses to act even if eye-contact interest has developed, he must be accorded three more chances to initiate the moment of truth, even if he must at times be helped along. Deeply impressed by the royal blue speckles, Lundquist saw himself face-to-face with the premonition that his life was about to undergo a dramatic but inevitably positive change.

Lundquist flew into Orly the morning of the opening day of the exhibition and was escorted to the embassy by the third secretary. De Bellemaire prudently decided not only to abide by the protocol but also not to expose herself to a direct hit in the airport reception lounge by one of Cupid's arrows. Art-women had no business acting like receptionists even in matters of the heart and especially not if they were out to move up to the unique and exclusive plateau of the Queentessence market. Instead, she would wait for him at the main entrance hall to the embassy, wearing a Givenchy dark blue pantalon silk suit with light gray trim and a medium gray high-collar blouse with a necklace of three strings of natural pearls. But unlike his wife's classic hairdo, straight and with a central parting drawn back and gathered into a tight knot at the nape of her neck, de Bellemaire decided to arrange her hair in soft waves so as to bring out better the full luster of the natural chestnut glow with its purple highlights, tied in a loose knot and secured with a matching natural-pearl hairpin.

Cupid did not need three opportunities to accomplish his task. As a matter of fact, he didn't even have to let loose the first arrow because the blue-gray of Lundquist's Nordic ice eyes first crystallized and then melted into free-flowing anticipation as he disembarked from the official motorcar and caught sight of that ever-so-slightly bowlegged Canadian woman standing in the entrance portal. Her attire revealed that she had the courage to challenge the rigid formalities of diplomatic standards, while her choice of the blue confirmed to him that she understood that color was both an esthetic and an emotional experience. For a moment, he wondered if she had Swedish blood or had been to Sweden, for the hue of the medium gray of her blouse could have originated from the Carstens steel mills, famous for the texture and resilience of its alloys and possessing a worldwide monopoly in the unmatched mellow colorings of their high-tech products. Her eyes confirmed his disquiet concerning the perfume; this woman knew the best of France and of its genius and was able to make her own choices. Inevitably, he did kiss her hand and was then bemused to discover that her pupils had instantaneously and noticeably widened. How slender she was—a perfect size eight, tall. She would certainly not have to expect a man to bend down in order to kiss her, but it was curious to notice that she was wearing medium-high heels as if she weren't certain about how tall he really was, a crucial consideration for their first direct eye-to-eye contact.

De Bellemaire would have ample time to study every feature and line in his face during the exhibition and the deliberations concerning the prize-winning artists. Fleetingly, she noted the remaining grief, especially around the corners of his eyes and what looked like a recent but unusually stern line between his eyebrows. But his whole mannerism, from the hand kiss to the litheness of his movements revealed not only an exceptionally fine sense of touch but also a gentleness which is characteristic only of those men who possess the four basic requisites of quintessence and are therefore in full control of all their facilities: wisdom, knowledge, authority, and tenderness.

After the festive opening of the exhibition and during most of the official part, which would eventually include the prize-winning ceremonials, de Bellemaire devoted most of her time to catering to the presence of the invited dignitaries, which included the three judges of the competition. She was able narrowly to avert several mob scene–like moments around the person of Lundquist, who was signing numerous autographs. During the 5:00 p.m. tea, she finally managed to sit down by his side; only then did she notice how haggard he was, well-nigh undernourished. His suit appeared a custom tailored Pierre Cardin, but it was not the most recent cut and it also seemed too loose, as was the collar of his shirt. Neither were his hands, so typically bearing traces of many oil colors, able to lie still. Supercreativity or hypersensitivity? Her heart suddenly turned upside down, letting loose a warming and caring energy beam and transmitting it toward this man who did not even perceive of his need to be looked after by a loving woman. But she managed to control this outburst of feeling and went on to think ahead—the prizes, the evening reception, and his announced departure the following morning.

Several times during the formalities, their eyes met, the initial defensive alertness being gradually replaced by an expression of curiosity and then by the display of confidence. The official part of the evening was suddenly turning out to be much longer than foreseen or desired. Finally, just after 1:00 a.m., Cupid shifted into high gear: "Madame de Bellemaire, I now find that I must postpone my planned departure by at least twenty-four hours. An unanticipated situation has arisen which I must absolutely look into. With my profound congratulations for a magnificently arranged official part of the exhibition, may I count on your help, most of it concerning my work?"

One of the "pieces of business" was Lundquist's desire to meet in person with the first-prize-winning young French Canadian and to invite him to stay in Saint-Raphaël for a few months and attempt some postimpressionist work. The other concerned his desire to stage a very private exhibition in London and also to contact Sotheby's through her contacts. A very large aid project had arisen from Hurricane Hugo's swath over Saint Kitts, destroying all elementary schools and orphaning quite a score of children. He wished to set up a special fund of one million dollars and would have to sell, as quickly as possible but without suffering a significant discount, two of his very personal paintings which he had never planned to sell and which were in the vault of his villa in Saint-Raphaël.

De Bellemaire arranged to take off the following morning and met Lundquist and Jules Lagace, the talented French Canadian, for brunch. She then contacted the Paris representative of Sotheby's and brought her guest to the Gare du Sud. Parting at the terminal, he took hold of her hand, touched every one of her fingers, and looked into her eyes with the gentleness which only quality men who had suffered a great deal can muster: "At the proper time, you will come to Saint-Raphaël, won't you?" Hanging on to her lips like a little boy who will die if there is not even a crumb of cake left on the plate by the time it is passed on to him, de Bellemaire once again felt the vertigo effect open up a huge abyss all around her except where he was standing. She had difficulties remembering which basic principle of the Sexonomic Institute applied to this particular precious moment at the Gare du Sud. She looked back at him and then at her fingers. He had kissed only one of them, the ring finger. "I will at the proper time. Depending on the arrangements by Sotheby's and on whether you will feel safer if I act as the carrier." After many years of numbness, the glow she had experienced only once before was beginning to permeate her being as a woman. It was highest time that he had boarded the Riviera Express.

While driving back to her office, she had extra time to sort out and analyze her feelings—quite a task in the mayhem of Paris traffic. At the Sexonomic Institute, she had passed several major tests concerning her inborn talents and state of sexonomic happiness. The test results and eventually the quality of her work and examinations placed her into the highest range of Art-women. Her having wasted that time in the commune and the following abortion caused her such anguish as to make her, for a while, even lose the sense of belief in herself. She knew that some members of the order of Art-women will seek to compensate for very stressful periods by engaging in unusually frequent intercourse, mainly with those Vulpine-men who are very good "at it" and are extremely pleased to provide for free this sexual shake-up service. A few Art-women would even seek to compensate by turning to drugs but rarely for longer than three months. Lotus-women would never use drugs, but Art-women would. But unlike many Conch-women, Art-women never become addicted. The fact that de Bellemaire was unable to resist taking drugs in seeking to solve her problems after her father's death was the proof that, in spite of her many superb innate qualities, she lacked the perfection of a Lotus-woman. She did not become addicted, but her using them when she should have known how to refrain left her with an enormous feeling of guilt. Bedding with the men in the commune, studying at the institute the practical art of lovemaking and its many detailed techniques, and marrying the law professor were, in hindsight, intimate linkages with men who were inferior to her—even her husband—but were a price that had to be paid in her attempt to understand her sexuality and its role in her life as a woman. But fully grown up, she realized that she would never again compromise herself with such men because they left her empty and cold, in spite of the regular occurrence of orgasms in the purely technical but vulgar erotic sense, during her lab sessions at the institute and then at the hands of her husband.

Only recently did she get to realize that sexonomic fulfillment cannot be achieved except with a man who would be an extension of herself, a man with whom the naturally earthy human biology of lovemaking would attain a heavenly glow and with whom the togetherness of mind and spirit would take on a forever creative dimension. Such a man could only come from the order of Quintessential-men. With such a man, it is never love at first sight but a slow and premeditated process of learning how and why to love him. But this process would have to be triggered upon first seeing that man by an initial intensive meltdown in her innermost being as a woman, a meltdown which her reason would have to prove capable of controlling. That moment arose when she saw Lundquist for the first time in New York. She was twenty-eight then and had to leave in a terrible hurry because she did not want him to see that she was experiencing that meltdown right there and then and for the first time in her life. She had since matured into a thirty-year-old Art-woman who knew, by experience, that her overall qualities and exquisite femininity would arouse the attention even of the men of the highest order. But, longing with her body for Lundquist, her mind was wondering whether those exquisite men would ever understand her escapades as a teenager. Would Lundquist only understand, or would he also forgive?

In the spur of the moment, de Bellemaire decided to tell him everything when the proper time arose. If he were only a Lace-man, she might lose him there and then. But he was Quintessential in that he possessed wisdom and spiritual wealth, which meant he would manifest the quality of generosity. Whenever he looked at her, she knew that he would understand and forgive. He would because he must have observed her truly ladylike appearance and must have discovered that she had most of the requisites to qualify for a Lotus-woman, *his* Lotus-woman. However, even if he did all this, she would still face a major personal handicap; several times since that initial meltdown, urged on by the burning sensation in her loins, she has caught herself tempted to take the first step toward him. But she did not because she knew only too well that a Lotus-woman would never run after a man. Being a Lotus-woman, she would expect even the highest-quality man to take up the pursuit. She had ample evidence that no woman, including a Lotus-woman, could retain her sexonomic valuation if she reversed the roles and overtly attempted to become the hunter. Her natural disposition of a most finely attuned sexonomic rationality complemented by sexonomic training and experience, a Lotus-woman and top-level Art-woman will instinctively know how to entice men of quality to commence the bidding. Clearly, if she was to have any chance of playing a winning game with Lundquist, she would have to convince her control quality that, for the time being, her passion had to be checked—absolutely.

By the time de Bellemaire parked her car in the garage of the embassy, she had convinced herself that Lundquist's curiosity had been aroused at the Silverstein Gallery and that she could henceforth anticipate the second stage, the arousal, to take its ideal course toward sexonomic fulfillment. She entered her office with a radiance which an observing cognoscente of human intimacy would refer to as so much more than a woman in love—a woman in love who knows that her strategy cannot possibly fail.

No one at the embassy or among her friends noticed during the following week de Bellemaire's increased disquiet about the lack of communication from Saint-Raphaël. Sotheby's London responded on the third day after his departure; no auction would be necessary as a reliable buyer was standing by to see the said paintings, possibly within the week. On the following day, a fax was received outlining the conditions of Jules Lagace's visit. It was addressed to de Bellemaire with the request that she should accompany the French Canadian and remain a few days to review and classify those paintings, which had never left the villa and which he was now willing to put on the market. Except for "mes meilleurs voeux," the fax contained no greetings. De Bellemaire would have preferred a concluding personal touch, but as an Art-woman wishing to move up, she knew that Quintessential-men could and should never be prodded. Since she really desired this man, she needed to exercise extraordinary prudence in her strategic follow-through. She had no choice but to reassert the primacy of her control function in order to neutralize and keep in check the threat of her pleasure-quality needs turning her Lady LUSSEY into blazing unmitigated passion.

Saint-Raphaël. Stage Three: A Story of Sexonomic Success, First Act

Even though living a very private life and feeling very comfortable in his state of voluntary isolation, Lundquist liked mixing with crowds, especially if made up of numerous individuals. Unlike colonies of ants on the hunt for food, none of which would ever step out of line, individuals moving in a crowd bear a unique quality and manifest a sense of purpose of their own. Unlike a mob, who have a common goal that makes them fall into step and threatens to consume them all, an assembly of individuals on the move appears as a kaleidoscope of uncoordinated acts, of motion without an ultimate goal—in fact, a giant chessboard on which the pieces move at random rather than at the command of the opposing players, a set whose players will neither win nor lose. Lundquist had never had the urge to find out the supreme powers of a chess queen since, had he wished to, he would possibly have had to consent to subject his freedom to the will of the queen and to the rules of her game, the "royal game." His wife had understood and left him to be himself, with his French ultramarines, cadmium deep reds, and Windsor emeralds. But never the brown and ivories or the black and whites of the traditional chessboards.

On both occasions, de Bellemaire had appeared in his life, dressed in two of the three colors which were typical of his first two periods, the red and the blue. Arriving in Saint-Raphaël, would she be dressed in the pastel green that was also Lagerfeld's sensational and so totally unexpected choice for the 2001 season?

He recalled de Bellemaire's summertime dress at Silverstein's—fire-red shantung skirt, loosely falling in a triangle down to her knees and revealing about one-third of her outside thighs as she made her way toward the auctioneer. Her stride seemed like a cross between a ballerina and a horsewoman—tippytoeing while, at the same time, moving her long legs forward as if in harmony with the gait of the purebred. He had seen and admired the poetry in some of the most exquisite legs of tall women, especially the Nordic women intending to leave their imprints all over the Riviera, but de Bellemare's legs were in perfect balance as well as in perfect control. The balance of a woman of extraordinary poise, the control by a top-order woman—a woman who knew what to do with men without robbing them of their freedom; a woman who, seeking to experience a mind-trembling meltdown for herself, would never open her legs for even the most superior male—not even while riding on her very own prize-winning stallion—unless he wore her very own colors, colors handpicked for each unique occasion.

On his return flight from New York to Paris, he was unable to detach his mind from those thighs and their inward extension toward her pelvic area. Firmness, resilience, resolution, authority—but also compactness, buoyancy, resonance, spirit. An extraordinary woman! Lundquist remembered reading up on the traditional qualities of Lotus-women: "a body soft as petals, skin tender and fair as fragrant pollen . . ." His mind momentarily shut off any other meanderings because he was still too committed to his dead wife. However, halfway across the Atlantic, an unexpected mental jump made him remember and even spell it out word by word: "a Lady LUSSEY resembling a lotus bud about to burst open . . . !" which revelation resulted in a shockingly sudden outburst of energy between the two pockets of his corduroy traveling trousers. From Paris, he then flew on to Nice, deeply stashed away for complete privacy in his business-class seat and wondering what kind of woman it took to ride her men the way she rode her stallion.

Arriving at his villa and feeling increasingly guilty about the wanderings of his mind, he literally ran to the portrait of his wife, hoping that she would scold him. Her eyes radiated their usual velvety warmth and looked at him with the serenity of a loving woman who understood that her husband was a living human being and, therefore, in need of something that she could never again share with him. Eventually, his acute feelings of remorse abated, while the curiosity of his mind and the excitement in his pelvic area also calmed down. Two years earlier, Lundquist had buried Dagbar van Soencken. Four years after New York, he left for home after the exhibition in Paris and waited for six days after sending the fax about the visit of Lagace and de Bellemaire. Two more days followed during which he tried to force himself to concentrate on his work. But his mind just would not cooperate. Instead, he started sorting out which paintings he would put up for sale in London—seven paintings, excluding the two from his vault. Those two would have to wait until de Bellemaire's arrival.

Finally, and after what had seemed like an interminably long forenoon, the confirming fax was received. London would be happy to make the arrangements for the following week. She could join him at Orly for the flight to Heathrow. On the return leg, they would pick up Lagace and her personal things and proceed to Saint-Raphaël. But she could not remain longer than two weeks—one half of her annual vacation allowance.

Lundquist would fly out from Nice on the following Monday in the morning. Touch down at Orly and fly on to Heathrow at 11:00 a.m. They could be at Sotheby's at 1:00 p.m. and fly back to Paris at 7:00 p.m. and would then decide whether to continue directly to Nice or to stay over until the following morning. In anticipation of her visit, he asked Magdalena Sophie to arrange for an extra helper, who would do general housekeeping and would get ready the two-bedroom guesthouse in the rear of the gardens and with a splendid view of the sunrise over the Mediterranean. Then he went to the vault and took out two of the three paintings. He carefully looked at each, one at a time, and then held on to the third one for a very long time—the first portrait of his wife, dressed in a fisherwoman's netting and with the disheveled and wet hair so typical of the wives waiting at the wharf at 4:00 a.m. for their fishermen husbands to arrive and terribly apprehensive on stormy days that they might never make it back.

They had been married for twelve years. Anticipating a lifelong marriage, he never did more than two portraits of her, and he knew all along that he would never part with either of them. The first portrait was done against the cadmium red backdrop which is so typical of the sunsets of the French Riviera and which was the basic color theme in his initial stage, the "red" period. He took this painting to his atelier, compared the two faces, traced out with his ring finger the lips on both paintings, and then rested his entire right hand on the heart of his wife's first portrait. For a while, he seemed engaged in a quiet dialogue, his face motionless and his eyes peaceful. He then took the first portrait back to the vault and returned with the other two paintings—one from his "red" period, the other from the "blue"—*Serenade to the Dancing Butterflies* and *Entrapment by the Royal Moth*. Both had been presents to his wife, recalling two amusing and unforgettable incidents on the occasion of their first and fifth anniversaries.

Lundquist was packed by Friday evening but, so totally unlike himself, spent an agitated night tossing himself around and feeling suspended between the haunting images of his wife and the enticing visions of de Bellemaire. He saw his wife come to life, shake piles of snow off her body, and reach out after him only to push him away and disappear back into the deep snow. Then he experienced a surge of heat permeate his whole body as he watched his hands move toward the thighs of de Bellemaire and move up toward her chest and come to a rest. Suddenly, her blouse parted, and her breasts became fully exposed and with erect nipples as if inviting him to touch them. Beautiful full life-approving breasts—breasts created to be nibbled at, to nurse children that are wanted—his children. By about 5:00 a.m., he had had enough and got up. Saturday morning, a perfect time to a take a five-mile run along the beach and to reestablish his internal balance. Getting back within the hour, he showered, shaved, had another silent conversation with his wife's portrait, took his breakfast, walked down to his boathouse, and sat down by the mooring. For a long time, he stared at the sea and then shifted his focus on to the *Lady Dagbar*. In the mild rocking motion of his yacht responding to the rising tide, he perceived a beckoning and felt tempted to board and take the vessel out to where the swimming waters were unpolluted. But all of a sudden, he felt lonely and turned toward the villa, stepping out with deliberate slowness.

Entering the alcove, he stood still for a moment and proceeded to his studio. He took the nine paintings, rearranged them according to size, and inserted them into two of the crates standing by the rear wall. He then washed his hands, entered his bedroom, and commenced packing his carrying case. A few moments later, he stopped, walked over to the telephone, and dialed Paris. No answer. Then he remembered that embassies were closed on Saturdays. Looking quite disturbed about not being able to put through his call, he stepped out toward his car, got in, and drove to his service station. He absolutely needed to get to Paris before Monday.

Paris. Stage Four: A Story of Sexonomic Success, Second Act

Lundquist flew into Orly on Sunday at 4:25 p.m., confirmed his flight to London, and booked his crates with the paintings. He then took the CNCF into Paris and stepped off at his usual hotel, the Adelbert in the 4e arrondissement, whose owners had been his friends for more than twenty years and whose cuisine had always been in perfect accord with his flavor buds. After settling in and not having de Bellemaire's private number, he called the embassy on the chance that she might be working, but there was no answer. His intuition told him to try the riding club. "Oui, monsieur. Madame de Bellemaire vient d'arriver. Mais elle est déjà en route avec Poseidon pour faire la course d'obstacles."

What distinguishes Quintessential-men perhaps the most from the lesser orders of men is their exuberant spirit and apparent eternal youthfulness. Unlike other men, Quintessential-men's energy field radiates an abundance of strength that will serve the multitude of those who need to tap it. This abundance accords to these men a unique dynamism and propels them to incessant creativity. Yet they never trespass because they need not ever live off anyone else or anyone else's energy supply. Such is their spirit that, upon hearing that the woman who had by the sheer magnetism of her femininity—but still unknown to herself—discovered the key to his own being, this particular Quintessential-man jumped out of the hotel's telephone booth and performed, right there and then, the first five paces of the Swedish royal quadrille, floating on a cushion of happiness and almost tripping over his slightly disabled left leg. Forty years of age and yet still adolescent enough to rediscover that the buds of loving, inborn in humans and forever ready to start sprouting, constitute the bridge between the eternity of our spirit and the immortality of our personal and physical identity. His hosts were observing this unusual interlude with the condescending airs that are so typical of the Gauls when confronted on their own soil with foreigners and their incomprehensible habits. "N'oubliez pas, le dîner est servi à 9:00 heures!" "Mais Alphonse, j'ai dû partir!" And off he went, dancing down the stairs and across the square on his way to the Métro, direction Bois de Boulogne.

De Bellemaire had indeed gone to her riding club for the weekly dressage of Poseidon as well as for her own physical conditioning. However, on this day, she also had a feeling of frustration to burn off since she was finding it much more difficult than her sexonomic schooling had ever implied to cope with the increasingly erotic presence of Lundquist in her sublime life since arriving in Paris. What annoyed her most about herself was the fact that her Lady LUSSEY had gone ahead to indicate that she would henceforth receive only that man's sexuality to the total exclusion of any other, even though her very personal owner had just met him and knew very little about him. When living in that commune, de Bellemaire ceased believing in miracle men or knights galloping on their white steeds. She did not even know if Lundquist had ever sat on a horse. But she did find out that he had indeed been an Olympic silver medalist in épée and that a man who knew how to swing a sword would certainly be able to handle even the purest-bred mare!

Custom has it that the Riding Club of Paris absolutely insisted on proper attire on arrival and the appropriate gear for the dressage. She crossed over to the ladies' lounge, went in, entered her compartment, and changed into her colors—red and blue, diagonally divided, with a turquoise scarf and rider's cap; black low-heel boots with a turquoise trim. While changing, she looked at herself in the mirror even more critically than usual. Becoming thirty years old had never caused her any anxiety, but this glorious-looking man couldn't possibly be older than forty-five—an urgent cause for special concern. Her horsey legs would outcompete even those of horsewomen in their early twenties; she had absolutely no trace of cellulite; neither was there a single line in her face that might indicate the onset of middle age. But lowering her eyes and stepping very close to the stand-up mirror, she first scrutinized her breasts with utmost attentiveness and then focused on her pubic area. There definitely was cause for uneasiness—a barely perceptible sagging just below her nipples, a softening along the inside of her thighs. Lotus-women would not show any of these early deficiencies before turning forty-five. She tried to console herself. She hadn't had sex since the seventh month into her marriage; neither had she been lusting after anyone until her first meeting with Lundquist at the Embassy. Would he notice these imperfections?

Her mind's brief moment of pessimism struck an innermost chord as her Lady LUSSEY spoke up with clarity and determination: "De Bellemaire, stop thinking nonsense. We both know only too well that we really want this man. This one and no other. For life." De Bellemaire responded calmly: "I've seen him only twice and talked to him only once. On first sight, I recognized his select qualities. I have sixteen days to find out if I want him for much more than just to satisfy your needs—one in London, one in Paris, and fourteen in Saint-Raphaël. During those days, you'd better not be too impatient, else you'll get absolutely nothing!"

Mounting Poseidon, she rode out to the oval and broke into a canter. Five circles. Then a long gallop, halfway along the racetrack. After a brief rest, she then took her stallion into the Bois and rode him hard for twenty minutes. How he loved it—his rider in perfect harmony with his rhythm, her thighs totally responsive to the heaving of his massive chest while also holding him tightly enough to perceive of the power of what he felt was a complete woman. In the kingdom of horses, just as in the realm of humans, there are five orders of stallions and of mares. Poseidon never had any doubt that he was the horse equivalent of a Quintessential-man, even though he had been sired unto his mother—an Arab pure thoroughbred whose lineage went back to the Ottoman siege of Vienna—by the prize stallion of far lesser birth, who belonged to a band of Gypsies passing through the outskirts of Deauville and on whose speed the band depended for fast getaways before the law—a horse whose charms, manliness, and advances his mother simply could not resist when he managed to break through the eight-foot-high walls that surrounded her stall.

Turning around for a leisurely gait back to the club, de Bellemaire rested for a brief moment, sitting upright on Poseidon and stroking his neck. Suddenly, a thought hit her, and she broke out smiling. "When Lundquist proves to me that he can handle a real horsewoman, I might just permit him to take Poseidon out for a ride." She rode back pensively, wondering about his superior qualities and the reasons for his tremendous attractiveness. Was she about to commit the error of many women, even of the higher orders, who throw themselves into the arms of men known to be philanderers in the expectation of outbidding all other competing women and yet unable to recognize such men's ultimate egotism?

During the shower, the last traces of her uneasiness vanished. She even smiled as she visualized Lundquist trying to mount Poseidon but not succeeding. Getting dressed, she felt aglow and decided to stop for a martini on ice with two razor-thin slices of lemon. Sitting down, she suddenly perceived a shadow of someone standing tall in front of her. She raised her eyes and once again felt that instantaneous outbreak of the vertigo. Lost for words, she raised her hands while trying to hide the glow of her royal blue speckles. He took both of her hands, kissed each with the gentleness of an artist whose unique natural talent enabled him to make apparently floating cumulus clouds look so real on his impressionistic paintings, and spoke quietly but with the resonance of a quality man who had made a binding decision: "I need you!"

Inseparable from the moment of their leaving Paris, de Bellemaire and Lundquist sold the paintings in London and took care of the legal formalities pertaining to the fund. Returning to Paris, she asked for all of her vacation time and took Lundquist to the racing club to meet Poseidon. Standing in front of this beautiful animal, Lundquist reached into his pocket and retrieved two lumps of sugar, which he offered to the stallion. The horse looked at de Bellemaire, sniffled at the open hand, and gently pressed his snout into the palm of the Swede, taking hold of the lumps of sugar. He then rubbed his nostrils against the sleeve of the Swede's blazer and asked for more. "He has already taken a liking to you, but I will not ask you to mount him tonight. We'll have other things to do." She then took him by the hands and asked him to race her to her Jeep. The one who'd get there first would do the driving.

De Bellemaire and Lundquist did not make love until the sixteenth day of her stay at the villa. Lagace had left after the end of the first week claiming that he had had an urgent call to return to Montreal. For sixteen days, this magnificent man and this exceptional woman were fighting to hold back their intimate needs while seeking to conform to the code of the highest orders: Until you know about the totality of the person to which your being feels so emotionally attracted, your reason will remain in full charge of your enticement-and-control quality and will guide your passion quality. Only when you have realized that the merger of your two beings has become inevitable (because it had been ordained by nature) will you proceed to make your reason fully and truly the substantive part of your loving. This is so because only such loving will last forever and because only such loving can fully occupy your sexonomic hearts.

Seven days into her visit, de Bellemaire knew that their union would be a complete one. But there was still so much to learn about him and about his dreams. On the eighth day, he asked her if she would marry him, which she accepted with their first kiss. But instead of hopping into bed, they got the urge to swim to the yacht and take her out to where the waters of the Mediterranean were pure and cool. They remained on board overnight, cuddling and shivering with anticipation, and did so seven nights in a row. Somewhere during those soul-merging moments, they touched each other. Never had she realized that being sexonomically liberated would give her such natural joy and fulfillment in their mutual quest to find to each other and to explore each other's mystique. And then, in the second hour after midnight on the sixteenth day, she experienced the overwhelming totality of her first complete meltdown as a woman truly in love. "I will indeed marry him, for this man and only this man was meant to be the father of my children."

Sexonomic Games in the Lower Orders: The Banality of Sex for Cash

Eliza: Fashion show director. Unmarried because always on the run, and has an ease with which she can obtain sexual gratification from the best-looking and effectively performing male models—a condition for their renewal of contracts yet with the added advantage of earning double income (one half of which tax-free). In the language of Sexonomics, a Conch-woman bordering on Vampire-woman.

John: Recently engaged for the first time to model men's underwear, sleepwear, and leisurewear. Loves women and lives off them, must therefore keep in female mind–arousing shape. For his first-ever appearance with Eliza, he wanted to look his most charming. He had heard of her sexual moods and preferences and is looking forward to cashing in on them. In language of Sexonomics, a Girandole-man descended from the order of Vulpine-men.

Eliza tried to pinpoint the vague feeling of anxiety that had plagued her since that morning's eight o'clock sales meeting. It wasn't the fact that everyone had rushed from the comfort of their beds to the stifling and sterile atmosphere of the reunion without so much as a cup of coffee to recharge their batteries nor was it the gnawing realization on both her and her coworkers' parts that they had been on a workaholic marathon for the last ten days in a row (without even the slightest chance at lovemaking suffused with the expectation of tintinnabulating eroticism). Although the "design team," as they had been labeled by the company's directors, had been through similar situations in a variety of other postings, this particular sales union was different.

She walked down the sunny hallway of the little auberge on her way to a fast lunch before the next meeting and couldn't help noticing through the expansive bay windows how the sun seemed to catch the crystals of snow on the ski hill—mid-March in the Laurentians. Everything looked crisp and pulsating with little darts of color sparkling off the moguls in the distance, the skiers themselves like festive ants scurrying down the slopes. There had been talk of an afternoon trip up to the hills, but as she had remarked earlier, it was more likely an alternative for the salesmen who viewed these meetings as "one more party." Her friend Anna had hinted conspiratorially that maybe it wasn't such a bad idea to strap on a pair of skis, get someone to give a good shove from the top, and roll all the way down to an unmarked ambulance waiting below—at least it would get them out of the dreaded fashion show.

A fashion show. Now there had been the winner of all ideas blurted out at practically the last moment by their ever-flighty president. As if they didn't have enough to do in preparation for the annual five-day sales meeting, they were now obliged to participate—yes, actually model—in a fashion show that was for no one's benefit but the salesmen and the salesladies. From music to choreography to makeup samples of the latest line, it was one more headache in a long list of tasks that had to be professionally accomplished. "We don't want to look stupid," the president had said. And so a list was drawn up of the thinnest and best-looking people in the company, which amounted to nine—not nearly enough to keep the pace moving for the show. The staff receptionist was added, along with the daughter of another employee and Anna's cousin, John, who had had fashion model experience and had been engaged a few days before this event.

Eliza, being somewhat more Rubénienne than the others on the design team, had been relegated the duty of makeup artist and dresser for that dreaded evening. At first, she had been slightly insulted; after all, she did fit into the samples and was far from ordinary-looking, but as the sales meeting had drawn nearer, she had silently thanked her stars that she would play only a backstage role in the whole affair. What really bothered her was that she was now forced to run directly from her presentation to the big dining hall where preparations were under way for the show—two hours to countdown.

Anna greeted her at the door with a proffered glass of wine in her hand: "You look as though you need this—it's a Château Margaux!" After taking her first sip, Eliza glanced around the room—the stage had been set up in the shape of a T, and in a semicircle in front were small round tables where all the salespersons would sit. Everyone seemed in a sort of giddy preshow stress, the girls all scooting around like frenzied chickens wondering where to put the rack of clothes, and the credit manager and Anna's cousin battling with some quirky inoperative part of a stereo system. It seemed best to start on the girls' makeup as they required the most attention to detail; besides, if she ran out of time, the men would be more than thankful that they didn't have to undergo such tribulations.

Face after face came under her delicate hands and was transformed by late spring shades of shadow and deft strokes of eyeliner into that generic "healthy" model look. Eliza took a long draft of wine, looked at her watch, and decided to corner the men into their bout with the makeup artist. She realized as the minutes ticked how little we explored people's faces. Up close, they were all big pores and little lines, bad skin and uneven complexions. Those she had thought to be clean, clear, and healthy from a distance looked, at kissing distance, sun-damaged or frostbitten and badly aging.

John quickly jumped in anticipation when she told him it was his turn in the chair. He wasn't bad-looking in a rakish sort of way, with that boyish charm she knew came from living as a bachelor for extended periods of time. Dirty blond hair—what was it that attracted her to blonds when she had never any luck with them?—and good clear skin with only the faintest hit of a tan, and as she leaned over to smooth foundation across his cheeks, she looked at the bluest of eyes that had crossed her path in a long while. Eliza moved closer between his open legs to be able to apply the eye pencil and realized that she had been holding her breath. John looked up at her as if he had been studying her expressions and had a little smile. She started to blush, a reaction she hadn't experienced since she was about fourteen, and exhaled. Maybe it was the wine that was making her feel flushed! That must have been it since she hadn't been drinking much lately owing to all the overtime. In one respect, she was glad that his makeup was finished, for she had the sudden urge to lean down and do some exploratory surgery on his full mouth with her tongue. On the other hand, it was a bit of a shame to let him get out of her grip, for who knew if she would ever get him back in that chair!

In any event, they had to hurry to the dining room to start dressing for the show, so Eliza informed John that he had been the easiest and by far the most fun to make up as he had been the most relaxed of the lot. She found out as they walked down that he had done other fashion shows for Anna but never had found someone else who had such a soft hand.

The sun had set while Eliza had been occupied with her duties, and the dining room looked less barren than it had earlier. All the tables were set with silver and crystal, the linen napkins were folded in exotic shapes, the lights were low, and the room actually had quite a romantic atmosphere. There had been no provision for where the models would change, so one corner of the room had been transmitted by huge greenery planters into a more private area. The racks for the clothes were jammed against the windows to block the view from the outside, and luckily, the girls had found a huge storage cupboard that would serve as their dressing area, while the men would have to change among the racks as they had at the real shows. Even though there would be a musical soundtrack for the show, they would have to keep quiet behind the scenes. The audience didn't need to hear shouts of "Where are my pants?" in the middle of the show.

All the girls felt quite capable of dressing themselves, so Eliza was relegated to the task of dressing the male models. It was fortunate that everything had been labeled in advance as all she would have to do would be to pull off their clothing, throw them into the corner, and get them buttoned, zipped, and snapped into the next outfit. Not a bad job the more she thought about it. How many times in a girl's life did she get a half a dozen men stripping down in a frenzy before her, literally all them at the same time? John!

The next forty-five minutes were spent in a whirlwind of straightening collars, tucking shirts down pants, diving for missing running shoes, and grabbing for the right outfit in the grand procession of things. Eliza didn't have a second to look at the runway, and even if she had, she wasn't tall enough to peer over the shrubbery walls. The next thing she knew, the music was winding down and the sound of the applause was coming from the tables. All the models were crammed into the rear of the room, the girls jumping up and down kissing each other, the men somewhat more restrained, grinning and slapping each other on the back. Eliza watched the spectacle from the sidelines feeling somewhat left out, when suddenly, John came up to her, wrapped his arms around her, and planted a big kiss on her unsuspecting lips. "Thanks for your help," he said, grinning. "I would have been out there without my pants a few times if it weren't for you."

Dinner was served by candlelight with all the girls on the design team at one table, with John wedged between Anna and Eliza. Both the main course and the conversation were delicious, and as their glasses were repeatedly filled, everyone started to relax in ways they hadn't done in months. The jokes started to be bandied about—funny anecdotes about other meetings, other trips. Eliza could feel John's foot close to hers under the table but didn't want to think anything of it until she felt the gentle pressure of his hand on her knee under the table. That was one way to accentuate a story!

His small touches, casual to an observer, continued through dessert, and each time she felt his fingertips on her skin, she quivered. Normally inviting a man when she wanted him, it wasn't like her to just let someone be so forward since they had just met that afternoon and had barely an hour's worth of conversation between them. Apart from Anna, who had told her in passing about him, the only thing that made them familiar was the fact that she had made up his face, put on his pants, and laced his running shoes. This might have something to do with the sense of intimacy she felt. However, she also recognized that the deep inside of her being was rapidly heating up . . . all these fashion shows and all these pressures . . . she had been without "it" far too long . . . and John felt like a man who would certainly know how to please her!

All that French food had stuffed them to sleepiness by eleven o'clock, so Anna and Eliza decided to go for a walk in the surrounding countryside. John volunteered to be their chaperone and offered each one his arm. It was crisp and cold outside, the stars just starting to peep out from behind the clouds and the silvery trace of a crescent moon lighting up the path before them. They laughed and made comments on the houses, each one remarking how they would change this or add that; they told of what they really wanted to do, how they planned to get out of the job ruts they were in, how they felt about the next few days. John was by far the luckiest of the three of them; while they would be involved in presentations the whole next few days, he would be on the slopes. After a good hour's walk, they circled around and headed back to the auberge. As they were going up the steps, Anne claimed exhaustion, saying the only thing she wanted was her pillow. Eliza was still revved up from all the fresh country air and asked John if he'd join her for a drink at the bar.

They just managed to get the last call at the near-empty bar and sat down beside a few of the female salespersons playing backgammon near the windows. It was now as if John and Eliza had known each other for a long time; they sat and sipped their soda water, making small talk and looking off into the distance as though nothing really had to be said. He slipped off his loafers and put one foot under her thigh and the other in her lap as if he had been doing it for years. She looked down at the designer socks as she stroked his instep and wondered to herself whether this was really such a wise move on her part . . . the boiling point was just about to be reached. John mentioned how tired he was, and they bid their good nights to the ladies still battling at the backgammon boards. As they walked down the hall toward their rooms, he put his hand at the small of her back, a comforting yet guiding sensation that made Eliza feel as though she didn't have to make any decisions at all. He stopped in front of his door, inserted the key, and led her into the darkness.

She had been right—nothing had to be said, nothing was really that complicated. John seemed to know how she felt, how she wanted to feel as they kissed. It was a slow and sensual dance in the dark as they moved toward the bed, still wrapped up in exploring each other's mouths softly and silently as they lowered themselves down onto the feather mattress. She could make out the outlines of his face hovering above her, something a little more animal now sharpening the features that had been soft earlier on, and she knew that he would be a perfect lover. Hard and fast when she allowed, gentle and submissive when she wanted to dominate. They peeled each other's clothing off slowly, reveling in each new layer uncovered, caressing until impatience would hit them and the next layer would be stripped off.

Eliza and John spent hours making love together, discovering each other's bodies like mapmakers charting the New World, lingering over crevices and hidden places until they were both exhausted. John lay in Eliza's arms like a child, head curled in toward her chest, his breathing slow and shallow. She knew that, at any moment, he would fall asleep and that she would have to extricate herself from his grip. How hard it was to leave him, to tell him that she had to go back to her shared room with Anna and back to work in the morning. She dressed slowly in the dark, caressing him longingly as though, at any moment, she could start their lovemaking again, telling him to call her when they were back in the city. Eliza pulled the disheveled covers up around John, kissed him softly, quickly took two one hundred dollar bills from her purse, placed them under his jeans, then silently pulled the door closed behind her.

As she lay in her own bed going over the events of the day, reliving the pressure of the fashion show while still filled with every pleasurable moment of her being with John, Eliza suddenly realized that she didn't even have his phone number. This time, the aftereffect felt different . . . deep inside, warmth, an enduring glow, an esthetic high that she hadn't experienced for years. Also, unlike numerous times in the past—when she would normally have picked up the bar check and left behind a cash check for the amount that had been decided upon in advance—this time, her cash donation was voluntary, which made her feel much better. How did John really fit into all this? For a change, a less demoralizing end to this sort of short but exciting game? Or possibly the beginning of a most curiously titillating adventure?

Dear readers: You are now invited to reflect on the four persons and the course of events in these two accounts of "sexonomic strategies and games" and to take a position with respect first to de Bellemaire and Lundquist and then to Eliza and John. How do the two strategies and the two outcomes compare? If you found yourself in a similar situation and had the opportunity to pursue your own strategy, which of these two male/female partners would you prefer? Can you explain your choice? Would your choice involve only pure emotion, or would it also (and discreetly) be linked to material considerations? If the latter, can you explain why and what form it would take? If the latter, would your material consideration have rendered your lovemaking less fulfilling (more inferior)? If you had been in Eliza's place, would you have given John less money or more money? Or would you have left without giving him any? Finally, would you wish to share your personal horse (stallion or mare) with the man you love—love because he never had and never would ask you for any kind of payment in return for his continuous commitment to provide your Lady LUSSEY with the ultimate romantic and masculine lovemaking?

The Art of Sexonomics: Promise and Fulfillment

Having defined Sexonomics as an inquiry into the relationship between sex, money, and power (i.e., the marketing of human sexuality), we then proceeded to describe the societal framework within which this particular form of competition among humans takes place. To reveal the overt and covert rules of the sexonomic game, to engage in a detailed discussion of sexonomic strategies, and to present one particular case study of sexonomic "success." Underlying this effort is our basic theme, viz. that human reason, in all five orders of women and men, seeks to maximize overall human happiness but that such maximization cannot be achieved equally by each of the participating individuals. This is so because of their widely differing talents and natural endowments, their dissimilar sociocultural backgrounds and affiliations, existing social constraints and discriminations, and most of all, the inability of the ultimate control center of human behavior, reason, to keep in check the enticement function and the passion quality. We ascribe this problem to the women and men of the "lower orders" in particular, a predicament which is seen as the singularly most important cause for low sexonomic valuations, inadequate degrees of competitiveness, and unsatisfactory levels of sexonomic utility functions (i.e., for the prevailing general degree of unhappiness in the relations between women and men).

Our reasoning rests on several major postulates concerning the character of humans and interactions between them: rationality; freedom of thought and action; horizontal and vertical mobility unrestrained by class structures; naturally preordained equality between women and men; absence of ideological, religious, or political indoctrination or oppression; healthy emphasis on the material component of life; and the willingness to improve upon one's conditions in life and state of sexonomic happiness. While material wealth is presumed to have influence over lifestyles, the quantity of material wealth is not deemed significant to the structure of the five orders of women and men. Much rather, it is the willingness and the ability to handle material wealth and to dispose of it for a general improvement in the welfare of society that is seen as the primary requisite for belonging to the higher orders; a self-centered sexploitative rich narcissist or egotist is necessarily seen as a human being of low sexonomic value, as are those women and men who would sell their sexuality exclusively only in return for material wealth.

Our inquiry has confirmed our belief that most women and men may expect to increase their total sexonomic happiness if they "work at it." Except for the lowest order of women, Vampire-women, and the lowest order of men, Girandole-men, whose naturally negative inclinations and singular emphasis on material values prevent them from ever achieving the love-induced component of sexonomic utility. All other orders of women and men are deemed ideally capable of realizing their full sexonomic potential and even to move onto the next higher order of women or men. "Working at it" means that most women and men are viewed as individuals who not only have the potential but also the desire to maximize their sexonomic happiness. This is the course of action they are presumed to wish for in order to achieve success by learning to discover themselves, to understand their potential, and to recognize the primary role of their reason as the control instrument over their passion. By enrolling in appropriate specialized programs, they will seek to develop expertise in achieving and maintaining a perfect balance between human rationality and human sexuality and between the spiritual and the material aspects of life.

In our reflections concerning the potentiality of positive outcomes in the quest by individual women and men for sexonomic happiness, we have, to our regret, discovered three major impediments which might inhibit the quest of any woman to maximize her sexonomic happiness. First, the evidence of the increasing disparity in numbers between women and men, which has resulted in the significant sexonomic devaluation of women vis-à-vis men. Second, the replacement of the traditional doctrinaire attitudes with respect to women by the perhaps even more debilitating propagations of some of the "representative" groups in the women's rights movement, ranging from negativism to extreme forms of hatred of men. Third, the increasing and almost singular concern of the younger set of women with the attainment of material wealth and materially-induced means of power—often by the blatant display and crude exchange of raw sexuality—in exchange for immediate monetary gain and to the total exclusion of an equal and balanced development of their spiritual values.

We have also found, very much to our dismay, that the enormous promise of women's liberation, of rendering women truly equal to men and assuring them of never again having to have sex against their will, has resulted in a universal emphasis on material values and has thereby led to a significant sexonomic devaluation, especially of the women of the lower orders. Human freedom misused? Or rather, the failure to coordinate the realization of the promise of human liberty and equality in the envisaged time frame with the appropriate development of human reason?

Can Sexonomics be of any assistance? Can it render any contribution toward the quest of individual women and men to achieve the yearned-for equality and to assure all of us of that the maximization of our sexonomic happiness is not only a desirable goal but also an attainable one? Evidently, it can—in the short run, the normal run, and the long run—by inducing women and men to fully develop their capacity to reason and to use this capacity not only for the purpose of keeping in check the instantaneous outpouring of unmitigated sexuality but also and primarily by removing, over the course of time, all those societal constraints, prohibitions, and institutions which have been the major historical causes of this rising disparity between men and women and of the tragically visible worldwide sexonomic disequilibrium.

Since sexonomists view themselves as biosocial scientists, who are fully committed to human freedom and human progress and are therefore optimistic about the evolution of human society, let us recall our assessment with respect to the long-run evolution of mankind:

In the long run, the time period is deemed long enough to allow for profound changes in the public perception of individual liberty and its codification. The evolution of standards of behavior will become equally binding—even upon the socioeconomic elite—and will force the gradual and officially endorsed withdrawal into the backdrop of their own frustrations concerning the linkages between human sexuality and material gain, of the self-appointed enforcers of public morality. In the long run, the individual is seen as moving toward the attainment of increasing freedom and liberty in her/his personal choices on the road to sexonomic happiness.

Sexonomics constitutes the intellectual expression of this entitlement. It provides the objective means toward the rational pursuit (versus the manipulated fear of "sin") of natural sexual enjoyment and the maximization of material welfare. In this run, equilibrium means two things: for the individual, a lifestyle that will enable any pair of two consenting adults to seek and to attain their maximum sexonomic happiness—without ever again having to fear condemnation, persecution, death, or the so-called wrath of God (or that of His "enforcers"); for society, it means the recognition that there cannot be human progress unless the so-called moral imperatives from the bygone era of ignorance and superstition will have finally been discarded and replaced by the freedom of humankind to use their reason in the quest to fill their sexonomic happiness hearts to highest possible levels—from the regimentation of the many by the self-seeking few, progress toward a single set of rules of conduct for everyone. Long-run equilibrium cannot be attained if there continues to be one legal system but two sets of moral conduct (i.e., if society does not allow itself to adjust to and to grow along with our perceived intellectual, physical, and sexual needs and if it fails to align these needs with the dictates of the laws of nature).

PART TWO

The Fascinating World of Sexonomics as a Science

In this part, we provide a generalized hypothetical explanation of how millions of sexonomically involved women and men behave in their quest to secure for themselves their ultimate male or female partners. Commencing with the specific analysis of the sexonomic hearts of each of the five orders, both female and male, we shall then name and explain those sexonomic terms which serve as our principal measures of sexonomic interaction between women and men.

This treatment is a requisite for our specific understanding and practical handling of how the five sexonomic markets decide upon the respective sexonomic values and sexonomic prices of the women and men that participate in them and also how these parameters may be quantified. This analytical treatment is also meant to provide the theoretical foundation for empirical fact-finding—of how the women and the men in their respective five orders proceed to implement their strategies concerning the acquisition of the "user's rights" over their partners' sexuality and of the role material considerations play in their aim to maximize their lifetime sexonomic utilities.

CHAPTER ONE

Female and Male Sexonomic Hearts:
An Analysis of Each of the Five Orders

Illustration F-2: Sexonomic happiness heart—Lotus-woman

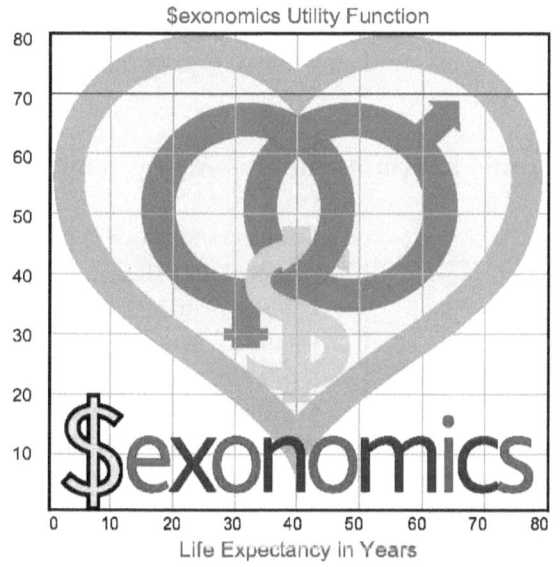

- Entire sexonomic heart is filled (100 percent sexonomic happiness).

- All value are positive; range is zero to one hundred sexons.

- As a top-quality woman throughout her lifetime, the Lotus-woman is the happiest of all women.

The Lotus-woman's sexonomic happiness heart ranks the highest by far. This is so because the women belonging to this order offer the ultimate value and command the highest price from the world of (Quintessential) men and accumulate in this process the highest possible level of sexonomic satisfaction. The Lotus-woman's lifetime sexonomic happiness heart line attains two peaks: the first during her transition to young womanhood and the second when she blooms into full maturity at the age of about forty-five years. Lotus-women age much more slowly than do women of the other orders. Even during her postmenstrual years, the slope of her sexonomic happiness heart line descends only very gently downward and to the right, and there is no break at the end of her menstrual life cycle, even though she experiences a short period of uncertainty concerning her "complete" femininity. This is so because she soon discovers that her overall supreme qualities will never abate and will more than offset the initial pessimism over the quality of her postmenstrual years, thereby entering the road to a very happy and fulfilling old age.

In the enclosed illustration, our readers will notice that Lotus-women's sexonomic happiness heart line is smooth and continuous, filling each bit of space in her sexonomic heart. This is so because the few women belonging to this order have a fulfilling lifestyle and without any of the noticeable short-term downs which are so much the scene with the lesser orders of women. Since the entire area of the heart is filled with the lines which appropriately measure Lotus-women's sexonomic happiness, we shall use this particular illustration as the standard for lower-order women, a guide which will assist the readers in their attempts to establish the position of their own sexonomic happiness heart line as well as to estimate their relative level of lifetime sexonomic happiness (which insight will be deemed of enormous significance if the readers desire to improve on their sexonomic performance and standing).

Illustration F-3: Sexonomic happiness heart—Art-woman

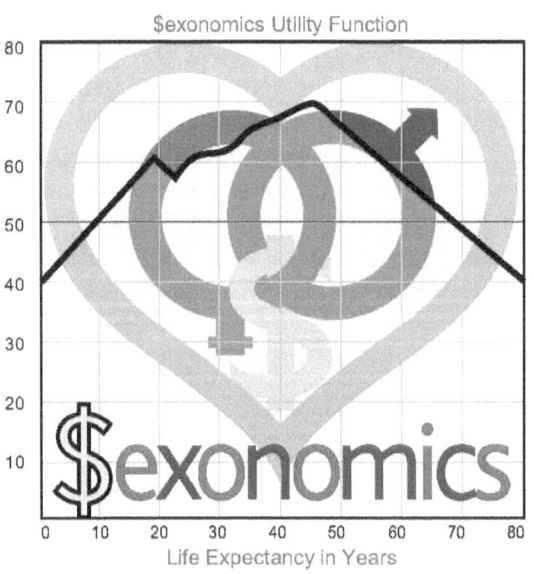

- Sexonomic heart is less filled than that of the Lotus-woman: less lifetime sexonomic happiness.

- All value are positive; range is zero to eighty-five sexons.

- The Art-woman maximizes her sexonomic happiness when she is between thirty-five and fifty years of age.

As we can observe from this illustration, the level of sexonomic happiness of the Art-woman fills a distinctly smaller part of the sexonomic heart throughout her lifetime but still with a gently declining slope in her later years. At first, in her state as a virgin, the Art-woman is given very favorable consideration by the competing (Lace-order) men, an appreciation which will be carried over to her professionalism and similar creative involvements during her adult years, all of which will lead to the apogee of her mature years. But with the commencement of her postmenstrual years, her sexonomic happiness line takes a perceptible dip, indicating that the aging-induced devaluation of the three qualities of her Lady LUSSEY is not quite offset by her material assets and her significance in the web of social hierarchies.

Notice that the Art-woman's sexonomic happiness heart line is not a continuously and totally smooth line; the several slight dips are explained by the occasionally manifested desire of the Art-woman to reach down to the Vulpine-man—a consequence of her Lady LUSSEY's passion quality prevailing in intensely longing moments over her enticement-and-control quality. Notice also how much lower the overall height of the Art-woman's sexonomic happiness heart line is than that of the Lotus-woman; in comparison with the latter's totality of sexonomic happiness, the Art-woman loses about 20 percent during her lifetime, a loss which she can avoid only if she succeeds through sheer personal striving in moving up to the ranks of the order of Lotus-women.

Since the sexonomic valuation range of Art-women involves about 15 percent of the female population and spreads over fifteen valuation points, Art-women—quite unlike Lotus-women—show a significant variety of types and endowments. They include very diversely individualistic women, from those who are almost at the Lotus-woman level of reason but with less exciting sexuality to those whose intellectual capacity places them just about at the level of Conch-women but whose sexuality borders on the unique exquisiteness of Lotus-women.

All in all, Art-women are a very challenging hunting ground for those demanding men who are willing to experiment with diverse types of women and who insist on high standards and are, in return, capable of furnishing their best personal characteristics and highest material inducements.

Illustration F-4: Sexonomic happiness heart—Conch-woman

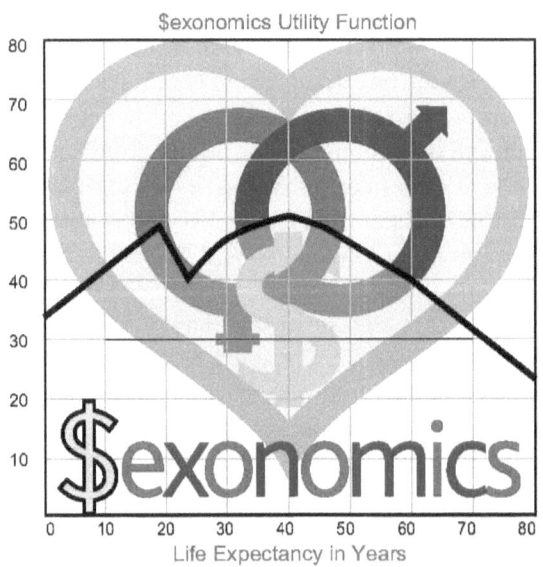

$exonomics Utility Function

Life Expectancy in Years

- Sexonomic heart is only about half-filled with happiness (much less so than the Art-woman's).

- All value are positive; range is zero to sixty-five sexons.

- The Conch-woman will reach her highest sexonomic happiness when she is between thirty and forty-five years old.

This order of women represents a large number of women with average qualities. Consequently, the average sexonomic happiness heart line of this order reflects a valuation that, for its entire length, lies well below that of Art-women (see illustration, page 136). It also declines more rapidly after reaching the first peak, which connotes the fleeting but discernible virginity premium, a bonus which her order counterpart, the Vulpine-man, is always willing to pay in seeking to swap cash and assets for this assertion of his self-possessed masculinity.

In her years of full bloom as a woman, the decline of the Conch-woman's sexonomic happiness heart level is explained by the fact that her state of happiness reflects her concern about the diminution of her sexual appeal while recognizing that she had not really achieved any of her maidenhood dreams (including the yearning for a permanent affiliation with a male from the order of Art-men). In her postmenstrual state, her unhappiness rises rapidly (as seen on that rapidly declining section on her sexonomic happiness heart line) because she finds herself increasingly unwanted even by Vulpine-men and outcompeted by the set of younger women not only of her own order but also by the somewhat less uncouth ones from the order of Elephant-women. One of the particular drawbacks that Conch-women suffer in their mature years is the debasement of their sexonomic valuations, which is due to their sudden massive outpouring of the enticement quality and engagement in frequent fornication, both as an attempt to compensate for their inferior traits and as a desperate last attempt toward achieving maximum sexonomic happiness.

However, Lace-men and top-ranking Vulpine-men, who are the presumed beneficiaries of this outpouring of Conch-women's still quite refined sexual skills, will have no remorse turning to the rising numbers of competing younger Conch-women and thereby contributing to the older Conch-women's increasing unhappiness in their mature years. It is specifically in the order of Conch-women that the infighting between the younger set and the older set takes on a brutalizing expression. All of the Conch-women recognize the advantage of being with men of a higher quality than that of Vulpine-men, but they are forced to compete in a sexonomic market in which the numbers of women are far too large relative to the number of available Lace-men. In addition, the older Conch-women also lack the educational levels of their younger order sisters and are, therefore, unable to provide literary or intellectual stimulants as effective counterweights for their diminishing sex appeal.

Yet overall, the future lifetime sexonomic happiness heart line of Conch-women is expected to move up slightly, mainly owing to increased access to postsecondary education and gradual adaptation to more refined cosmetics and insistence on health care. Conch-women's increased participation in the labor market will also secure for the more acquisitive Vulpine-men an increasingly satisfactory material situation, a positive expectation that may be even enhanced by the occasional (and very much coveted and forever remembered) sexual encounter with the Lace-man.

In comparison with the overall level that the Art-woman's happiness fills in her sexonomic heart, the Conch-woman occupies much less heart space, which attests to a significant loss in total lifetime sexonomic happiness for the order of these women, a loss which only those very few Conch-women will make up by managing to move up to the order of Art-women. Otherwise, it would appear that the case of Conch-women demonstrates most clearly that women are their own worst enemies.

Illustration F-5:
Sexonomic happiness heart—Elephant-woman

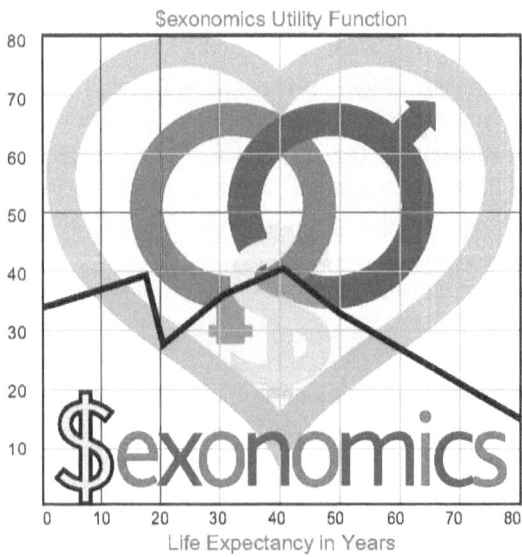

$exonomics Utility Function

Life Expectancy in Years

- Sexonomic heart is filled only about 25 percent (she is envious of the Conch-woman's happiness).

- All value are positive; range is zero to forty sexons.

- The Elephant-woman experiences a rapid decrease in sexonomic happiness after she turns forty years old.

The sexonomic happiness heart of Elephant-women bears out the lack of sexonomic appeal of the typical members of this order (see illustration). Throughout the lifetime of the women making up this order, these happiness lines literally hug the horizontal axis, with a downward trend and with two short upward trend discontinuities. The high first occurs in her adolescent years, when the future Elephant-woman may collect a small virginity premium from this kind of pleasure-seeking suitor from the ranks of Vulpine-men. The second peak reveals the few years in her twenties, when older Mob-men reach out to satisfy their lust for perverted copulation.

In Elephant-women's postmenstrual state, the sexonomic valuation will approach zero, which means that their sexuality ceases being marketable—a disheartening predicament, absolutely, as well as relative to the fortunes and status of the three higher orders of women. In sexonomic terminology, the lot of Elephant-women, in their more mature years, will have to be termed sexonomic "subsistence" living since, even in their prime years, their sexonomic marketability is limited by their coarseness and the manifestly demonstrated forever lust for raw sex—a situation which only Mob-men can cope with in the long run. Historically unaware of the fact that sex by itself cannot buy a permanent improvement in their social state, Elephant-women have been unable to secure a move up to the next higher order of women. Even in modern times, when Elephant-women too enjoy increasing access to education, they are expected to continue having great difficulty recognizing that modern men prefer sharing their sexonomic qualities with women who can offer them so much more enjoyable sexual togetherness than the Elephant-women's lustful but primitive kind.

An additional difficulty for Elephant-women is posed by the relatively increasing number of women from her own order, to which are added the several scores of "dishonored" Conch-women. All of these women seek to secure for themselves "their own" male from the forever smaller proportion of the materially better-endowed Mob-men in a setting in which the latter prefer reaching up for the relatively much more intelligent (but normally not so well-off) younger Conch-woman. In consequence of all these impediments, even the small remaining area of the Elephant-woman's lifetime sexonomic happiness is destined to diminish to zero in her old age.

Illustration F-6:
Sexonomic happiness heart—Vampire-woman

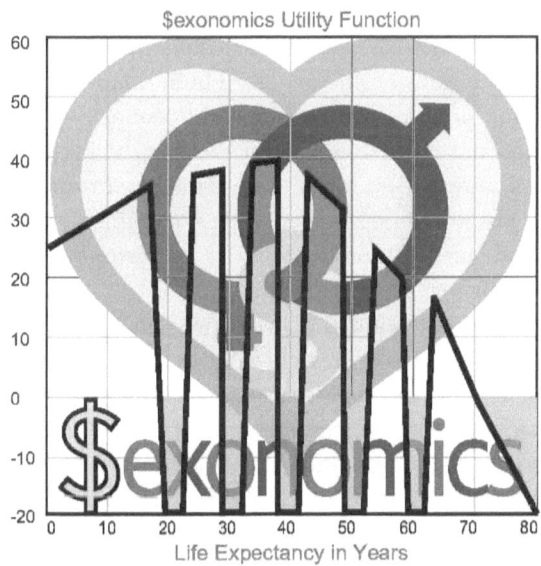

$exonomics Utility Function

Life Expectancy in Years

A victim of her own success as a professional in postmodern Western society, this selfish and unfortunate woman has neither the time for nor the desire to understand men; she is incapable of loving. Not being able to hold on to any man, she is forced to cohabit with sex-for-hire men (of the Girandole order). She barely, if ever, enjoys sexonomic happiness and repeatedly sinks into negative sexonomic valuations. Her lifetime sexonomic happiness is almost zero—an almost empty sexonomic heart.

The sexonomic happiness heart of the Vampire-woman portrays her capacity to generate enormous short-term enthusiasm with men of the orders below the Quintessential-man, with the resulting respectively high-level sexonomic valuation in her adolescent years (in the vicinity of young Art-women). However, since the Vampire-woman cannot help quickly revealing the predatory nature of her true self, the momentary elation only too soon takes on the expression of disgust, which makes her sexonomic happiness heart line rise and fall discontinuously—revealing that her several "ups" are matched by an equal number of "downs" right through her best years and into her postmenstrual age. As we can observe from this illustration, Vampire-women's sexonomic happiness heart line has these breaks and dislocations because she is compelled to keep on moving from post to post and between different social milieus as well as among differentiated entertainment, business, and government environments.

Vampire-women's lifetime sexonomic happiness heart line has but one apogee and will then decline; professional successes are always followed by dismal sexonomic failures that are caused by her inability to attract any higher-order man into a long-term relationship. In consequence, her scope of sexonomic strategies and games becomes more and more limited because the number of eligible and willing candidates decreases rapidly as soon as these men discover Vampire-women's scheming and manipulative ways. After a number of rises to and falls from posts of power and prestige (for a lifetime average of about four for a typical woman of this order), in her postmenstrual stage, she descends into a state of prolonged ostracized and lonely existence in spite of often owning a significant number of real assets. Her sexonomic valuation descends toward zero, whereby her sexonomic happiness heart line declines to a permanently negative value of −20 right into her old age. Still having money but never having prolonged friendships, the Vampire-woman eventually becomes totally unhappy and often thinks of suicide, but she keeps on living in the hope for just one final miracle—even from any of the lower orders of men. But this yearned-for miracle just would not happen, not even at the hands of any member of the order of Vulpine-men. Becoming less and less sexonomically marketable, she will then start disbursing her accumulated wealth by paying for the services of Girandole-men with the illusion that true love can be bought. Growing older, the cash cost of these copulating services will rise rapidly, and she will eventually be drained of her funds without the miracle ever having happened. Without any funds, her sexonomic valuation will descend to zero and will render her worthless in all sexonomic markets, unloved and sexually undesired even by Mob-men. Clearly, Vampire-women's lifetime sexonomic utility function will express minimum net valuations and happiness, the outcome of the vertiginous experience of the egoistic, self-seeking, debilitating, and destabilized lifestyles of the members of this order.

Illustration M-2: Sexonomic happiness
heart—Quintessential-man

$exonomics Utility Function

Life Expectancy in Years

- Entire sexonomic heart is filled (100 percent sexonomic happiness).

- All values are positive; range is zero to one hundred sexons.

- As top-quality man throughout his lifetime, the Quintessential-man is the happiest of all men.

The Quintessential-man's sexonomic happiness heart level ranks highest, by far, of all five orders of men, a situation which guarantees the members of this order a lifetime's enjoyment of the most refined pleasures and the most remarkable achievements in the material sense. This is so because women of highest quality know that the Quintessential-man's sexonomic valuation has a coefficient value of ninety to one hundred and are willing to pay the exclusive lifetime price which getting such a man would command. This market being restricted only to very few men (a "pure monopoly"), only those women have access—those who belong to the order of Lotus-women and/or whose combination of the highest-quality Lady LUSSEYs with the appropriate exclusivity—may be considered irresistible even for members of this exalted order of men, a form of behavior found only in the *Queentessence* market (see illustration). As you can observe, the sexonomic heart of the Quintessential-man is completely filled. Since the qualities of the members of this order become discernible during their adolescence, their sexonomic happiness heart line commences high, moves up rapidly, and ascends continuously to the apogee after the age of about sixty years without even a hint of a downturn.

This is so because the Quintessential-man's quality of potency in its diminishing stage is still more than offset by his renown as a man of the highest moral caliber as well as by his status in his community—without, however, also requiring ownership or access to vast material endowments. As a matter of fact, this function for a large number of men of this order may even keep on rising right into their old age—an indication of their exceptional wisdom and of the wonderful presence of their remarkable personality.

Illustration M-3: Sexonomic happiness heart—Lace-man

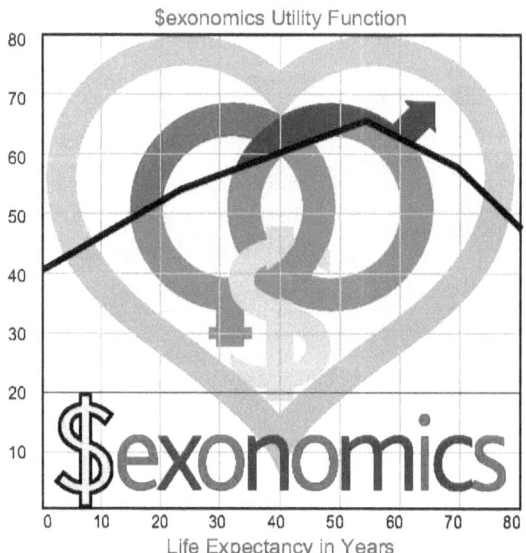

$exonomics Utility Function

Life Expectancy in Years

- Sexonomic heart is only about three-quarters filled with happiness (lesser degree of happiness than that of the Quintessential-man).

- All values are positive; range is zero to eighty-five sexons.

- The Lace-man's sexonomic happiness is highest when he is between forty and sixty years old.

Sexonomic Happiness Heart: Lace-man

The determinants of the sexonomic happiness heart level of Lace-men have high values, reflecting their sexonomic valuation index in the range of sixty to sixty-five. Even though not having first-order status, most Lace-men are happy with their lifestyles, knowing that their qualities and their presumed linkages with the highest levels of power are appreciated by Art-women and the more select of the order of Conch-women.

The Lace-man also knows that these women admire his suaveness and silky touch when sharing in his cohabitation patterns, which more than helps to offset the lower valuation of his lifetime sexonomic happiness heart line relative to that of the Quintessential-man. As we can discern from the illustration, in the case of the Lace-man, this line rises more slowly than that of the men of the top order, and it also attains an earlier peak at the age of about fifty-five. Then the gradual demise follows, attesting to the fact that women will tend to take an increasingly critical view of his decrease in sexual prowess, a situation which will likely make the Lace-man apprehensive and unhappy in spite of the fact that he normally considers himself materially secure and, therefore, always in demand by Art-women and the many adventurous Conch-women.

Illustration M-4: Sexonomic happiness heart—Vulpine-man

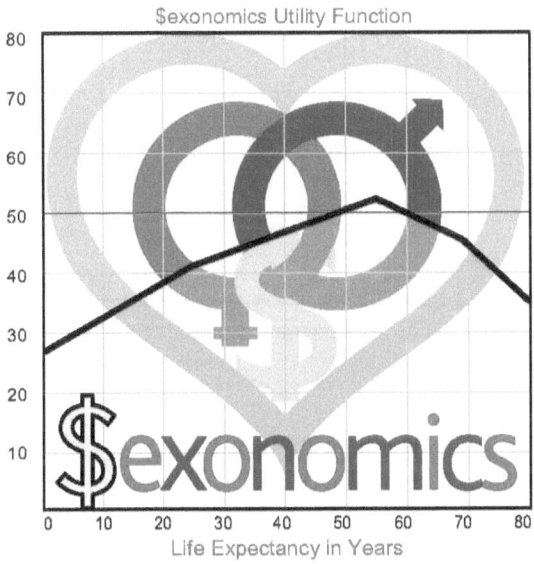

- Sexonomic heart is only about half-filled with happiness (much less so than the Lace-man's).

- All values are positive; range is zero to sixty-five sexons.

- The Vulpine-man is happiest when he is between forty and fifty-five years old.

The sexonomic happiness heart level of the Vulpine-man lies in its entirety well below that of the Lace-man, but it also manifests a rising trend through adolescence and until the age of about forty-five years, after which it starts descending, with a sharp break when he turns about sixty. This is so not only because his sexonomic valuation in the eyes of women falls only into the thirty to fifty-five range but also because Vulpine-men worry about the possible loss of their potency, trying to make up for this possibility by relying more and more on their innate energy reserves and by resorting to an increasing use of muscle—an attitude that not only brings them to the brink of exhaustion in their mature years but also makes them resemble on numerous occasions the crude and vulgar presence of Mob-men. As we can see in the illustration, Vulpine-men too experience a first smaller peak during their adolescence and the final higher peak in their middle years. But on the whole, they are a contented lot because Lace-men treat them well and because they do occasionally have their highlights by copulating with some members of the order of Art-women.

Illustration M-5: Sexonomic happiness heart—Mob-man

- Sexonomic heart is only about one-quarter filled (the Mob-man would love to reach the Vulpine-man's level of happiness).

- All values are positive; range is zero to thirty-five sexons.

- The Mob-man's sexonomic happiness decreases rapidly after he turns thirty-five years old.

Generally speaking, the value and the acquisition price of the Mob-man reflect his low valuation assessment by women, a situation which can be clearly seen in the location of his lifetime sexonomic happiness heart level (see illustration). From its peak during late adolescence (young Mob-men are, for some mysterious reason, very popular not only with the Conch-woman undergraduate crowd but also with the well-heeled coeds from the order of Art-women), this line inches up very slowly, reaches its apex at the age of thirty-five years, turns around, and experiences a decline in his early fifties. Since the Mob-man's main sexonomic asset is crude and brutalizing sex (as is his tasteless disposition of wealth as a nouveau riche), a commodity which may even provide shortest-term enticement to some women from the higher orders, he cherishes his sexuality and convinces himself that, in bed, he is second to no other man. This (false) perception generates a few highlights in his life and keeps him contented with his lot, as indicated by the relatively smooth shape of his sexonomic happiness heart line.

Mob-men belong to one of the two lowest orders whose sexonomic happiness heart level will descend toward zero by the time these men reach their old age. In fact, their sexonomic heart shows how far removed these men are from enjoying a life of full sexonomic happiness. These men grow bitter and resentful in their old age because they recognize that, having lost their potency and not having the wisdom to hold on to whatever material wealth they were able to accumulate during their working years, their fate is to become sexonomically totally unwanted.

Illustration M-6: Sexonomic happiness heart—Girandole-man

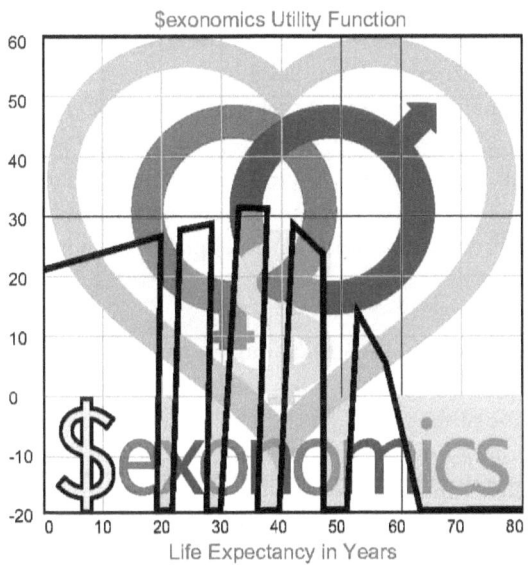

- In spite of hedonistic inclinations and a narcissistic attitude, the Girandole-man ends his life after barely experiencing any net sexonomic happiness.

- His Sexonomics utility function has frequent negative values: -20 to +60 sexons.

- His early sexonomic successes are offset by increasingly prolonged negative valuations after he turns fifty years old.

In women's perception, the sexonomic valuation of Girandole-men is linked directly to the ups and downs of the economy, the fortunes of the executive women who are their main clients, and the conspicuous spending pattern of the parasitic women of the wealthy class. In consequence, their sexonomic happiness level is reflected by a discontinuous line over time, with a prolonged period of smaller peaks and deep troughs which start in their late adolescence toward the apogee when they are about forty years old and with a subsequent rapid decline toward the absolute sexonomic zero (negative value sexonomic valuation coefficient which indicates that the male in question has definitively nothing left to offer to any bidding female person).

As we can see in the illustration, the Girandole-man's demise comes when he turns about forty-five years old, when he becomes mercilessly exposed to increasingly vicious competition by the incoming younger members of his order. The increments in his happiness heart levels are explained by the fact that Girandole-men are in great demand in prosperous times when their income increases by leaps and bounds and his sexuality is primed up—in short, when he feels great. But in economically poor times, his clientele vanishes upon having no purchasing power, and this situation cuts off his primary sources of income and makes him feel unappreciated and unwanted; even the semblance of minimum requisites in civil society (a touch of manners, a bit of tact, an expression of politeness) will then tend to disappear with catastrophic effects, especially on his otherwise well-manifested sexuality. In his later years, his sexonomic happiness heart level irrevocably descends into a negative valuation.

The readers will by now have noticed that, in our discussion of the five orders of men and of their sexonomic happiness hearts, no reference was made to Indian mythology, the reason being that Indian mythology failed to accord to men the distinction of orders of men. Instead, it classifies men according to their sexual characteristics—three kinds of men who are differentiated by the physical sizes of their penises and whose different forms of male behavior arise from these differences. The omission to classify men into orders and their qualities is an unfortunate state of affairs since women throughout history have sought in men so much more than just superbly endowed penises. Even the lowest orders of women demand the minimum of the three qualities of the MOJJ plus the minimum requisite qualities as a human being.

Our own sexonomic analysis of the evolution of mankind (versus womankind), from ancient Greece to modern industrial society, has led us to conclude that women view men as belonging to one of the five orders of men and that women will do their utmost to secure for themselves, by applying their full rational sexonomic calculus, not only their men's sexuality but also—depending on the requisites for that particular order—the full complement of their men's other characteristics, qualities, and endowments. Equally for women and men, each and all of these are considered to constitute the rational bases for a fundamental, interesting, futuristic societal pastime: *the fascinating world of sexonomic marketing and success.*

CHAPTER TWO

Theory of Sexonomics Marketing: Demand, Supply, Equilibrium

As specified in the introduction, we have named three main methods of human sexual interaction: instant gratification (the "haystack effect"), pure love (the most romantic art of loving), and "sexonomic loving" (applying sexonomic rationality to our choices of sexual togetherness).

In our analysis of sexonomic marketing, we shall be using the inductive and deductive reasoning of traditional (Western) economics, with its postulates of price determination by the interaction of suppliers and demanders in what are deemed to be "free markets." While the producers are driven by the profit motive, the consumers respond to them to maximize happiness—to maximize their total utility—from the purchase of their preferred goods and services. This presumably free interaction will enable the markets (goods, services, financial instruments) to establish their respective equilibrium positions, where the demand curves intersect the supply curves (the quantities demanded equal the quantities supplies). These free market–determined equilibrium situations are viewed as fundamental for the establishment of social harmony in a dynamic setting—the image of horizontal and vertical symmetry. In traditional economic reasoning, each and all of these activities revolved around the production and consumption mainly of manufactured products (industry) and of produce (agriculture), both of which are considered as "inert" (they cannot by themselves create an offspring). Concerned about the market of real goods, mainly because their output could be measured objectively and therefore subjected to rational economic analysis, traditional economic reasoning failed to address the question of the "economics of human sexuality" not only because it was considered a "subjective" matter (and therefore impossible to measure and to count) but also because of not wishing to be linked with the "immoral and irrational" forces in society. To cite an interesting example: early in its appearance on the Internet, my website, www.sexonomics.com, was listed by Google as "pornographic." Only after the official launching in 2001 of my treatise

The Golden Triangle: Sexuality, Money, Power—Sexonomics that was quickly followed by several books—by renowned academics (e.g., on sex and law, on economics and prostitution, on the economics of sex and love)—that the subject of "sexonomics" suddenly became à la mode at the university level, even though most of the articles and treatises involve the analysis of prostitution as a market phenomenon, with its demand curves and supply curves, price setting, and equilibrium conditions and situations, finally moving away from the tradition of regarding prostitution as a sin.

While lauding this evolution toward considering human sexuality as subject to objective rational analysis, sexonomic reasoning views prostitution as being but a minor part of "sexonomics as the fifth social science." Sexonomic reasoning involves all aspects of human sexuality. It names (as explained in the introduction, page 1) three main methods of human sexual interaction: instant gratification ("fornication," mainly prostitution), application of sexonomic rationality to choices of sexual togetherness (sexonomic marketing), and the art of romantic loving ("pure love").

Clearly, in human sexual interaction, we speak of the rational quest of a minimum of two persons—equal women and men—to seek out a partner with whom they would share their sexuality, hoping for a satisfying and long-lasting relationship. Unlike in the product market, sexonomic markets involve not a finished inert product but living, pulsating, dynamic human beings who expect to share reciprocally and equally in their loving—an entire course of action (from courtship, to preplay, to stimulation, to marriage proposals, to petting, and finally, to sharing in a mind—and soul-participating union). This course of action may be very short-term, but it may most likely be linked to longer-term planning—sexual choices as a long-term investment. This reciprocal relationship differs totally from happenings in the product market. In the latter, we are involved in a continuous triangular linkage—from the producer, to the finished product, to the consumer—that is horizontally and vertically detached in space and results in an inert good, whose cost and perceived valuation then finds expression as its market price In the former, we view the interaction (usually) between woman and man as a sharing of their sexual needs, a process in which they seek, together, to achieve the "end product" of their desire, be it simple sexual gratification, confirmation of their love, or even to beget a child. In this very personally experienced sense, the process of "making love" involves woman and man at the same time as both consumers and producers. Instead of separation in distance and space, woman and man are joined, unified, merged—just briefly, in the middle run, or even in the long run. In the product and produce markets, we consume the item—subject to the economic law of diminishing marginal utility. In our sexual togetherness, we do not speak of a product that will be produced only physically (subject to the law of diminishing marginal productivity, which results in increasing costs) in order to be consumed (subject to the law of diminishing marginal utility of consuming an inert good) but of sharing in the simultaneous production of the joy of sexual pleasure (not necessarily resulting in procreation). Sexonomic reasoning submits that the laws of decreasing marginal productivity and of decreasing marginal utility do not apply in sexual sharing that emanates from "pure love." On the contrary, as human experience has amply demonstrated, if both partners are involved in "pure love" and therefore always seek the full sexual contentment of one another, then those two "laws" are reversed; during the course of a simultaneous reciprocal loving togetherness, both the "marginal product" and the "marginal utility" keep on increasing until they reach the highest possible level as perceived by the physical, emotional, and mental needs of the partners. "Pure love"—a togetherness that is not adulterated, diminished by any material, financial, or powerful political interests or manipulations.

Since, in traditional economic reasoning, most demand curves are negatively sloping (with varying degrees of decline) while supply curves are positively sloped (with various degrees of incline), sexonomic reasoning—at its most objective and rational—submits that most sexonomic demand functions are positively sloping (with various degrees of incline), attesting to the presence and the functioning of the law of increasing marginal sexonomic utility. The simultaneous sharing in loving also has its effects on marginal productivity; it keeps on rising, which means it results in diminishing costs per additional unit (i.e., in true love sharing, a unit increase in pleasure is achieved with a relatively smaller increase in effort). The expression "Floating at the seventh level of heaven" implies that the "true lovers" have achieved ultimate bliss with a minimal level of physical and mental exertion.

The determination of sexonomic prices and sexonomic values in a situation in which only human loving is involved (especially what sexonomic reasoning labels as "pure love" or "true love") necessitates additional theoretic exploration, starting with the sexonomic definition of "pure love"—a love that involves neither any material, financial, or powerful political considerations nor any religious constraints (both on the demand side and the supply side).

Engaging in "pure love," the partners share their reciprocity fully and equally during the time of their sexual togetherness whereby they add a third dimension to their particular sexonomic demand curve and sexonomic supply curve—the dimension that commands no price, even though it is a very powerful motivating factor. "Pure love" is viewed by sexonomics as the highest level of value of a particular sexonomic linkage. Unlike prostitution, in which the price is deemed equal to the value received—a value that is discounted by the absence of human loving—"pure love" is considered a situation in which the "value received" is higher than the "price paid," leaving the two partners with a unique net gain in happiness. More specifically, in a situation of "pure love," the marginal utility of consuming the final unit will always be higher than the marginal price—the difference between these two measures that we shall label the "pure love bonus" that elevates both partners into the higher regions of total utility (the higher levels of happiness) in which both partners will share equally. Long-lasting happy marriages provide us with the real-life examples of the existence of such situations, a natural consequence of their equal sharing in their pure loving.

In our "sexonomic hearts," pure love is deemed the sole sexonomic linkage that will fill to the brim each partner's sexonomic heart. Loving. It is only in pure love that the loving partners—uninhibited by materialistic considerations (money, power)—will be able to experience the highest level of sexual contentment (the "seventh heaven" level), a state that will last for their lifetime. The steep positive slope of the sexonomic demand curve is explained by the power of human imagination in the act of sharing one's loving sex drive with that of one's partner. Diagram VII/1 portrays pure love situations as expressed by the combined sexonomic demand curves and the combined sexonomic supply curves.

Diagram VII/3: Pure Loves

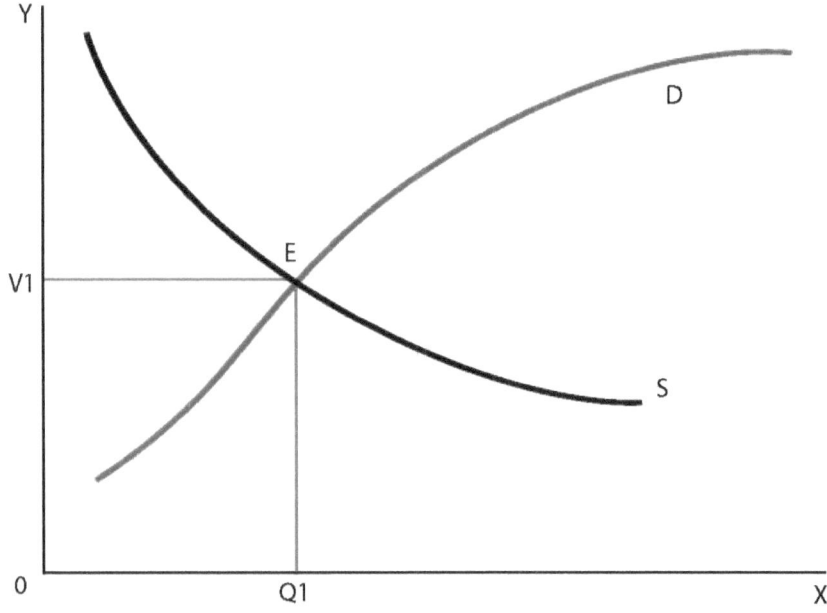

- The sexonomic demand curve (in red) is positively sloping.
- The sexonomic supply curve (in blue) is negatively sloping.
- Point E: equilibrium, where the lovers share equally in their togetherness
- Distance 0–q1: duration of a particular sharing in love

- Distance 0–v1: level of the perceived sexonomic value (in pure love, there is no pricing)
- The flat part at the end of the sexonomic demand curve: in the long run, the factor age results in sexual linkages of continuous contentment with the existing level.
- The flat part at the end of the sexonomic supply curve: in the long run, the factor age results in continuous contentment with the existing level of sexonomic interaction capacity.

Note: In traditional economic reasoning, in diagrams involving demand curves and supply curves, the horizontal axis (the x-axis) normally measures "quantity demanded," while the vertical axis (the y-axis) denotes the "price." "Marginal utility" and "total utility" also involve quantity of the product along the horizontal axis and the quantity of derived utility along the vertical axis. In sexonomic reasoning, we use, in a similar manner, the horizontal axis as measuring "quantity," but the vertical axis shows "price" only in the prostitution market (be it street-level or "high-class") since such market prices are market-determined. However, sexonomic reasoning prefers using the vertical axis to measure the perceived value of sexual togetherness, moving upward along the axis, signifying higher and higher levels of reciprocal contentment for the sexually partnering women and men (a situation that is typical of "pure love" situations). This being so because, in sexonomic reasoning, "pure love is never for sale" because it is considered "priceless."

The one exception from the positively sloping sexonomic demand function is presented by the prostitution market. Street-level prostitution is viewed by sexonomics as cash-and-carry sex ("fornication" as defined in "Definition and Purpose," page 1)—an engagement in which the sex organs are used to play a role reminiscent of the operations of machines (i.e., devoid of any feeling of love). As cash-and-carry sex acts, prostitution results in market prices that are deemed "objective" in a setting in which many sellers and buyers act rationally, albeit always in a hurry; instead of sharing in and enhancing loving, the sex organs are called upon to engage in the repetitive mechanical motions of an inert product, a mass-produced motor.

The buyer is a Mob-man who is seeking repeated "instant gratification"; the seller is an Elephant-woman who makes her living as a street-level prostitute. In return for a fifteen-minute session, she demands a cash payment of fifty dollars. Not seeking love but only "quick relief," the buyer willingly accepts. A professional sex worker, the seller is not expected to offer love but only skilled locomotion whose mechanized rhythm will result in the buyer's quick climax. Sexonomic reasoning views the prostitute's LUSSEY as a "product" with no loving and therefore no need to reciprocate, no desire for highest-level sexonomic contentment. In this sense, as cash-and-carry sex—the lowest level of sexonomic marketing—prostitution is considered only as the equivalent of the sale and the purchase of an inert product. However, the marketing of it will—corresponding to situations in real product markets—still result in equilibrium situations; at the intersection of the sexonomic demand curve and the sexonomic supply curve, the "equilibrium market price" will be established, where the quantity (of sexual servicing) demanded equals the quantity (of sexual servicing) supplied—direct consequences of the use of human sexual organs as if they were "production inputs" and "merchandise."

In the street-level prostitution market, the valuation of these inputs as merchandise is the lowest because both the quality of the inputs and of the outputs—in the absence of human loving—is inferior, resulting in low satisfaction levels. Yet even these low valuations and low prices are deemed "fair" assessments of market reality. In this sense, sexonomic reasoning views cash-and-carry sex (that involves women and men both as inputs and outputs) as transactions that are comparable with "pure competition" in the product markets—large quantities of cheaply produced merchandise sold to large numbers of buyers determining quantities and prices in a manner in which the producers need to cover all costs of production and to secure a small profit margin, while the consumers can only attain levels of total utility that are significantly inferior to those in the higher-quality markets. In the long run, both cash-and-carry sex and "pure" competition involve transactions that are premised not to have subjective roots (e.g., human loving) but to emanate from objective rational reasoning. Even though prostitution normally directly involves two persons at a time, overall goings-on in both of these markets are similar. Prices and values are determined in the same manner; there are large numbers of demanders and suppliers, with free entry and exit; the output quality is low; and profit margins and levels of satisfaction are minimal.

It follows that the sexonomic demand function in the Mophant market manifests the same shape as the real product demand curve—slightly curvilinear and downward sloping to the right, except that it is more discontinuous. The mass consumption of a purely competitive product continues without interruption, whereas in sexual linkages involving street prostitution, shorter or longer time periods are biologically required for both the street workers and the johns. In both of these markets, we never speak of the emergence of a "consumer surplus" (a surplus of real benefits over real costs that accrues to the consumers yet does not have to be paid for since there is no expectation by the users that there might be even the slightest bit of loving on the part of the server during the course of the sex act).

Diagram VII/3: Prostitution

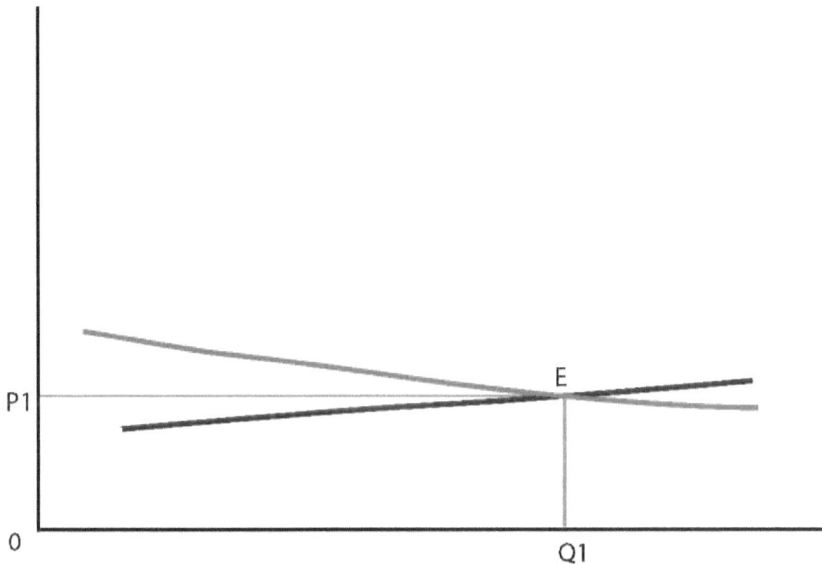

Turning our attention to sexonomic marketing at the "midlevel" sexonomic orders (Art-women and Lace-men, Conch-women and Vulpine-men) as well as the lowest-ranking order (Vampire-women and Girandole-men), we consider that they are similar to those actual market structures in the capitalist economic system that traditional economics refers to as "imperfect competition" or "monopolistic competition"—smaller numbers of buyers and sellers, somewhat restricted entry and exit, some influence over pricing and price setting, some product differentiation—in a situation in which, unlike the purchase and the sale of an "inert" good, the marketing of human sexuality becomes a service. In these sexonomic markets, we speak of a rational reciprocal exchange involving the pulsating, lively, sensuous, active LUSSEYs and MOJJs—a more than just physical merger of a female body with a male body in anticipation of as well as the consequence of the participating female and male's desire—and the appropriate level of sexual effort to reach the highest possible levels of sexual fulfillment as well as material and powerful political gains—a quest that may involve increasing expressions of caring and even of genuine human loving.

Why a "service" and not anymore an "inert" product?

In reality, unlike street-level prostitution, members of these orders are educated women and men who have equal backgrounds and experiences in monetary and powerful political matters. As mature human beings, they seek, during their private hours, to enrich their contentment as professionals by linking it with the biological, the spiritual, and the loving—and even the lustful—needs in their lives. As described in part 1, in their quest for material gains or political influence, such women and men will attempt to have their reason become the primary rational decision maker in their choice of sexual partners. In fact their chief control agent of the intensity of their sexual needs as well as of their compatible partners, sexonomic reasoning refers to the combination of all of these considerations as the "rational calculus of reciprocated sexuality and loving," its applied purpose being the quest for maximum sexual enjoyment between the respective—and usually monogamous—partners. The participation in the "rational calculus" of sexonomic merchandising in the quest for material gains and political influence cannot attain the level of happiness that is experienced in "pure love"; however, emanating from the desire by the respective two partners to merge into a fully aroused, vibrant, and absorbing union, it will rise beyond the biological and the sexual, also touching the soul and even making their reason sparkle with happiness.

The sexonomic demand curves of these midlevel orders demonstrate the phenomenon of reciprocation. They portray the partners' attempts at sharing, in full, every impulse and every motion during the act of loving, one that—unlike in the lowest orders—is always followed by longer moments of contented reflection and feelings of togetherness. They also imply that the partners are—at the same time during the act of loving—both demanders and suppliers who have decided to give as much as they wish to obtain in response and who—even though still imbued with materialistic considerations—are in complete physical, emotional, and spiritual accord about the meaning of their union. In a reciprocal union, sexonomic happiness is elevated to its second highest level of physical, psychological, and mental contentment, a level that reflects itself in a much higher level of total utility. This type of a "combined" demand curve differs from both the cash-and-carry sex one and the one that is typical of the "purely competitive" product market.

Diagram VII/3: Sexonomics Equilibrium

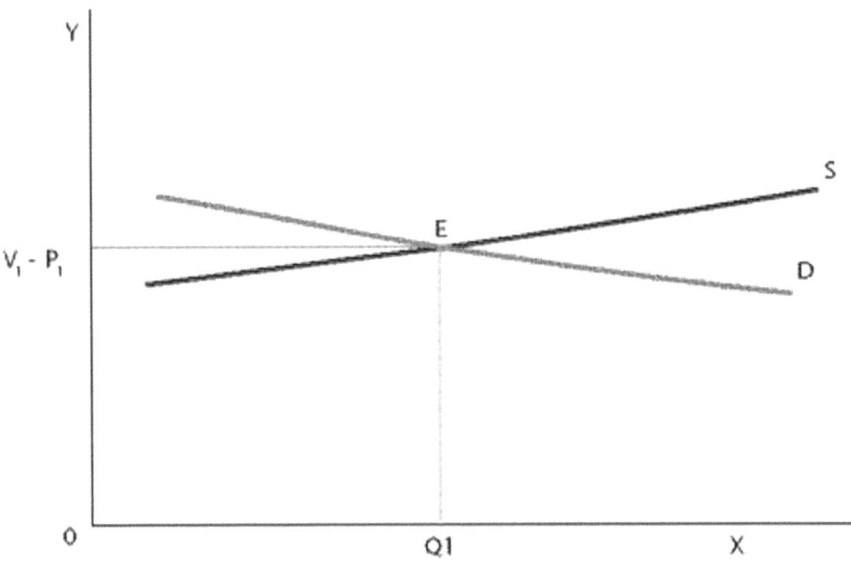

The difference in the levels of happiness and well-being that arise in the sexonomic markets as explained above is clearly demonstrated in Diagram VII/4:

Diagram VII/4: Pure Love

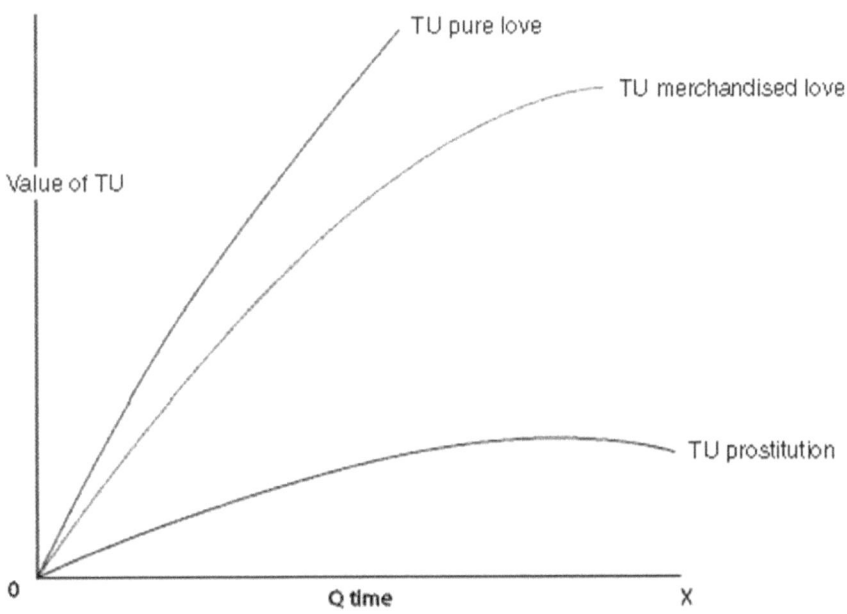

- The pink line expresses the maximum happiness that accrues from pure love.
- The green line expresses the intermediate level of happiness of the midlevel orders; it also includes the "high-class" prostitution market.
- The brown line demonstrates the low level of contentment for those who make up the street-level prostitution market.

Concluding our attempt at creating an initial theory of sexonomic demand, sexonomic supply, and sexonomic equilibrium as the main determinants in the process of sexonomic marketing, we wish to reiterate that sexonomic marketing refers to individuals in our society who engage in it in the expectation of material, financial, or powerful political gains. In this sense, we also wish to reiterate that "sexonomic marketing"—unlike pure love togetherness—does involve material considerations like money and power politics as means that are expected to enhance the chances of "sexonomic success." In sexonomic marketing situations (those in which material, monetary, and powerful political considerations are involved), sexonomic reasoning suggests the following:

A sudden increase in income or in wealth will not increase the quantity demanded for sexual interaction, more so for men—because of their biological makeup—than for women. However, there will be, over time, an increased desire for higher-quality sexual interaction (suddenly, much wealthier single women and men will find the "high-class" prostitution market an affordable luxury).

A sudden acquisition of political, financial, or bidding power will also not result in an immediate increase in the quantity demanded for sexual interaction, more so for men—because of their biological makeup—than for women. However, it will result in an increase in the supply of persons, more so younger women than men—who, attracted by the promise of sharing in these kinds of "powers" will make themselves available for sexual partnering—causing a decrease in their sexonomic valuations.

Let us also be reminded of the significance of the biological and cognitive determinants of successful sexonomic marketing, both on the demand side and the supply side (please refer back to part 1, chapter 2):

Women
　　　　Biologically innate: conception-and-delivery quality
　　　　Innate as well as cognitive: enticement-and-control quality
　　　　Mainly cognitive: pleasure quality
Men
　　　　Biologically innate: dimension, prolificity

Innate as well as cognitive: pukkacity, erethism, sensitiveness, perseverance, enticement-and-control, pleasure.

In addition, we must also account equally for men and women the external factors that shape the participating individuals' sexonomic choices and have direct influence in marketing capacity, strategies, and success—customs and the legal system; cultural, sociopolitical, and socioeconomic structures and environment; religion; education; population density; mobility; natural as well as induced competitiveness and combativeness; preference for peace rather than war.

CHAPTER THREE

The Magic of the Golden Triangle

As we have seen, the "sexonomic heart" is the copyrighted trademark (1988) of Dr. Adalbert Lallier's first reflections in *The Golden Triangle: Sexuality, Money, Power—Sexonomics*. As an illustration, the "sexonomic heart" reveals a two-dimensional concept, equally for women and for men—an attempt to measure the level of "sexonomic happiness" of each of the five women's and men's orders over their entire active lifetime. Visually, the highest levels of "sexonomic happiness" are those of Lotus-women and Quintessential-men; their entire hearts are filled with the color of happiness because they are the only ones who have experienced "pure love," the highest, the ideal, form of human loving. The subsequent lower-order sexonomic hearts are filled with gradually lower levels of happiness, as we have shown by demonstrating the "sexonomic utility functions" for the average of each lower order. As we already know, it is only for the two lowest orders, Vampire-women and Girandole-men, that the value of sexonomic happiness drops below zero in the course of their respective lifetimes since those women and men, throughout their lifetimes, engage in situations of "cash-and-carry sex" and are incapable of ever experiencing "pure love."

Sexonomic reasoning as portrayed in its author's *The Golden Triangle* is closely linked to Indian mythology and philosophy that date back from the fourth to the seventh centuries AD. Its definition of "pure love" is derived from Indian mythology. It reflects the ideal form of human loving (i.e., one that excludes any notions of material and monetary interests or power plays). In his view, only Lotus-women and Quintessential-men are capable of experiencing that exalted (heavenly?) level of loving.

However, reflecting upon the evolution of the other major world civilizations, we must reach back to the much earlier antiquity to well before the rise of Christianity and include even certain pagan views and rites about the linkages between human sexuality, divinity, and the (presumed) "divine" nature and destiny of human beings. Ancient times in which, in numerous instances of regional cultures, much more emphasis—relative to the views of the Vatican since about the sixth century—had been put upon the nature and role of the female gender—the cult of female deities, of "goddesses," and with terms appropriate to their state of "supreme beings" and "central characters," with very strong emphasis on the "divine nature of their sexuality." These terms are specific to their exalted status—the *sacred feminine*, *sacred matrimony*, *sacred marriage*, *sacred union*, and *divine mother*. Each of these antiquity or early Christian reflections which involved the repeated use of the term *sacred*—implied that, at the level of male gods and goddesses, sexuality was "sacred," and "sacred marriage" constituted the desired, highest moral norm, one that was expected to apply to all of humankind and equally so to women and men. Sexual union, at that level, represents the highest level of union between woman and man, a union anchored in spirituality, consciousness, and wisdom (character traits that, in sexonomic reasoning, are exclusive to Lotus-women and Quintessential-men).

Recalling the earlier philosophies' emphases on the four fundamental elements/ forces in nature that rule over the lives and destinies of human beings—air, water, fire, and gravity—sexonomic reasoning confirms that each of these make up, individually and jointly, the pillars upon which our continuously evolving social structure is built, with its apex as—in the language of ancient pagan cults—"the royal throne from which . . . the chosen kings, anointed by and united in 'holy matrimony' by the priestess-queen, would reign and wield absolute power . . ." (Lynn Pickett, as described by Dan Burstein's *Secrets of the Code*, page 19). Each of these four fundamental elements/forces exerts its own influence on human beings as composites of the physical and the spiritual, with particular emphasis on human sexuality (the urge to procreate and thereby to propagate our species). However, while taking account of the four fundamental natural elements/forces as representing the laws of nature in our universe, sexonomic reasoning prefers viewing the concept of "holy matrimony" (*hieros gamos*) as involving a basically triangular situation that reflects the three primary determinants of human behavior—reason (consciousness), sexuality (*carnalis*), wisdom (*sophia*)—a three-dimensional relationship, which has found its expression in what was termed in ancient times the "sacred union" between female deities and male gods of war. Reflecting the modern secular-oriented rational pattern of thought, the language of Sexonomics will undertake to "bring down to earth" these ancient preoccupations with the "heavenly" in the attempt to apply the concept of the "sacred union" to female and male behavior in contemporary society. Rationalizing about this concept, Sexonomics envisages it as a *golden triangle*, a geometric structure that represents the (gradual but eventually complete) fusion of the eternally feminine with the forever masculine as illustrated by two symmetrically perfect triangles, the red-colored (for the feminine) and the blue-colored (for the masculine). Rooted in the orthodox tradition of ancient Israel and the "Star of David" as its eternal heavenly symbol, the merging of these two triangles expresses a vertical pattern of movement—at the same time from the top down as well as from the bottom up (historically, in the later Christian tradition, the masculine is seen as descending upon the feminine). Sexonomics will disregard the question of "who starts from the top" since sexonomic reasoning accords completely equal status to both the female and the male component in its final stage, the "sacred union."

Since, in this portrayal, the two sides of the two triangles are equal in length (they are "isosceles"), we also assume—following the original dimensions of the "Star of David"—that the base line is of equal length, which gives us the image of a perfect symmetry. Sexonomics will view this situation not only as one of perfect harmony but also of a perfect balance and perfect symmetry between the feminine and the masculine—a stable equilibrium situation. A perpendicular from the apex down to the center of the base line conveys the impression of the longest distance between the top and the bottom of the graph, a measure that will help us in the analysis of the consequence of any movement along any of these three lines.

Now looking at Illustration S-1 (page 150), we shall insert a perpendicular that cuts through the baseline exactly at its center. The length of the baseline signifies the amount of resources and time that a sexonomic player plans to use in seeking to increase the level of her/his sexonomic happiness. Starting with point A on the extreme left of the baseline and moving to the right means that the player wishes to allocate more resources and time in the pursuit of greater *material or financial wealth* (even though such a decision also means that the player has fewer resources and time left for "pure love"). If the movement begins at point B on the extreme right of the base line, it will demonstrate the sexonomic player's desire to devote more resources and time in the pursuit of *more power*, assuming that "more power will buy more sex" (even though it will also mean that the player will have fewer resources and time left for "pure love").

The vertical lines (Fo-F1 in Illustration S-1 and Mo-M1 in Illustration S-2) are located in the very centers of each graph, which is of great significance in sexonomic reasoning because they are presumed to measure and to express the level of sexonomic happiness that is attained over the course of a player's lifetime—one that is unimpeded by any material, monetary, or powerful political influences. This level is the highest at the apex and is equivalent, in the sexonomic heart illustrations, to the sexonomic hearts of Lotus-women and Quintessential-men. In the mythologies of the antiquity, rising above the apex was not possible for human beings (since the apex and above were viewed as the exclusive natural habitat for gods and goddesses). Sexonomic rationality submits that the movement up along the perpendicular right up to its very apex is exclusive to the two highest orders, Lotus-women and Quintessential-men, and that movements away, to the left or to the right, from the perpendicular can involve only the women and the men of the lower orders (starting with Art-women and Lace-men), whose sexonomic decisions involve their desire to offer proportionally more and more material assets and/ or power benefits in exchange for loveless fornication—cruder and cruder forms of sexual intercourse—in preference to seeking "pure love." Moving toward the right expresses the swapping of instant sex for increasing quantities of money and assets. Moving toward the left indicates the swapping for instant sex of more and more means of power and control. While at the center of the baseline, we speak of a "balance," of a "symmetry," of an "equilibrium" involving the attainment of the highest levels of "pure love" by the rational use of reason, consciousness, and wisdom during the course of the players' lifetime. Any movement away from the center will result in rising instability, in a regression into increasing asymmetry, and eventually, in an ensuing disequilibrium.

What is the end result of shifting sexonomic decisions from the quest for "pure love" toward the pursuit of material wealth or power with the intention of buying sex? The "sexonomic happiness line" becomes shorter and shorter, implying a continuous decrease in sexonomic happiness because the idealistic quest for pure love is being replaced by intention to satisfy one's sexual craving by engaging in (vulgar) fornication—instant cash for the fleeting joy of a loveless sex act. We must note that the linkage between the quest for pure love, on the one hand, and the attainment of more abundant material or financial wealth, on the other, is one of opposites; putting increasing emphasis on the latter will inevitably have an increasingly negative effect on pure love. We must also point out that the linkage between attaining more material wealth and securing more power may be viewed as one of complementarity in the sexonomic marketing of sexuality. Historically, peddlers of instant sex for instant cash or instant access to sources of power have always used either as a backup for the other. While it is "natural" for Lotus-women and Quintessential-men to move up to the highest level, the ideal level, of "pure love" (moving from the center point upward along the perpendicular), it is equally "natural" for the women and men of the lower orders to seek greater happiness not by aspiring for "pure love" but by engaging in the pursuit of purely material or financial ends of power plays as a means that might enhance their success in marketing their sexuality.

Illustrations of Perfect ("Sacred")
Happiness and Sexonomic Reasoning

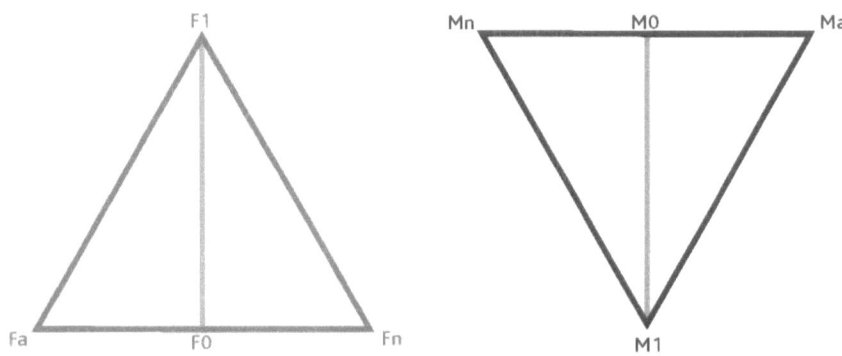

F0 > F1: Maximum potential happiness,   M0 > M1: Maximum potential happiness,
    female   male

Fa > Fn: Shifting from pure love to more   Ma > Mn: Shifting from pure love to
    money and power, female   more money and power, male

S3: Union of the feminine and the masculine

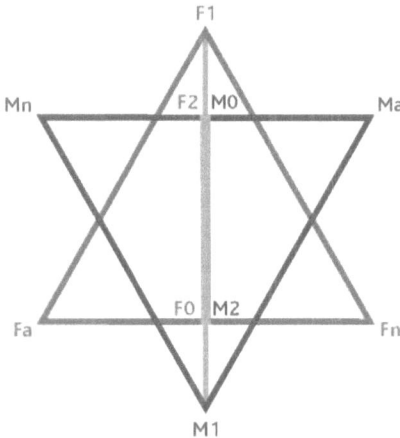

F0 > F1 = M1 > M0: maximum potential happiness from both the feminine and the
    masculine from their "perfect" union;

Fa > Fn: shifting from pure love to more   Ma > Mn: shifting from pure love to
    money; and power, female,   more money and power, male

Illustration S4: Perfect "sacred" union of the feminine and the masculine (and sexonomic deviation therefrom)

Female triangle:

Starting point for "perfect" happiness, female

Highest happinesse point, female

Happiness gain from union, female

Female time allocation for mre monety and power

Male triangle:

Starting point for "perfect" happiness, male

Highest happinesse point, male

Happiness gain from union, male

Male time allocation for more monety and power

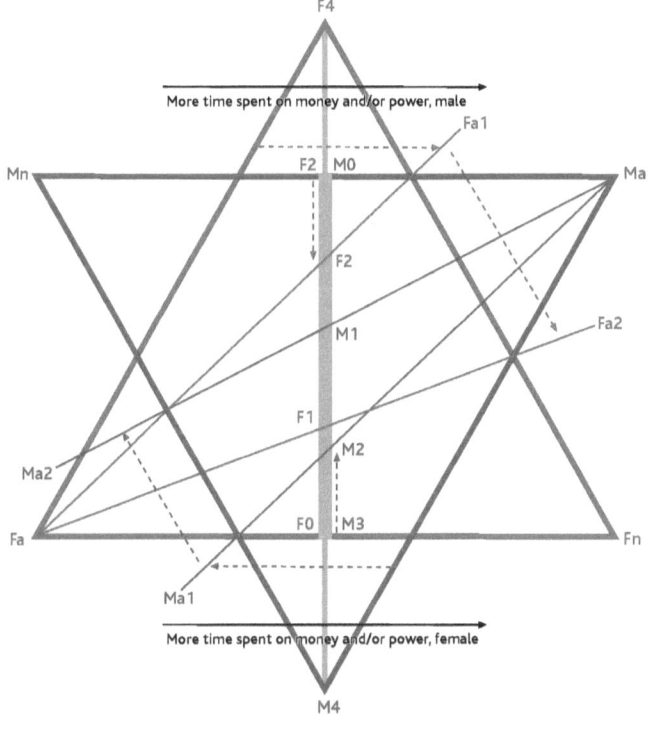

Line Fa > Fa1: more time on money or power towards buying sex, women;

Loss of happiness from first shift from pure love to buying sex, women;

First loss of happiness from shifting to line Fa > Fa1, women;

Total loss of happiness once down to line Fa > Fn,

Women

Line Ma > Mn: more time on money or power towards buying sex, women;

Loss of happiness from first shift from pure love to buying sex, women;

First loss of happiness from shifting to line Ma > Mn, men;

Total loss of happiness once down to line Mn > Fn,

Men

Except for its red-colored lines, Illustration S-1 is the upside-down version of S-2 (with its blue-colored lines), following the historical juxtapositions in several ancient cultures of the feminine and the masculine as symbolized by the "chalice" and "the sword" and reminiscent of the Star of David. Reflecting the presumed balance as expressed by the duality between the female divine force and the male divine force, their merger and union take on an exclusive deeply spiritual meaning, the male being viewed as the giver of life and the female as the receiver—the concept of the sacred union visually expressed by the harmonious symmetrical merger of the downward triangle with the upward triangle. The end result of the fusion of triangles S1 and S2 is presented in Illustration S-3 but this time with a perpendicular starting at the apex of the female diagram, cutting downward exactly halfway through the upper horizontal baseline of the blue male diagram, continuing downward exactly halfway through the lower horizontal line of the red female diagram, and ending at the apex of the downside-up blue male diagram. Sexonomic reasoning will proceed with its emphasis on this line in its entirety from the upper apex to the lower apex, by coloring it *gold* since moving directly upward along this line is presumed to keep on increasing the "pure love" content in the "sacred union" (the "perfect union" of the feminine with its counterpart, the masculine).

The sexonomic interpretation of the "perfect union" puts special emphasis on the nature, the determinants, and the overall effects of this union:

> —sexonomic happiness is maximized for both parties when the "sacred union" is achieved—the gold-colored perpendicular is the longest between the upper apex and the lower apex (i.e., between points F1 and M1);

> —of this total length, the part between points MoM2 and FoF2 represents the equal net gain from the union of the ("sacred") feminine with the ("godly") masculine;

> —any deviation from the golden perpendicular will result in a diminution of sexonomic happiness, in consequence of the decision of sexonomic players to engage in marketing their sexuality in exchange for cash or power. This situation is portrayed in Illustration S-4 (page 151); and

> —overall, the complete merger of the two triangles will result in perfect balance and symmetry and a stable equilibrium between the feminine and the masculine forces—with the appropriate unification of reason, consciousness, and wisdom—all uninhibited by considerations for material wealth or power for the purpose of purchasing or selling crude sex.

Illustration S-4 portrays a situation in which both the feminine and the masculine forces will pursue the quest for more money and other liquid assets. Resources and time will be shifted away from the attainment of pure love and will be put to use in the expectation of finding a sexonomic partner who will consider an instantaneously more opulent material lifestyle as more preferable than waiting endlessly for the ideal, pure-love partner to materialize. Using the feminine triangle (colored red), we draw a line from point Fa (the extreme left of the baseline of the feminine triangle) and upward and to the right, up until it intersects point Fa1. The new point of the joint balance is established, but it will become asymmetrical and will also result in a much lower level of sexonomic happiness (this new line intersecting the golden perpendicular at point F2, a point much lower than both points F1 and M1).

Illustration S-4: The Golden Triangle and Sexonomic Strategies—Explanations

We assume that the "perfect union" is disturbed by a major event (possibly the death of the female player's "ideal partner") that induces her to change her sexonomic strategy by shifting more time and resources into securing more material means and/or power, driven by the quest to survive this tragic situation. We are interested in her decisions as well as the consequences of her decisions, all of which we can trace by following closely their portrayal in Illustration S-4 (note that the red triangle represents the "feminine," whereas the blue triangle represents the "masculine").

Step 1: The decision to shift more emphasis from the purely spiritual to the more material is shown by the movement to the right from the initial point Fa toward the endpoint Fn. This greater emphasis on the material (away from the spiritual) changes the initial time proportion between "pure love" and "money and/or power, which is expressed as a change in the slope of the initial line (in red) between point Fa and F1; the new line becomes flatter because more time is now spent on material goods, as can be seen moving along the (new) line Fa–Fa1.

Consequence: The change in sexonomic strategy will disturb the initial equilibrium (the initial "perfect symmetrical balance" as expressed by the golden line Fo–F3) toward the right. Moving along the (new) line Fa–Fa1, we note that it intersects the golden line at point F2, which lies below the initial equilibrium point at F3. This new intersection means that a shift toward more material means (and away from the initial highest level of happiness point at F3) will result in an overall lower level of happiness because of the added emphasis on money and/or power in exchange for sex. This new equilibrium point (F2) will be established by the intersection of the new line (Fa–Fa1) with the red line F1–Fn (on the right-hand side of the red triangle). This new point is asymmetrical and expresses a lower level of overall sexonomic contentment that is borne out in similar conditions in real life.

Ultimate consequence. Experiencing a lower level of happiness, the female player will likely put even more emphasis on the material, which will shift even more time away from the "pure love" apex and will result in a further decrease in sexonomic happiness (just follow the second new line, Fa–Fa2, to discover the new equilibrium at point F1). In response, even more time will be shifted to the material since concern for money and/or power will prevail more and more over the spiritual; the quality of human loving will keep on deteriorating as the sentiment for "pure love" will be replaced more and more by the increasing urge to "buy love" . . . a deterioration toward the dismal lifestyles of the lowest-level sexonomic orders, Vampire-women and Girandole-men. Dropping all the way to point Fn will mean that the highest level of human loving, "pure love," will have been totally replaced by an attitude of "love for cash" or "cash for love"—that is, by lowering ideal human loving to the base level of a marketable commodity.

Should this "bidding" female person (even if only trying to find a way out of a personal tragedy) come across a male sexonomic player who enters the sexonomic market in seeking to take advantage of such vulnerable female players, "he" would also put more and more emphasis on the material (charging a forever higher material price for his services), as shown by "his" blue lines shifting from the initial Ma–M1, first to the left toward Ma–Ma1, and eventually even more to the left to Ma–Ma2, with the result that the level of sexonomic happiness of the female player will decrease even more rapidly to her point Fo, the level of zero sexonomic happiness . . . a situation which expresses, in contemporary society, the tragic fate of many millions of older women.

The process of sexonomic decision making in increasingly dismal situations, as described above, will ultimately lead to a general deterioration of overall happiness for increasing numbers of human beings . . . a direct consequence of seeking to convert the naturally imbedded yearning for "pure love" into a vast outpouring of human sexuality as a marketable commodity.

Any additional transfers of sexonomic decisions in attempting to secure yet higher material benefits will inevitably result in rapidly lower levels of pure love—a process that, if continued, will result in the complete destruction of human loving capacity—a negation of human reason, consciousness, and wisdom and a major step toward the disintegration of the moral fiber of our society.

The "sacred union" illustrations allow us to view sexonomic analysis as a means to reflect upon situations that—unlike the concept of the sexonomic heart—are more than two-dimensional. In particular, they are very useful in the attempt to measure, with a greater degree of precision, the private and social losses that will arise if increasingly more pure-loving time is transferred into the quest for greater material wealth or the attainment of more power while debasing the spiritual quality of human sexuality toward its lowest common denominator (at the level of interaction between Vampire-women and Girandole-men, the two lowest orders in contemporary society).

In this sense, we in Sexonomics wish to express our hope that the spiritual in human beings will eventually succeed in having them seek to move progressively up to the highest possible realm of loving, that of the "pure" or the "ideal" love, the earthly equivalents of the classicals' concept of "divine" or "sacred" love. In this spiritual sense, we wish to submit that, even though our lives are physically determined by the four fundamental natural forces as described above, we shall be able to reach that spiritual and emotional level of happiness if, in the course of our lifetimes, we learn how to apply to their fullest extent and conditions of the full equality between the feminine and the masculine our reason, consciousness, and wisdom.

Chapter Four

Sexonomic Terminology

In this chapter, we shall proceed to define the following terms and measures that are pertinent to sexonomic reasoning and its quest to assist the millions of women and men who are active in the five sexonomic markets in seeking to secure for themselves their ultimate male or female partner and to realize their respective highest levels of sexonomic happiness.

> Sexonomic valuation index (female and male);
> Sexonomic utility function (female and male);
> Sexonomic value (female and male);
> Sexonomic price (female and male); and
> Sexonomic equilibrium (short-run, normal-run, long-run).

Note: Those readers who may find this part too analytical for their liking are advised to skip it and to proceed directly to the appendices. But they may wish to back-check later since a thorough understanding of its technical terms will most likely enhance our readers' long-run chances of success in their own sexonomic strategies and games.

Sexonomic Valuation Index: Female

The sexonomic valuation index of a human female measures the perceived value of a woman's being (which includes the Lady LUSSEY's three qualities) as viewed by the competing males in her particular sexonomic market. Expressed as an index, this measure applies to all five orders of women, with the highest coefficient for the top-level order and the lowest for the lowest orders.

This measure serves the purpose of assessing how men view women in their desire to avail themselves of their "ultimate" choice in their quest to experience maximum sexonomic happiness. We expect that this measure will also assist women in their own quest to improve on their sexonomic "rating" if they wish to share their sexuality and material means with men of the higher orders. In its essence, the sexonomic valuation index provides the foundation for women's sexonomic strategies and games; in fact, it is a reliable and objective measure of a woman's chances to succeed (or to fail) in her attempt to secure for herself the coveted quality male from her order equivalent or even to "conquer" a male from the next higher order of men.

The overall range (involving all orders of women and men) of the sexonomic valuation begins at -20 and rises as high as +100. This index is derived from three essential sexonomic "characteristics" and also presumes the presence of eight sexonomic "imbedded conditions."

In each of the five orders of women, each of the three "characteristics" attains its own market-determined sexonomic weight:

- capacity to reason (involving both intelligence and education);
- propensity to arouse the sexual drive of men (power of sex appeal); and
- experience and aptitude to handle material wealth (power of the Midas touch).

The eight naturally imbedded conditions are ranked as follows in descending order of significance:

- feminine touch
- maternal instinct
- competitiveness
- poise
- comradeship
- natural aptitude to grow things
- horizon
- cleanliness

It is understood that a serious deficiency of any of these naturally imbedded conditions will seriously inhibit the successful portrayal of the major characteristics and will therefore strongly diminish the chances of success in a woman's sexonomic marketing.

Intuitively, the valuation index of the Lotus-woman is expected to involve coefficients (that is, average numerical weights for each of these characteristics) of much higher value than would the indexes of any of the four lower orders of women, the specific range for each of the orders being as follows:

Order of women:	Sexonomic valuation coefficient:
Lotus	90 - 100
Art	70 - 85
Conch	40 - 65
Elephant	20 - 35
Vampire	-20 - + 60

The overall sexonomic valuation of Lotus-women adds up to the highest total for all women: 90–100 SEVACs (units of the sexonomic valuation coefficient). Of these, 60 percent account for the "characteristics" (reason: 25 points; sexuality: 20 points; Midas touch: 15 points), while the remaining 40 percent are composed of the respective shares of the imbedded conditions.

For Art-women, the scale of weighting is correspondingly lower since high-quality men know why Art-women's valuation needs to be discounted by an average of about 15 percent for all characteristics and imbedded conditions. The high end of the range amounts to 85 SEVACs, which includes the maximum of 4.25 points for each of the imbedded conditions and the highest SEVACs for Art-women's reason, sexuality, and the Midas touch, viz. 20, 18, and 13. The bottom of the range for Art-women totals 70 SEVACs, with the corresponding lower valuations of each of its constituent parts.

Conch-women's sexonomic valuation is correspondingly lower since their overall characteristics and imbedded conditions are significantly inferior to those of Art-women. The highest value for each of the conditions averages out at 3.50 points for all eight, but the first five suffer a greater proportionate decline than the last three. For the three sexonomic characteristics, the Conch-woman's valuation also suffers a sizeable discount down to 14 SEVACs for reason but still as high as 15 for sexuality (do you recall our discussion of the Conch-woman's delightfully appealing sexuality?), and the big drop to 8 is for the clearly evident alchemy in her Midas touch. This range of Conch-women's medium-value SEVACs expresses the lower-quality desires and cravings of the average type of male in the order of Vulpine-men.

The sexonomic valuation of Elephant-women comprises vastly inferior sets of characteristics, especially with respect to reason and the crudeness of her sexuality. Even though Elephant-women may be quite wealthy, their overall valuation cannot amount to a total higher than 35 SEVACs, which includes the low valuations of their imbedded conditions. The latter will average out to a maximum of 2 points (competitiveness ranking by far the highest while she literally lacks the aura of femininity and poise); the former is made up of a total of 10 SEVACs for shrewdness (reason) but not more than 5 for sexuality (mainly because of the thoroughly salacious nature of these women) and only a maximum of 4 for her heavy-fisted and avaricious attitude with respect to income and wealth (even the most unsavory of alchemists would never hire an Elephant-woman as his laboratory assistant).

The order of Vampire-women falls into the lowest sexonomic valuation range. This is so because the women of this order represent the ultimate self in sexonomic relations—human beings who cannot love and who seek to satisfy their own sexual desires in return for instant cash payment or other material considerations. Even though often very well-to-do, these women have no feeling except when lusting for intercourse. Originally possessing an otherwise superb brain, the Vampire-woman finds herself exposed to the alternating cycle of periods during which she has a continuous craving for sex and times when she manifests total aloofness with respect to fornication. This destabilizing situation renders her behavior extremely unpleasant over time in that she seeks to compensate for the lack of loving capacity by recourse to pecuniary manipulations. For money, anything goes, especially offering sex for free or even buying or selling, if it can be turned into gain or profit. When young and having the appearance of poise and quality, she will succeed in attracting quality men even into marriage. But incapable of loving, she will proceed to exploit and to suck them dry of their material means, only to drop them when a better opportunity comes around. But eventually, she becomes unmarketable at a crucial stage of her life, in her midthirties, when her self-seeking evil reputation finally catches up with her. Desperate, she then goes around seeking to buy men with less and less success until her sexonomic valuation gets debased below even that of the Elephant-woman.

Vampire-women's three sexonomic valuation characteristics manifest the consequences of her unpredictable behavior; her reason is valued at the Lace-woman's high of 20 SEVACs when in the state of professional competence but at the low of 0 when she is hit by the frenzy of the urge to fornicate. Her sexuality accounts for 10 SEVACs when she manages to refrain but drops to a negative valuation of -20 when she repeatedly resorts to paying cash to Girandole-men, her eventual and final partners in fornication. Even her disposition of wealth and income reveals a destructive cyclical pattern. When times are prosperous, she spends all her income both on seeking to qualify for the status and distinct lifestyle of the Art-woman and on desperately but unsuccessfully trying to attract and keep men; when times are bad, many Vampire-women are out of jobs, and their overall valuation decreases to a net of 0. A sexonomic valuation of 0 SEVACs clearly indicates that the women in this order offer no value whatsoever to any man above the order of Girandole-men; it also explains why Vampire women repeatedly go through those periods of sexual frenzy. As younger women, they cannot cope with the fact of no man wanting them for permanent relationships; growing older, they recognize that they will most likely never have a family of their own.

A Note on the Sexonomic Valuation Coefficient of Women

At this time, and pending further empirical research, the sexonomic valuation coefficient is presented as an abstract measure. But this coefficient is known to exist in the minds of experienced men, who will thoughtfully look at a woman and be able to tell to which order of women she belongs to and will even place her into her approximate valuation range, just as a perceptive woman will recognize a man of "style and substance"—a man who she knows "will behave." A man's assessment of a woman will express itself in his mind as a valuation coefficient and will tell him whether a woman is worth the price he would be expected to meet (the equivalent of his own opportunity cost) in the market for her particular order. Clearly, a man's "capacity to pay" represents the ultimate limit beyond which he will not be able to reach, however much he may be lusting after her. Only very few men in any of the lower orders will possess the means and the qualities that will be required if they were to reach up successfully for women coming from an order higher than their own.

The sexonomic valuation coefficient will also inform a competing man about the basic qualities of a particular woman as a lifetime "investment"—her combination of reason, sexuality, and the touch of Midas. The science of Sexonomics will postulate (as discussed in "Male Sexonomic Players: The Five Orders of Men," above) that men will, during the acquisitive period in their lives, seek to move up to the order that they deem commensurate with their natural talents and market-tested sexonomic qualities. These men will also seek to create the institutions that will be required in order to guarantee for themselves a free entry into any of these sexonomic markets (orders)—institutions that will also sustain their desire for self-protection and self-perpetuation. Once in their appropriate market for a few years, these men will proceed to develop a clear perception of the quality of women in their order counterpart and will know what kinds of short-run or even lifetime costs and prices they will have to incur to secure for themselves the enjoyment of that particular woman with whom sharing in sexuality and creating a joint lifetime sexonomic utility function would not only be a lot of fun but also the reasonable thing to do.

For example, the Quintessential-man will know why the Lotus-woman's sexonomic valuation coefficient ranges in the nineties and why he would be enticed, without hesitation, into matching her sexonomic valuation with his. The whole process of thought involving the getting together of woman and man in the higher orders not only involves reason but also reveals itself as a highly meaningful human experience; it also bears out the expectations concerning a lifetime's worth of happiness.

This thinking process demonstrates that there is much more to women and men "falling in love" and wishing to build a life together than only their outpouring of loin heat–generated feelings.

Sexonomics cannot visualize a situation in which higher-order men will seek to affiliate permanently with lower-order women (neither, for that matter, a permanent linkage between a higher-order woman and a lower-order man!). Yet we are faced with the need to explain the frequent sexonomic ritual of higher-order men seeking to fornicate with lower-order women and of higher-order women seeking the same experience with lower-order men (both at a cost always lower than that involving women/men of their own orders). Is it lust and curiosity rather than reason? Or could it not possibly be the uncontrollable remnants of a primeval force which will break out from underneath the thin layer of modern civilization as a volcanic outpouring of passion, with which even Lotus-women and Quintessential-men may have difficulties coping—a situation that is beyond "sinning" or "immorality" (terms whose subjective meanings do not permit an objective testing in any of the five sexonomic markets)?

Sexonomic Value: Female

The sexonomic value of a human female is the subjective measure that underlies the calculation of her sexonomic valuation coefficient (the *objective* measure being the sexonomic price).

The human female's sexonomic value is her intrinsic capacity to satisfy the human male's sexonomic needs. In its basic essence, the female sexonomic value reflects the following qualities of women, as viewed by men:

- esthetics
- commitment
- steadfastness
- material well-being
- creativity
- approbation
- capacity to grow
- sexuality (the Lady LUSSEY's three qualities)
- tenderness
- sympathy
- multidimensionality

Higher-order men will always know the value of the women in their order counterparts, but they will also be cognizant of the values of lower-order women since all these qualities reveal and reflect the women's breeding, upbringing, and sexonomic experience. The perceived sexonomic values of women are a subjective assessment, but they may be measured because they are revealed by the experience of the real-life linkages between women and men in the sexonomic markets and, therefore, of their successes or failures. These values are different for the different orders of women; in fact, each of the orders of women has a range of variations of its own. When faced with a woman, an experienced man will recognize which particular sexonomic market is her own domain.

However, men's perception of the sexonomic values of women is subject to all kinds of manipulation on the part of the women themselves. Women, starting in their adolescence, will consciously seek to develop their talents and bring to full bloom all their endowments in attempting to take on the men in the various sexonomic markets. They will also wish to move up to the next higher order of women—an undertaking that may last a lifetime and may require not only the acquisition but also the demonstration of the ability to convince the bidding men that a woman's perceived value is a fair reflection of that woman's particular sexonomic price.

Sexonomic Price: Female

The sexonomic price of a human female is the equivalent which the men must disburse in seeking to secure for themselves the enjoyment of the sexonomic utility of their particular female partners. This price may be measured in outright pecuniary terms (so many dollars in a particular relationship or during an individual's lifetime), but it may also properly be thought of in terms of opportunity cost—that is, the total cost to the bidding male. This cost includes the following major items: the use of a man's material means, the wear and tear of his person, the need to compromise, and the negative psychological factors, viz. curtailment of his freedom with respect to other women, pressures arising from finding himself tied down, aggravation from her higher development capacity over time, and the whole set of worries which emanate from a long-term relationship (including children and what to do with them).

Clearly, for a man to select a woman and make her his longtime mate, the benefits must prevail over the costs, a rationalization which is centered in reason but which may be heavily influenced by the "irrationality of the heart." Sexonomic reasoning proposes that these net benefits derive from the quality of the three major characteristics and the eight imbedded conditions of women. For the men of the two highest orders, intercourse is never the primary objective, even though begetting offspring may be a major consideration, especially if both partners are somewhat older and still without children.

The sexonomic price of a human female is a function of the scarcity and quality of women (particularly those of the two highest orders), of the number of available substitutes (also among adjoining orders), of a particular woman's own personal mystique (which is rendered visible in the marketing of her person), and of the bidding male's personal sexonomic utility needs. Evidently, this price will be the highest for the Lotus-woman and ordinarily the lowest for the Elephant-woman but on many occasions lower still for the Vampire-woman (especially, as we have already noted, in her state of reoccurring sexonomic market depression).

This price may be short-term or long-run, the former always being the lower one, since nonpermanence is implied (as well as the acute possibility of a woman's sexonomic interest in other competing men). This lower price is also explained by the lesser commitment, on the part of the bidding male, of effort, of personal and material means, and of fealty (for what may turn out to have been only a temporary liaison).

There is a range of prices for every order of women since, even within a particular order, qualities are different and relative scarcities also play an important role (clearly, in cities where women outnumber men by a ratio of two to one, women's sexonomic prices will be lower than, say, in pioneering areas in which the men vastly outnumber the women). But in the short run, these prices may vary quite significantly, depending on the relative numbers of women and men and on the ease or difficulty of entering a particular sexonomic market. The long-run price itself may be termed the "natural price"; it is expected to correspond to the true valuation of women within each of the five orders. This is so because, in the markets for sexonomic linkages, human rationality will preclude the possibility of overpaying or underbidding; in the long run, the men will have to expect a fair or adequate return, or else they will not wish to commit themselves.

Interestingly, however, a dichotomy has developed in modern society with respect to the sexonomic valuation of women. On the one hand, the quality of women's natural endowment and acquired skills has vastly increased (at least high-school education and therefore most likely higher-quality partnership and motherhood), illustrated by rising expertise and professionalism (including regular salary checks), higher-level culture (including general hygiene, body care, and dietary habits), and better health. On the other hand, the expressly more libertarian attitudes of women have brought about a general depreciation or devaluation of almost all women's sexonomic values and prices. This is so because, unlike about two generations ago, men no longer need to put as much effort into "conquering" women; in consequence, the sexonomic valuation coefficients of women have experienced a decline. Almost all women have, by now, engaged literally in massive sexual activity as if they were attempting to catch up with the men. As a result, men's opportunity cost of securing for themselves the desired woman in the respective sexonomic market has decreased (with the possible exception of Lotus-women).

However, this trend may well reverse itself in the near future; a novel situation has arisen which has already caused the depreciation of women's sexonomic valuations to slow down and even to be brought to a halt in the case of Art-women—the increasing participation of women in the labor force as a function of their desire to secure for themselves independent sources of income and to liberate themselves from their historical bondage and reliance on the men's earning capacity. This evolution has become an important consideration for competing males and represents an inducement for them to intensify their efforts (and even to expend a higher material or personal opportunity cost) in seeking to secure for themselves their particular females. However, as we have seen in our study of Vampire-women, a notable exception from this general slowdown or even reversal of women's sexonomic valuations has become visible; a significant percentage of professional women, especially in corporate ranks and in the entertainment industry, have manifested an increasing inability to attract permanent male partners and have had to resort to the purchase of sexual services provided by male drones, of men who are typical of the order of Girandole-men with their single-minded sex-for-sale view on life.

The pricing of women's sexonomic valuations in the long run forms part and parcel of the "great societal bidding strategy," which may take the form of brides-for-sale arrangements in "traditional societies" to dowries in former empires and nineteenth-century bourgeois circles, and in the top layers of contemporary capitalism, to participation in sexonomic games, with the following characteristics on the part of both women and men—expressed theatrical performance, rising expertise in marketing one's sexuality, rationalizations about successes and failures, schools and research centers for human sexonomic behavior, and continuous empirical testing (dating agencies, the bar scene, blind dates, "one-night stands," wife—and husband-swapping, outright "gang bangs," and a massive public outpouring of pornography).

At present, we are, in fact, evolving toward a society in which an educated and experienced adult female will be expected to know by the time she is twenty-five years old the makings of her own sexonomic valuation, component weights (as well as those of her competing lady friends!), and the expected level and range of her lifetime sexonomic utility (happiness) function. And starting at about the age of fifteen, she will "have had" scores of men. By her midtwenties, the modern woman will have learned that a "high price" means a "high exchange value," which valuation may take an enormous effort to achieve and an incessant need to demonstrate and to market (in the face of forever tougher competition). But they will also know, if ranked at the "low price" end of the scale, that they will not only have to keep intercourse in check but will also have to work awfully hard in order not to fail to develop and to market the natural endowments with which they were born and to secure for themselves the highest possible sexonomic valuation.

We also observe that the sexonomic price of younger women will be higher than that of older women (all their qualities and all other circumstances considered equal), even though the set of older women is more likely to be wealthier than the set of younger women. This phenomenon may be as much the consequence of all men preferring younger women (with their supposedly less utilized and therefore better "preserved" LUSSEYs and with the younger women's "fertility premium" monopoly) as the effect of the increasing disproportion of older women to older men in all of the respective orders. The interest which older men will at times have in younger women will be a well-noticed addition to the younger men's demand, but it will not significantly increase the sexonomic price of the whole set of younger women, even though the older men of the higher orders are well endowed and willing to spend a lot in seeking to play out this illusion of youth and of forever enduring performance. All younger women are aware of the fact that they represent potentially precious "hunting grounds" for the wealthier older men of the higher orders, and many female university graduates and aspiring professionals will make themselves available, even though only the exceptional ones will succeed in *permanently* swapping their sexuality for instant wealth. Even so, what used to be an exquisitely played sexonomic strategy by Madame de Pompadour types has, by now, developed into a massive attempt at "social climbing," especially by young Conch-women whose assortment of women's "wiles" will secure them remarkable success with all men except those of the Quintessential order. Clearly, these younger women will command an instantaneous significant sexonomic price increment for their conception-and-delivery quality if these wealthy older men absolutely insist on securing for themselves at least one heir.

The Sexonomic Utility Function: Female

The sexonomic utility function of a human female measures and reveals the lump sum total of sexonomic enjoyments and benefits which accrue to her during her lifetime. Quantifiable in pecuniary terms, this measure demonstrates the human female's biological and material success (or lack of thereof) in marketing her sexuality. Generally speaking, this function starts at a high level in reflecting the men's sexonomic valuation of a female adolescent. However, this function is then expected to decline, slowly or rapidly, depending on the particular order of women—beginning with the metamorphosis of the virgin into full womanhood, this decline will go on gradually until menopause and will then fall more rapidly. We must note, though, that every woman may, by sheer personal effort, succeed in slowing down this rate of decline; as a matter of fact, she may even raise the level of the whole function above the average for her particular order, and she may even move up to the level of the next higher order of women (particularly if she proves exquisitely astute in marketing her enticement-and-control quality).

Sexonomic Valuation Index: Male

The sexonomic valuation index of a human male measures the marketability of the estimated value of a man's sexuality (including his Sir MOJJ, the Three Ps) and material circumstances. This index refers to all orders of men, with the highest coefficient for the Quintessential-man and the lowest for the Mob-man.

Arriving at this measure, we must emphasize that it serves the purpose of assessing how women view men in their desire to avail themselves of their "ultimate" male partner and to experience maximum happiness. This measure applies in sexonomic markets in which the respective women order counterparts make up the demanders. This measure is also meant to assist men in their own quest to improve on their sexonomic "rating," with the intention to qualify for higher-order women and their sexuality and material means.

In its essence, the sexonomic valuation index for men forms the basis for men's participation in sexonomic strategies and games; in fact, this measure also constitutes an objective indicator of a man's chances to succeed (or his chances of failure) in his attempt to secure for himself a quality female of an appropriate caliber or even to aspire to "move up to and secure for himself" a higher-order female.

The sexonomic valuation index of human males ranges from a low of –20 (minus twenty) to a high of 100 (one hundred). The valuation index comprises three major characteristics as well as a set of imbedded sexonomic conditions. Clearly, each of these has their own sexonomic market–determined weight for each of the five orders of men. The major sexonomic characteristics of men are as follows: capacity to reason (intelligence and education); enticement to arouse the sexual desires of women (sexiness); and endowment in material assets, viz. wealth, liquid assets, productive inputs, expectation of high-income flows, and astuteness in managing them (Midas touch).

The set of ten imbedded sexonomic conditions for quality men involve the following (much more so for higher-order men than for lower-order men):

Masculine elegance, charm, touch, goal-getting competitiveness, comradeship, cleanliness, natural aptitude to grow and to be on top of things, control of horses and other men, desire to make and feed his babies and to wash their diapers.

Expressed in terms that are empirically verifiable, the sexonomic valuation index of men is presumed to exist in every informed woman's mind, in particular of those women who had gone through shorter or extended periods of courtship in one or several sexonomic markets and had proceeded to the ultimate goal—consummation. Viewed in this sense, the SEVAC of a particular male, or the average SEVAC of an order of men, will inform a competing woman specifically about the quality of a particular man or of the average male in an order of men and will, therefore, permit her to assess whether it will be worth her while to engage in the whole range of sexonomic strategies and games and eventually proceed to pay his "acquisition price."

The range of the sexonomic valuation coefficients which includes all orders of men is as follows:

Order of men:	Sexonomic Valuation Coefficient:
Quintessential	90 - 100
Lace	70 - 85
Vulpine	40 - 65
Mob	20 - 35
Girandole	-20 - +60

The overall valuation of the sexonomic characteristics and imbedded conditions of Quintessential-men has been market-tested and adds up to the highest total for all men—90–100 SEVACs. Of this total, 60 percent constitute the main sexonomic characteristics, while the remaining 40 percent account for an unequal proportion of the total value of the imbedded sexonomic conditions. Interestingly, Lotus-women's ranking of the main characteristics of Quintessential-men differs quite significantly from that of Art-women. For the Lotus-woman, Quintessential-men's reason and the Midas touch are about of equal significance, 25 SEVACs each; whereas she accords her man's sexiness at only a paltry value of 10 SEVACs. In comparison, the Art-woman's valuation of the Quintessential-man's sexiness is much higher—25 SEVACs—the consequence of her conviction that the highest-order men are the world's greatest lovers. The Lotus-woman explains this discrepancy by declaring that (her) Quintessential-man's sexiness is always perfect, for which reason they do not crave it as much but that they can also "do without it" and still be totally happy since "this is what they have their control function for" while fully enjoying his other superb qualities.

For Lace-men, the scale of weighting is correspondingly lower; women of the two highest orders know the difference between the absolutely highest valuations of Quintessential-men and the lower valuations of Lace-men. The three main sexonomic characteristics make up exactly one-half of the total valuation, reason accounting for a maximum of 20 SEVACs, sexiness for 16, and the Midas touch for 15. The imbedded sexonomic conditions make up a maximum total of 34 SEVACs or a value of 4.25 points each. The lower end of the scale amounts to a total of 70 SEVACs (the components of which are correspondingly adjusted for the lower-valuation limits in this order of men).

Vulpine-men's sexonomic valuation is lower still since their overall qualities are substantially inferior to those of the Lace-men. In consequence, the weight of all three major sexonomic characteristics constitutes a diminution—a maximum of

12 for reason, 13 for sexiness, and 10 for the Midas touch. These lower relatives express the valuations of the sexonomic market-tested experience of the bidding females from the order of Conch-women. These women know what kind of value they are "buying"—a high valuation of the Vulpine-man's sexiness (remember, he is very good "at it" and also so "marvelously robustly enduring"!). The relatively low valuation of Vulpine-men's Midas touch is due to his financial uncertainties; these men tend to sacrifice substantial funds and assets running after the rarely available Lady LUSSEY of those Art-women who desire the experience of a Vulpine-man's vehemently masculine pukkacity as well as an occasionally remarkable sensitiveness but still insist on a very high "courting fee."

Lacking the top-order qualities of "masculine elegance" and "charm," the maximum of the remaining imbedded sexonomic conditions of Vulpine-men amounts to a total of 30 SEVACs; of this total, the remaining top five (touch, goal-getting competitiveness, comradeship, cleanliness, and natural ability to grow) suffer a higher discount than the bottom three (to be on top of things, to wash diapers, and to wash dishes). Nevertheless, Conch-women typically enjoy the presence of Vulpine-men (their natural sexonomic partners), possibly because the majority of the women of this order usually suffer with the (non-market-tested) illusion that Vulpine-men are in all respects equal to the members of the order of Lace-men.

The sexonomic valuation of Mob-men is based on the evidence of visibly inferior talent and forms of behavior. In spite of the accumulation of significant assets on the part of the shrewd and ruthless Mob-men of business, entertainment, and government, their overall sexonomic valuation coefficient cannot rise higher than the total of 35 SEVACs. Of these, shrewdness commands not more than 10, sexuality not more than 5 (mainly because of its disgustingly vile nature), and only 5 for their incessant but crude striving to provide themselves with the brutalizing means of economic and financial power.

The Mob-man's low sexuality coefficient is explained by the fact that even Elephant-women know that Mob-men, in their insatiable greed, will cause intercourse to be an unpleasant and often painful experience. In regard to the imbedded conditions, the Mob-man, on the whole, will never reach the maximum SEVACs of 15; this is so because he is completely lacking in four of the primary imbedded qualities (masculine elegance, charm, touch, and natural ability to grow and be on top of things), barely possesses even a semblance of any of the additional three (cleanliness, goal-getting competitiveness, desire to feed babies and change diapers), and scores only on comradeship by sticking closely to his own kind. Moreover, he will never reject the opportunity to swap his sexuality for a gain in income.

The order of Girandole-men has the lowest sexonomic valuation range, which is explained by the fact that these men make their livelihood by bartering their sexuality for instant cash, whereby Vampire-women constitute their primary source of income. Even though very intelligent (for a potential weight of 20 SEVACs in their rarely attained highest sexonomic valuation of 60), their coefficient for reason is usually heavily discounted because sex for barter constitutes their primary mental preoccupation; often, they lose all of these 20 valuation points because, as lovers for hire, they represent poor investment and because the bidding women simply do not wish to have a permanent relationship with this kind of man. In addition, and unlike their main sexonomic clients—Vampire-women, some of whose members can accumulate significant wealth out of their various business engagements—typical Girandole-men have no assets to speak of because their earnings are fully taken up by their vicarious consumption of luxuries in their periods of high income (when, in years of economic expansion, Vampire-women indulge in sexonomic spending sprees), while they disburse their meager savings during the prolonged dry seasons of economic recessions.

Perceptive of Girandole-men's dronelike lifestyles and knowledgeable of the forever uncertain state of their problems of sustenance, Art-women and Conch-women would never accord these men more than the lowest long-run negative valuation of –20, even though the overall range of 80 SEVACs in itself indicates that these men have the potential to generate happiness. When times are good, they command premium prices from free-spending Vampire-women, when their SEVAC for sexuality hits a peak of 15, while their suddenly increased cash flow generates the illusion of real wealth and accounts for the remaining 13 points. However, their civility and charm are but an illusion and are recognized as such by the women of the higher orders, with the appropriate valuation discount in their sexonomic utility function.

A Note on the Sexonomic Valuation Coefficient of Men

Clearly, for a woman, the sexonomic valuation coefficient represents a basis for perhaps the most important rationalization of her life, a thought process truly reminiscent of a calculated investment decision. A woman's capacity to pay the equivalent in seeking to secure for herself an individual male from a particular order of men involves her own personal traits and talents, which reflect her order affiliation. But it also derives from her rational use, especially of her own enticement-and-control quality. Her capacity to pay also includes material assets (formerly in the form of a dowry but presently more and more as her own capacity to earn independent income). An intelligent woman will never wish to extend herself beyond the limits of her capacity, however much she may be lusting after a particular man (if she did, her act would amount to an overvaluation of that man's sexonomic qualities). An intelligent woman's sexonomic rationality will simply not allow such a devaluation of her own sexonomic qualities because she would inevitably suffer a general decrease of her sexonomic valuation in the eyes of all men. If a woman continuously seeks to compensate a man with a sexonomic price that is higher than his sexonomic valuation coefficient calls for, she would, in fact, give away far too cheaply the three qualities of her Lady LUSSEY.

The science of Sexonomics recognizes that there are still enormous constraints on women's upward mobility and that women will have much greater difficulty rising to the next higher order of women—unless they decide to take a calculated risk by making their Lady LUSSEYs more readily available to the bidding men while covering their position by strongly reasserting the primacy of their reason over their enticement quality.

Sexonomics postulates that, unlike the men, many women in the orders lower than that of Lotus-women are not comfortable in their particular state and that they have a tremendous urge—which often expresses itself in the quest for the accumulation of material assets—to move up to the next higher order, in the course of which strategy they only too often and too willingly open their LUSSEYs to higher-order men, with the consequence of devaluation and even lifetime tragedy. But really intelligent women know the true value of their personal sexonomic valuation coefficient as well the valuation coefficients of the men who constitute their primary source of supply; in fact, these women know exactly what quality of men to bargain for and in which sexonomic valuation range. They will also know the cost to themselves of the realization and enjoyment of their personal lifetime sexonomic utility functions.

For example, the Lotus-woman knows why her valuation index falls in the highest range (90–100), and she will, therefore, realize that only the Quintessential-man can give her true equivalent exchange value. But unlike the Lotus-women, who are perfectly knowledgeable and wise in matters concerning men, lower-order women's valuations of orders of men will not be as perceptive or accurate because they simply do not possess that quality of knowledge. But they do share in the offsetting advantage which is not only germane to all women but also constitutes a very important strategic consideration—the premise that no man (which includes even the Quintessential-man) can resist the desire to indulge in a (delicately served) Lady LUSSEY—a natural inclination even in the most refined of men, which will guarantee the respective successfully scheming woman rapid advancement into the next higher order of women. All thinking lower-order women will always first seek to secure for themselves a man from the next higher order of men. Only if they prove unsuccessful will they settle for men from their own respective order equivalent.

By their natural instincts, experienced women seeking to "conquer" men that they desire will eventually offer to them their whole set of endowments, which will include any and all of the three qualities of the Lady LUSSEY. Unfortunately, the sheer disparity between the large number of women wishing to move higher and the small number of men still available in the higher orders will enable only the most talented (and possibly the most predatory) women to advance.

Faced with this enormous predicament, the individual woman from the lower orders will have to settle for the occasional bedding with a man from the higher orders, be it out of pure loving or just to satiate lust or in the quest for material gain. Since higher-order women will only very rarely seek to fornicate with lower-order men, this massive intrusion by lower-*order* women into the "proper hunting grounds" of higher-order women will not be tolerated by the latter, with the consequence of increasingly vicious infighting about accessibility and the eventual diminution of the sexonomic valuations of *all* women.

These reflections lead us to the recognition that women in general rationalize much more about the material means and total qualities of men (including their Three Ps) than most men do about the total qualities of women. This is so because, as we demonstrated above (see "The Fascinating World of Sexonomic Marketing and Success"), in their thought concerning *men as sex subjects*, quality women demand of men much more than just their sexuality—a fact that has not gone unnoticed in the world of quality men and has initiated a grand strategy toward improving the sexonomic valuation index of men in general.

Can this valuation be raised? It most certainly can, especially for Lace-men and for some Vulpine-men. How? In the purely biological sense, by seeking to enhance the performance of their Three Ps and, in the sexonomic sense, by the acquisition of substantial material assets or by exemplary success and leadership in the corridors of corporate or political power.

Sexonomic Value: Male

A human male's sexonomic value expresses his capacity to satisfy a human female's sexonomic needs. Higher-order women will always recognize the true value of the men in their order counterpart, but they will also be cognizant of the value of lower-order men—a matter of breeding, general experience in the ordinary business of life, and the lessons learned from being with the young men during their wild oats seeding years.

In its basic essence, male sexonomic value postulates the existence of a number of essential qualities. These qualities will either be inborn or will have been inbred through education, linkages in society (networking), or prolonged training in specialized institutions (the Sexonomic Institute). Sexonomics presumes that these qualities are "true and unadulterated" as the end effect of an upbringing which reflects the values and the freedoms of our kind of society, with its intellectual origins from the philosophers of ancient Greece, in particular of Aristotle. These fourteen fundamental qualities are specified as follows:

- esthetics
- charisma
- leadership
- sympathy
- optimal Three Ps

- tenderness
- creativeness
- courage
- understanding
- appreciation of material well-being

- relaxed casualness
- sense of commitment
- sense of approbation
- sense of chivalry

The perceived sexonomic values of men are subjective, but they are measurable because they are confirmed by the experience of real-life ties between women and men as well as by the women's forever thoughtful preoccupation with the lifestyles of successful men. The views of the women in their five orders concerning the men's sexonomic values differ from those of the men in their five respective orders. This is so because, in the minds of women, all men will likely be rendered accessible by the appropriate handling of the women's enticement-and-control function. When faced with a particularly interesting man, an experienced woman will not only instantly recognize to which order he belongs, but she will also have no apprehensions, feelings of insecurity, or qualms in making her approach and in playing up to the very best of her feminine mystique, her enticement-and-control quality.

Evidently, an intelligent male will seek to enhance his perceived sexonomic value. Starting in his late adolescence (always later for young males than for young females), he will consciously seek to develop his talents and will acquire experience in putting to best sexonomic use his natural endowments.

These preparations will specifically involve his Sir MOJJ and his Three Ps (let us recall that barely forty years ago, young men would normally go to whorehouses to part with their virginity and to learn "all about sex," which was then deemed the best preparation for instructing their future (and virgin) brides "how to do it"!. These efforts not only represent a man's lifetime commitment to health and exercise but also constitute an absolute requisite in needing to demonstrate to the bidding women that he is the "best buy." Seeking fully to develop his sexonomic qualities, a man will not only provide the bidding women with full value for the appropriate (and just) market price but will also maximize his own personal sexonomic utility by securing for himself the "best sexonomic deal." It takes so much more than just origin or breeding in order to become a successful competitor in sexonomic strategies and games.

Sexonomic Price: Male

The sexonomic price of a human male is the equivalent which a woman must give up in seeking to secure for herself the sole enjoyment of the sexuality and the material assets of a particular male—in other words, to share in a man's sexonomic utility function. This price may be measured in money or in terms of opportunity cost and is the function of the scarcity of men in a particular order and of their quality, the number of available substitutes, the market structure to which the order belongs, the numbers of competing women, and the particular women's sexonomic utility bouquet. The sexonomic price will be the highest for Quintessential-men and the lowest for Mob-men and Girandole-men. In the short term, this price may be higher or lower than the lifetime price (the long-term valuation coefficient), depending on the numbers of women and their intensity of demand for particular men's qualities of sexuality and for their material assets. But the short-run sexonomic price will normally bear a discount because nonpermanent links are implied (as well as the distinct possibility that a particular male's sexuality might also be used by other women). The price discount in the short run is also explained by the lesser effort on the part of the bidding female, which she will need to expend in seeking to secure for herself the short-term enjoyment of a particular male's sexuality "one-night stand" cost, at best; a few drinks and some tipping; vaginal spray; morning-after pill; cab fare; and perhaps also some strong mouthwash, not as a disinfectant but to rinse down the inevitable feeling of disgust with oneself.

Similar to the sexonomic valuation index for men, the range of prices for short-term liaisons as well as for enduring relationships will vary and will be highest for Quintessential-men and lowest for Mob-men and Girandole-men. But the price levels will be strongly influenced by the absolute numbers of women competing at any one time in the free sexonomic markets for the available number of men (an enormous social problem during and after major wars), which is true both in the short run and the long run.

Looking at the sexonomic valuations of women and men from the historical perspective, we note that the short-run and the long-run prices of women have, on the whole, been lower than those of men (as if women had always been less "precious")—a difference which may be attributed not only to the smaller numbers of men than women in each of the respective orders but also to the men's higher income-earning or asset-holding capacity. Simply speaking, it will always cost women more to secure for themselves a lifetime male partner than it has cost men to obtain for themselves their women. This higher long-run price of men is also explained by the overall improvement in the quality of men (physical: better food, more exercise, better health; mental: more education, higher skill levels, more entrepreneurial spirit; societal: more optimism, better organization). These qualities, as well as the longer life expectancy of women, have rendered women's investment into securing for themselves their own male partners a more expensive proposition relative to the investment costs to men of securing for themselves their women.

However, and contrary to our expectations, the greater liberalism in contemporary society has tended to increase even more (rather than equalize) the relative valuation of men versus women in spite of the latter's own increase in absolute valuations (for reasons similar to those of men, as explained in the above paragraph). The very combativeness of modern women has accorded to the Sir MOJJ a rising sexonomic valuation, which reflects his increasing relative scarcity value owing to the fact that increasing numbers of women now openly covet the Sir MOJJ as their ultimate object of pleasure. Unlike the surplus of available LUSSEYs that have been intercoursed with by many men, which has resulted in their devaluation, the Sir MOJJs' SEVACs are the highest ever.

In addition, we have confirmation of yet another consequence of contemporary liberalism—the deliberate road to nihilistic libertinism which most younger women have systematically chosen by engaging in sexual contact with large numbers of men before being hit by the urge to found a family. Except for its unforeseen negative consequence, most marriage-minded men will simply not adjust to this new situation, while the few remaining unmarried quality men will neither marry nor even cohabit with women whose auras are tainted by the whiff of "ill repute." In consequence, and in spite of their liberation from old forms of oppression, women appear today to be expending much more effort than ever before (absolutely as well as relative to men) in seeking to secure for themselves an appropriate and satisfactory partner for longer-term sexonomic linkages.

These reflections on men's sexonomic values and sexonomic prices lead us to one global conclusion: since the 1960s, the opportunity cost to women of "getting their men" has increased quite considerably in spite of the massive participation of women in the labor force and their acquisition of substantial sources of income and material assets. In addition, most women still remain mired in performing the triple duties of household, cohabitation, and husband-and-child care. Not only are women presently paying a much higher cost price in personal (e.g., free sex) and material goods in seeking to secure for themselves their "chosen mate," but their expending of all this extra time and energy has brought forth only a diminishing rate of success, as we shall attempt to explain below in the subchapter "Men as Sexonomic Subjects."

Sexonomic Utility Function: Male

The sexonomic utility function of a human male reveals the lump sum total of enjoyments and benefits which accrue to him during his lifetime as a result of the successful marketing of his sexuality. This function can be measured in quantifiable or pecuniary terms. Generally speaking, it starts low, indicating that women have little use for male virgins or otherwise inexperienced adolescent males, except for those young men who are known to own or to expect to inherit sizeable assets. But with late adolescence and the beginning of sexual activity as a young man, the human male's sexonomic utility function starts rising, at times even very steeply, for his manifestly untiring and uninhibited lower-order prolificity and wild boar–like rigidity of his MOJJ. In the life of a healthy and normally acquisitive male person, the sexonomic utility function will eventually level off in its rate of ascent and will hit the peak around his midfifties. Then, so much unlike the sexonomic utility functions of all *orders* of women in their respective members' postmenstrual state, the sexonomic utility functions of men will either continue to rise slightly or to level off but not decline significantly, depending on the material wealth of men in their respective *orders*. This is so because women below the order of Lotus-women will have always known how to express their preference and much higher sexonomic valuations for men with ample material means over those without such means. The respective orders' sexonomic happiness hearts portray visually the specifically quantifiable levels of female and male sexonomic utility functions.

Additional Insights

Those of our readers who have persevered with their reading and have by now become acquainted with the basic sexonomic terminology are now asked to proceed to assess their understanding by looking at our examples of sexonomic reasoning which follow below, after which we shall go on to draw a distinction between sexonomic reasoning and economic reasoning, sexology and Sexonomics, and sexonomic reasoning and philosophy.

Real-Life Examples of Sexonomic Reasoning

Shirley is not an ordinary woman; she has a law degree and works as a criminal lawyer. While doing law, she had quite a few affairs but has remained single. She has been planning to enter into politics and has already slept with a senior parliamentary assistant (who is married).

Michael is brilliant but of poor background. He is also very ambitious. He has no qualms using women to advance his career goals.

Mary is happy being a high-class prostitute and servicing "caliber" men because she wants to live well. Sophie is a street-level prostitute who has three children to support. Since both of these women are sex workers and pay their taxes, neither of them should be labeled "immoral."

Albert has an unusually potent MOJJ and earns very high income cohabiting with Vampire-women. In prosperous times, his sexonomic valuation coefficient is even one hundred, but it drop to zero during an economic depression. His long-run sexonomic happiness levels off at zero.

When the number of prostitutes doubles, their earnings will be cut in half (because their sexonomic valuation will be lowered by one-half).

If all wives in the lower orders withdrew their LUSSEYs from their husbands, the number and the incomes of prostitutes in those orders would inevitably increase.

The increase in the participation rate of women in the labor force boosts their incomes, which will shift upward their sexonomic utility functions. But working full-time will lead to their less frequent and less satisfying lovemaking and will therefore decrease their sexonomic valuations.

The feminist slogan "Women should be free to do with their bodies as they please" has nothing to do with morals, ethics, or equality since it reveals the intensive desire of women to secure the highest possible material return from marketing their sexuality without having to worry about unwanted pregnancies.

If men are compelled to do household chores after a full day's work in the office or factory, their passion quality will decline, leaving their wives discontented and inducing them to fool around.

Men and women who know how to enjoy exquisite sex and should pay a sexonomic excise tax.

While it takes only a little money to buy a lot of low-quality sex, pure love cannot be had for money—which is why it results in an exceptional quality of sexuality. However, the latter will experience a demise when the material circumstances of the two lovers suffers a deterioration.

Cheating on one's spouse is wrong—whether the "cocheater" is wealthier or poorer than the spouse.

"Thou shalt not covet thy neighbor's wife" is a commandment that makes no sense because it is contrary to human nature; clearly, disobeying this commandment makes practical sense as it leads to very satisfying sexuality.

Since the president is also the commander-in-chief, to appear credible as a male to his millions of soldiers, he must engage in continuous demonstrations of his potency even while on the job—a setting that is clearly contrary to the moral requisites for ordinary citizens.

The long-run increase in the proportion of women to men will inevitably diminish the sexonomic valuations of women and raise the sexonomic valuations of men, with dire consequences on women's equal rights to life, liberty, and happiness.

While women's sexuality is generally aroused when romanticizing about trysts with men in power, men's sexual impulses generally abate when faced with powerful women.

CHAPTER FIVE

Sexonomics, Social Sciences, and Humanities: Comparative Definitions

Sexonomics and Economics

In most instances of objective inquiry, Sexonomics is like economics; both are practical and theoretical fields of analysis, except that Sexonomics adds human sexuality to the economists' premise of material welfare. Both social sciences seek empirical verification concerning material means and welfare, but Sexonomics also researches human sexuality and its linkage with material means. Just like economics, Sexonomics seeks to provide the scope and the forum for objective debate, but its concerns are the quest for the attainment of both ample material means and fulfilling sexuality.

Just like economics, Sexonomics considers the lifestyles of human males and females as individuals who interact in the quest to maximize their happiness in competitive structures, which give rise to quantifiable magnitudes—values, prices, utility functions, valuation coefficients, private pleasures, and social costs.

However, Sexonomics is also very much unlike economics. Sexonomics does not assign to human beings qualities that they do not possess; neither does it consider human behavior as "perfect." Sexonomics is not ashamed to inquire into matters concerning human sexuality since it views the latter neither as moral or immoral but as a natural inclination as well as a primary driving force. As a modern original and innovative inquiry, Sexonomics does not suffer from the infighting between conflicting schools of thought; it bears no allegiance to apostles or prophets and is subject to no taboos or dogmas, and it wishes government not to interfere in the goings-on in the five sexonomic markets. Neither does it believe in saints or sinners; instead, it engages in the analysis of human feeling and human loving in a real world in which reason, sexuality, and material self-interest are viewed as natural complements.

Sexonomists have no qualms whatsoever talking about human sexuality and its material environment, and they believe that experimentation and an objective assessment of this linkage is not only privately rewarding but also socially and economically of great value. The analytical linkage between economics and Sexonomics is easily understood; while the former rationalizes about the market conditions and the behavior of individuals which will lead to value creation and price determination, the latter seeks to explore the human element, the goings-on in the sexonomic psyches of women and men, and the superstructure in which the subjective, the loving, is fused with the objective, the calculating.

Sexonomics and Sexology

Sexonomics is totally unlike sexology since the latter studies theories about human sexuality as a psychobiological phenomenon with emphasis on problems and disorders arising from this kind of human interaction. Sexonomics explores how human sexonomic welfare can be maximized. It recognizes that sexual activity is tied to materialistic considerations and advocates that human beings go on to consider the investment into enhancing their sexual marketability as one of the essential undertakings in life, one which is expected to lead to fulfillment and happiness. Studying Sexonomics and being trained in the arts of sexonomic behavior will most likely reduce the risk of ever having to go to and consult a sexologist.

Sexonomics and Philosophy/Religion

Sexonomics views philosophy and religion with a sense of detachment because they have often been used for manipulation and indoctrination. Sexonomics views humankind as they are and how they go about maximizing happiness in the secular world. Based on openness and trust, Sexonomics recognizes the primacy of the genius of the human mind and considers individuals fully capable of making their own choices and of being personally accountable for their decisions. Unlike the misrepresentations of the past, which led to prejudice and created in us enormous feelings of guilt, Sexonomics submits that human sexuality and human loving are natural inclinations that cannot be detached from our material environment. They are the individuals' private domain and must not be subjected to control by those who, in their own self-deception, claim to "know better."

But Sexonomics also represents a new thought pattern about life and the human condition, one in which sexuality and material values are not anymore viewed as sinful or immoral undertakings but are indeed considered part and parcel of our inner self and, therefore, as immensely powerful expressions of what is so truly human about ourselves.

Sexonomics and Equilibrium

In Sexonomics, the notion of "equilibrium" implies a balanced relation in the togetherness of two human beings of the opposite sex, with particular emphasis on two main aspects of human behavior—the sexual and the material. In the societal sense, sexonomic equilibrium means that human sexual preferences in the social context are free to find their balance with human materialistic inclinations and that there must be institutions that will make possible this balancing process.

In dealing with the notion of sexonomic equilibrium, we must distinguish between three sexonomic time zones—the shortest, the normal, and the longest. The shortest is the most restricted when viewed against the backdrop of the more permanent external factors, some of which have been severely inhibiting (for example, those which have made for deeply imbedded feelings of guilt). The longest is considered the most flexible period, one in which all factors making for sexuality and material self-interest are free to adjust. This is so because the time period is deemed long enough to lead to the disappearance of the inhibiting factors—on the assumption that, in the long run, human reason will be brought into balance with nature, natural freedom will win out over the manipulation of humans, and natural forces (which include human sexuality) will be allowed to find their balance with the human material environment.

Sexonomic Equilibrium: The Short Run

In the short run, equilibrium means that woman and man get together in order to engage in sexual intercourse, even though many external factors may speak or work against such action (moral, religious, legal, etc.). This getting together may occur on impulse ("reciprocal loin heat") or may happen over an exchange of material means (especially money) in return for sex. Whichever may be the motive, the partners' desire is the quick attainment of (presumably) joint pleasure and the instantaneous maximization of sexonomic utility. In the short run, factors external to a couple's need to fornicate are considered as given (income levels, background, education, religion, etc.) and are often viewed as inhibiting or prohibiting forces, even though they may be more than offset by the intensity of the lust and/or the monetary capacity to buy privacy and "do it" covertly.

In the short run, interorder fornication is a distinct possibility, especially between the lower-order women and men. We must note, though, that this run does not necessitate the allocation of significant funds or resources and that the incurred opportunity costs are small; women and men get together, fornicate, and seek to maximize their instantaneous sexonomic pleasures (often even without any commitment to induce pleasure in their partner), then the clean up and part ways.

We should note that Sexonomics will not view this situation as moral or immoral; rather, it implies that a voluntary contract exists between two consenting adults, a contract which is directly linked to sexonomic rationality (the expectations of gains in utility; the cost of motels, meals, condoms, douches, etc.) and the quest for both pleasure and material reward. Since humankind has always been "doing it"—an infinite number of extramarital relations included—we may conclude that we do these things because they lead to net gains in short-run private utility and may therefore be viewed as constituting a net increment in social welfare. In this sense, and unlike the many outdated but still enforced teachings and proclamations, Sexonomics views the attainment of short-run equilibria as a normal form of human interaction, especially if equal consent by the participating women and men may be presumed. Necessarily, Sexonomics views prostitution as a particular example of the rational human quest that seeks to experience short-term pleasure and short-term pecuniary gains which are equally shared between the participating individuals. Viewed in this particular sense, the prohibition of prostitution not only goes contrary to human reason but also abrogates human natural freedom.

Sexonomic Equilibrium: The Normal Run

In the normal run, individual equilibrium is the result of a woman and a man getting together with the intention of sexonomic interaction over a longer period of time, possibly in the expectation of founding a family. Such action implies a commitment to pool the material resources and to share in personal endowments since a longer-term sexonomic interaction is tantamount to a joint investment venture with its rationality and the tradeoff between benefits and costs. The term *normal* refers to a medium standard for the duration of such linkages, which begins with the initiation period (presently the time that elapses between the first sexual contact and the wedding ceremony) and ends with the dissolution of the marriage (through a divorce or the death of one of the partners). A longer linkage will clearly invoke a greater commitment of material resources and personal endowments and will also involve a higher opportunity cost (for example, the loss of the official freedom to mate with other partners).

In contrast to the short run's temporary or intermittent linkages, the normal run presupposes a maximization of sexonomic utility over time (an increasing function) since permanence is presumed and since marriage is (at least initially) considered a lifetime investment for both. In consequence, sexonomic rationality requires that compatibility between the partners be established (background, culture, language, education, income levels, growth capacity, religion, etc.) and societal sanction be obtained as expressions of moral codes of social conduct and, therefore, bases for social stability. Cultures in which prearranged marriages are customary are the best examples of applied social sexonomic rationality.

Unlike the short-run linkage, in which the woman's enticement function and pleasure quality are expected to win out over her control function, in the normal-run situation, the woman's control quality exerts the dominating influence. This function is conditioned by her affiliation with her particular order and its codes of conduct (see Lotus-woman versus Elephant-woman), her personal sexonomic valuation, her expectations with respect to the state of happiness concerning her sexuality and material benefits (that is, her sexonomic utility function), and the scarcity of competing men in her respective order counterpart. The men themselves will have to reflect the comparative status of their particular order as well as the Three Ps of their Sir MOJJs.

If all normal-run linkages (including common-law) were stable (requisites for normal-run stability: adequate material means, loving and caring attitude, trust, reciprocally equal giving, equivalent development capacity, a sense of joint investment into the adventure of a lifetime) and therefore enduring, then the ninth commandment would become redundant and moralists would be able to sit back and relax. However, stable linkages are of detriment to some sectors of the economy since stability means contentment and lack of dynamism and leads to decreases in consumption on sexonomic goods and services.

Until recently, marriages in general were expected to last through the entire normal run, which means that the official rules of the game were considered as given and binding, that couples were presumed to pursue virtuous lifestyles based on the work ethic and that the masses would consider the rules of behavior as given or as changing only imperceptibly. Looked at with the eyes of the officials of government, society was kept in equilibrium with a mix of religious and legal restraints. But while these moral standards were applied to the common woman and man, the leading circles considered themselves free to indulge in double standards—select markets for human flesh and its products, polygamy by kings and kaisers, debauchery and corruption by high-ranking churchmen, and eventually, the emergence of the universal view of women as sex objects with the appropriate markets and price tags, from the reigning queen to the lowest-class whore. The ruling classes permitted themselves to indulge in this system of double standards while they were officially adhering to canon law and the self-proclaimed social laws of morality. But with time passing, they were finding themselves unable to control the rapidly expanding underground mass market in "sin" and proceeded to enforce upon the masses the palliatives of confession, penance, and absolution, coupled most recently with fines and jail terms for soliciting, in the hope to enable society to maintain this dual system of morality in a delicate state of normal-run balance—even though at the cost of continuous repression.

Presently, however, these rigorous official standards have been relaxed in response to the relentless pressure on the part of the masses who wish to enjoy freedoms equal to those women and men who were ruling over them. By now, the number of enforcers of public morality has been diminished, and the notion that equal human rights have nothing to do with God, coupled with the emergence of the principles of free will and personal accountability, has been generally accepted and codified. The set of double standards—originally the result of the powerful few subjecting the many to fear and repression—has been gradually transformed into the political message of true equality. In the course of this evolution, the rise of feminism has accorded women equal political clout; penance has become the personal responsibility of the individual; and the relaxation of divorce laws has not only diminished the number of concubinages but has also become the main driving force of the rapidly expanding sexonomic markets.

Unfortunately, however, the rise in liberalism has not only brought to the surface the existence of the (previously underground) markets in "sin goods" but has also contributed to the vast expansion of their overt operations; size, volume, and dollar revenue have multiplied while large-scale prostitution has become rampant as a subsidiary means of gaining income during economic emergencies. This relaxation has brought the profit motive into this vast market and, with it, contemporary manifestations of rational business conduct in an otherwise illegal type of enterprise—efficiency, price-fixing, limited entry, monopoly control, bribery and protection rackets, extortion, money laundering, and the sexploitation of children.

On the one hand, even the individual from the masses has become free to make her/his choices with respect to sexual enjoyment and material self-interest; however, on the other hand, this transition from the era of prohibitions to that of permissiveness has left society with an enormous behavioral dilemma concerning the direction of this evolution. Even though individual sexonomic utility maximization in each of the recent normal runs has, by now, become the (new) societal norm, we are now faced with the question of the long-run purpose of this evolution. How do sexonomists view this problem? As biosocial scientists, sexonomists are optimistic; they are fully committed to human freedom and human progress.

Sexonomic Equilibrium: The Long Run

In the long run, the time period is deemed long enough to allow for profound changes in the public perception of individual freedom and its codification, in the evolution of standards of behavior that are now fairly equally binding (even upon the socioeconomic elite) and in the gradual and officially endorsed withdrawal of the enforcers of public morality into the backdrop of their own frustrations concerning the linkages between human sexuality and material gain. In the long run, the individual is seen moving toward the attainment of full freedom in her/his choice on the road to sexonomic happiness.

Sexonomics constitutes the intellectual expression of these freedoms, as well as the means, toward the rational pursuit (versus the manipulated fear of "sin") of natural sexual enjoyment and the maximization of material welfare. In this run, equilibrium means two things: for the individual, a lifestyle which permits two consenting adults to seek and to attain maximum sexonomic happiness without having to fear condemnation, persecution, or the so-called wrath of God (or better still, that of His "enforcers"); for society, it means the recognition that there cannot be human progress unless the so-called moral imperatives from the bygone era of ignorance and superstition have finally been discarded and replaced by the freedom of humankind to use their reason in the quest to maximize their sexonomic utility functions—from the regimentation of the many by the self-seeking few to a single set of rules of conduct for everyone. Long-run equilibrium cannot be attained if there continues to be one legal system but two sets of rules of moral conduct (i.e., if society does not allow itself to adjust to and to grow along with our perceived intellectual, physical, and sexual needs and if it fails to align these needs with the laws of nature).

APPENDICES

Appendix One: A Note on the Sexonomics Institute

The Sexonomic Institute is a privately funded organization whose main task is to explore and to disseminate human sexonomic interaction. When fully operational, the institute will function as an entity whose basic structure will be made up of four major divisions: the scientific, the educational, the applied-experimental, and the developmental.

The Scientific Division has research and exploration as its primary mandate. By "research" is meant "pure research," which is a composite of three subdivisions: research into the biology of human sexuality; research into the social structures as the external determinants of human sexonomic interaction; and research into the material, economic, and financial circumstances which are determinants of human sexonomic interaction. This mandate is performed by trained professionals, normally with advanced graduate degrees. In this division, special emphasis is put on researching the linkage between material self-interest and human sexuality. It is in the scientific division that norms concerning the various sexonomic functions will be developed and the original abstract postulates will be tested for their relevance to reality.

The Educational Division has as its main mandate the setting up and the conducting of courses and programs on human sexonomic interaction. These courses and programs are structured along lines similar to university education, and their attendance will require a minimum of high school education. Its programs are progressive (i.e., spanning a total of two years, for a diploma, and leading the students from the first courses in sexonomic initiation into advanced courses, seminars, and workshops on specific aspects of human sexonomic interaction). These courses are theoretical and abstract as well as practical and reflect real-life circumstances. They are academic in that most of their contents are subjected to scientific testing and analysis. These courses also represent the appropriate mix of subjects which are of primary interest to sexonomists—biology, hygiene, and medicine; interdisciplinary (sociology, economics, and psychology); blue bloods and blue chips; management, finance, and statistics; and history, philosophy, religion, and law. The academic courses also include laboratory sessions, with special emphasis on sexual interaction workshops, but these sessions are conducted under the auspices of the experimental division of the institute.

Of the nonacademic courses, the following four are core courses: civility and individual and social interaction; etiquette; gymnastics and dancing; esthetics, body culture, and beauty culture; scent and sensuality.

The Applied-Experimental Division has as its primary responsibility the conduct of workshops and laboratory sessions in applied human sexuality. Core courses in this division involve sexual practice, sexual experimentation, control of sexual impulses, and advance sexual practice. Perhaps the most significant practical aspect in sexonomic education, these workshop sessions are meant to "teach" the students the "art of sexual performance" in order to have them discover the full potential of their natural sexual endowment. Clearly, these workshops will be conducted by medical doctors, who are assisted by appropriately well-trained experimental staff.

The Developmental Division is mandated to do planning, finance, and development. Its chief responsibilities are threefold: administration and infrastructures; planning, marketing, and public relations; and finance and budgeting.

The hierarchical structure of the institute reflects, as its base, its divisional setup; but in line with the private enterprise nature of its organization, it is headed by its president/owner, who bears ultimate responsibility for the financial viability of the institute and the academic soundness of its programs. Collegiate by orientation, the institute's policies and priorities will be determined by the board, composed of the president, the three deans, the chief administrator, two representatives of the medical staff, and two representatives of the nonmedical professional staff.

Evidently, the institute charter and the institute's operation are subject to approbation by the provincial and/or federal authorities. But the institute's ultimate judge in the long run will be the public, whose interest and satisfaction are deemed to constitute the best guarantee for its survival.

Appendix Two: A Note on the Sexonomic Board Game

Since Sexonomics is about women and men and their fascination with the magic triangle of sex, power, and money, it also qualifies as a topic for amusement if not outright entertainment. It contains the five basic ingredients of a fascinating social pastime—less than perfect knowledge and less than perfect foresight, vertical and horizontal structuring, exclusive qualities and areas, innate human propensity to self-assertion and maximum happiness, and the chance factor.

The absence of perfect knowledge and perfect predictability are impediments that induce human nature to take on the odds (i.e., to gamble [if there is little knowledge] or to compete [in seeking to find out which of the opponents is best informed or possesses the highest skills]). The sexonomic board game provides this stimulus in that it offers the players the possibility to discover what their sexonomic valuations are, at the cost of severe punishment if they overreach or if they underestimate the counterplayers' abilities to play sexonomic strategies and games.

The basic framework of the sexonomic board game consists of the five orders of women and the five orders of men—the basic idea being to progress from the lower orders to the higher ones and to land in the top order. Each of these progressions implies that an increasingly heavy price will have to be paid for advancement into the next higher order—a price that, if the players' state of knowledge cannot bear it out, will relegate the player back to the beginning. Theoretically, part of the price to be paid for advancement into the higher order may express itself in the performance of sexual services in line with the reasoning that lower-order women and men will pay with "their bodies" if they really wish to advance along the sexonomic ladder. Practically, however, all prices and fees will be paid in "sexonomic funds" (i.e., the cash accumulated from earning income by doing the "right thing") or by providing proper answers to questions. If this price cannot be paid and the player has no funds left, she/ he will either have to mortgage some of her/his sexonomic properties at a reasonable rate of interest or have to obtain a loan (at a much heftier rate of interest, which may be paid either in cash or in services). Special incentives will be offered to players starting out as members of one of the lower orders and showing exceptional dexterity and intelligence in clearing all impediments and handling all handicaps on their way up; in return, players who start our as members of a higher order and who perform dismally in the assigned tasks may have to face "exemplary" punishment (or choose to pay a correspondingly high cash fine).

Evidently, no player is exempt from this predicamental situation, which puts extra pressure on higher-order players since higher-order women and men are presumed, in theory as well as in practice, never to offer their sexuality in exchange for either social advancement or material gain. A particularly interesting feature of the sexonomic board game is the permission granted to the players to buy "stock" (i.e., to invest into fellow players' capacity to play the game), benefiting from her/ his advancement or suffering the consequence of her/his failure. In case of an individual's "stock market" bankruptcy, she/he must leave the game, unless a player is found who wishes to "invest" into the bankrupt player (and incur the respective risk against the appropriate cash bailout payment to the "bank"). Players may even proceed to form "partnerships" with special bonuses for "winning combinations" or, respectively, special fines for particularly inept play.

The vertical and horizontal structuring of the sexonomic game makes for interesting and possibly mind-arousing systems of cross-linkages between higher-order men or women and lower-order women or men. Since being attracted by lower-order women or men is viewed as demeaning of sexonomic valuations, respectively higher compensation prices will have to be paid in order to make up for the difference in valuations (e.g., "a devaluation premium" or a "revaluation bonus"). The throwing of the dice will necessarily lead to mismatched couplings at an extra cost for trying to bail oneself out. For example, a Lotus-woman will have to pay a much higher price for her mésalliance with, say, a Mob-man than a Lace-man would have to for his dice throw–determined affair with a Conch-woman. As in real life, vertical and horizontal structuring is very difficult to bridge, and crossing these structures may often lead to anticipated and possibly severe setbacks. Except that in this kind of board game of chance, no throw of the dice can be predicted with any degree of certainty.

Exclusive qualities and areas are, once again, typical of human society. In this board game, they constitute handicaps that the players must attempt to overcome, which can be both a learning process (questions and answers of an increasingly difficult kind) and a system of rewards or punishments (wrong answers will slide you back, right answers will lead to tougher questions and the possibility of advancement). Evidently, the philosophy of advancement will reveal the basic intention of playing the sexonomic game—the conquest (possibly including the theoretical exchange of human sexuality or the actual transfer of sexonomic funds) of the reigning queen (Lotus-woman) or of the ruling king (Quintessential-man)—either of which may be well turn out to be one of the several really challenging aspects of this game.

The innate propensity of humans toward self-assertion and maximization of happiness are inducements that make most games of chance prosper. The basic structure of the sexonomic board game being hierarchical, the game will literally compel its players to play a winning game. Winning will move any of the players into a higher sexonomic order for the subsequent game (at the threat of a rapid demotion if she/he does badly), while losing will relegate the player to the next lower order, all the way down to Vampire-women and Girandole-men (which player—competitive, sane in his mind, and playing to win—would ever wish to see himself relegated to the lowest level of sexonomic beings?). Self-assertion and maximization of happiness also having to do with competitiveness in the material realm, a knowledge of finance, stock markets, and foreign exchange will also be requisites for high-quality stakes and advancement into the realm of the higher orders. For advanced players, a tempting sideline of the quest for self-assertion will consist of their possibility to offer, under clearly and tightly defined terms, the swapping of personalized services of the sexonomic kind in order to bail or buy themselves out of a particularly detrimental situation.

The fascination with the chance factor is that chance is neither predictable nor manipulatable. In the sexonomic board game, chance may equally be a blessing or a curse on all players. The chance factor's special charm in this board game will be its calculated multiplier effect (i.e., the possibility that a chance met with great success could propel the player over several other players and across several orders and right into the top order of women or men or, on the contrary, demote all the way down the top-ranking players who fare very poorly in their handling of the chance factor). Evidently, this board game having to do with Sexonomics and, therefore, with infinite imagination and a great number of choices, fines and retributions may be paid in material goods or in personalized services, and bonuses and remissions may also be received in same, depending on the majority will of the competing players. But clearly, a very explicit and detailed set of "the rules of the sexonomic board game" will see to it that what is essentially a fun game of chance will not be turned into a sinfully tempting but essentially corrupt attempt at Machiavellian conspiracy.

Appendix Three: Notes on Sexonomic Lifestyles

Already listed on the Sexonomics webpage, the individual components of Sexonomics lifestyles will be outlined with the progressive development of our organization. Please consult our webpage, in particular our discussion board, and e-mail us your suggestions at lieux0525@hotmail.com.

Appendix Four: Copyright on the Glossary of Sexonomic Terminology

We wish to remind our readers that the terms *Sexonomics, sexonomic, sexonomy, sexonomist,* and derivatives thereof have been registered, following the legal provisions concerning intellectual property, under the name of Dr. Adalbert Lallier.

INDEX

www.ingramcontent.com/pod-product-compliance
Lightning Source LLC
Chambersburg PA
CBHW030305290526
45785CB00001B/223